GUIDE TO REFERENCE WORKS FOR THE STUDY OF THE SPANISH LANGUAGE AND LITERATURE AND SPANISH AMERICAN LITERATURE

Second Edition

Hensley C. Woodbridge

with three indexes by Elline Long

The Modern Language Association of America
New York   1997

For information about obtaining permission to reprint material from
MLA book publications, send your request by mail (see address below),
e-mail (permissions@mla.org), or fax (212 533-0680).

Library of Congress Cataloging-in-Publication Data
Woodbridge, Hensley Charles, 1923-
    Guide to reference works for the study of the Spanish language and
literature and Spanish American literature / Hensley C. Woodbridge;
with three indexes by Elline Long. — 2nd ed.
    p.   cm. — (Selected bibliographies in language and literature; 5)
    ISBN 0-87352-967-7 (cloth). — ISBN 0-87352-968-5 (paper)
    1. Reference books—Spanish philology—Bibliography.   2. Spanish
philology—Bibliography.   3. Reference books—Spanish American
literature—Bibliography.   4. Spanish American literature—
Bibliography.   I. Title.   II. Series
Z2695.A2W66   1997
[PC4071]
016.46—dc20   96-35093

Printed on recycled paper

Published by The Modern Language Association of America
10 Astor Place, New York, New York 10003-6981

A la querida y admirada Kristin,
profesora ayudante de la Casa-Museo Pérez Galdós
y guía perfectísima de dos continentes,
con cariño y amistad

Contents

**Spanish Literature of the Western
    Hemisphere**

Acknowledgments

Bibliographers build on one another's work, and this bibliography is no different from others of its kind. I am grateful to the reviewers of both *Spanish and Spanish-American Literature* (1983) and *Guide to Reference Works for the Study of the Spanish Language and Literature and Spanish American Literature* (1987) for their kind comments, corrections, and suggested additions. This present book has profited from their efforts.

I gratefully acknowledge the assistance of book dealers in Caracas (Soberbia), Buenos Aires (Fernando García Cambeiro and Librería del Plata), London (Grant and Cutler), Madrid (Insula and León Sánchez Cuesta), Zaragoza (Pórtico), and Barcelona (Pulvill and Passim) who either personally or through their catalogs have kept me informed about the publication of new reference works. In the United States, Libros Latinos, Libros Centroamericanos (both Redlands), and the Latin American Book Store (Ithaca) have performed a similar function.

Justo Alarcón, Robert Roland Anderson, Jorge Eduardo Arellano, Kristin Becker, James Chatham, Jack Emory Davis, Dana Drake, Evelyn Irving and Thomas Irving, Mary Dolan Jiménez, Frank Nuessel, Geraldine Scanlon, María del Carmen Simón Palmer, Joseph Snow, Rudolph C. Troike, Lih-Lirng Soang Wang, and David Zubatsky, as well as numerous other individuals, have presented me with their books and reprints of their articles and thus have assisted in keeping me current in an ever-changing field or have assisted in other ways.

The Southern Illinois University Humanities Library staff of the late Al Cohn and Kathleen Eads, and Debbie Cordts, Marta Davis, Angela Rubin, and Loretta Koch have often succeeded over the past decade and a half in borrowing reference books for me on interlibrary loan, although many libraries are not anxious to do so.

My wife, Annie (1915–92), was for many years a member of the staff of the Humanities Library and often called my attention to new material in the field as it reached the library. She helped in the proofreading of the two earlier volumes. Her help on this edition is sorely missed.

A word of gratitude should be expressed to the anonymous readers who praised this version even while they meticulously corrected accentuation and spelling errors and recommended a handful of additions. The French have a proverb, "Qui s'excuse, s'accuse." The year this version was undertaken was a period of a good number of eye problems for me, which prevented my working over long periods of time on the project. What errors there are, are mine alone; it would be unfair of me not to credit the consultants for their assistance. They know who they are. I do not.

Elline Long has worked with me on various projects for almost two decades. She has continued, as in the past, to put up with constant additions, renumbering, and deletions with patience and good humor. She undertook the tedious task of compiling the three indexes, thus rendering this volume more useful.

Introduction

This book has a twofold purpose. Graduate students in Spanish can use it to learn about some of the most important reference works in their field of interest, and librarians can use it as an aid in developing reference collections in Spanish language and literature and Spanish American literature. The elaborate table of contents outlines this guide's arrangement and should, with the three indexes, help the prospective user.

The first, rather short section lists works that deal with the Spanish language as well as with literature in Spanish. Two sections focus on the Spanish language, one on peninsular Spanish and one on American Spanish. Each has a variety of subdivisions. Thus the subsection on Spanish dictionaries is arranged by types of dictionaries, then by chronological periods, followed by works on different linguistic topics. The section on American Spanish is arranged by country; each subsection lists important bibliographies that deal with the Spanish of the country followed by dictionaries of the country's Spanish.

The section on peninsular Spanish literature begins with general manuals and dictionaries that cover Spanish literature and sometimes even Hispanic literature as a whole and then lists reference works by chronological periods: Middle Ages, Renaissance and Golden Age, eighteenth century, nineteenth century, and twentieth century. Each period may have a variety of subdivisions, usually arranged by literary genre or theme. These are followed by bibliographies, concordances, and glossaries on individual authors, which are arranged alphabetically by author. In this way, all references about, say, Miguel de Cervantes will appear together. After the section on twentieth-century Spanish literature, material is listed on a variety of topics, including women authors.

The final section of the guide, on Spanish literature of the Western hemisphere, contains works that cover the whole area, usually arranged by literary genre or topic. Subsections on individual Spanish-speaking countries follow, with a listing of general bibliographies or dictionaries of the country's literature and then reference works arranged by genre and topic. Author bibliographies and, if available, reference works on the country's women authors appear at the end of the country's listing. A variety of other helpful reference works are also noted.

Three indexes complete the guide: an index of authors, editors, compilers, and translators; an index of authors and anonymous works that are the subject of a bibliography, dictionary, glossary, or concordance; and a title index.

This is a selective, descriptive, annotated bibliography. A volume many times this size would be self-defeating as a teaching tool. I have generally limited myself to works published in and since 1950. In that year, the first volume of José Simón Díaz's *Bibliografía de la literatura hispánica* was published. It is a landmark in Spanish literary bibliography. Where two reference works on the same topic exist, I have often listed both if one is published in Spain or Spanish America and the other published in the non-Spanish-speaking world. All bibliographical guides are selective. This bibliography includes only several dozen dictionaries, whereas there exist several full-length bibliographies of dictionaries. Simón Díaz lists over a hundred bibliographies on Miguel de Cervantes; this bibliography lists but a half dozen. It is therefore not a comprehensive bibliography of bibliographies or a comprehensive bibliography of dictionaries or other types of reference material. The several bibliographies by David Zubatsky are outstanding not only because they provide data on separately published author bibliographies but also because he lists bibliographies published in periodicals and as parts of books. The student and scholar may be able to study the contents of this volume and determine which areas, national literatures, genres, and authors need additional reference works. Reference works soon become dated; perhaps in the near future, as computer techniques become developed, a way will be found to update or keep current the most important bibliographical reference works on CD-ROM and online databases. Publishers often do not seem keen on publishing supplements to existing bibliographies; the three volumes on Gabriel García Márquez would seem to be an exception. Publishers also often allow a volume to go out of print not long after publication.

This volume is one individual's selection: what I consider to be among the most important reference works in the fields covered. Some that I list are here because I chanced on them while exploring a library's holdings or scanning the book lists that are regularly sent me. Earlier versions of this work were used with success in teaching a course in bibliography and research methods for graduate students in Spanish at Southern Illinois University at Carbondale. The work of several of my former students appears in this volume. The first edition was used as a text when a seminar was given in 1994 in the Casa-Museo Pérez Galdós, in Las Palmas, Gran Canaria.

I hope that this edition, with about three hundred new items and others corrected and updated, will continue to serve students and scholars in the field of Hispanic studies.

Hensley C. Woodbridge
Emeritus Professor
Southern Illinois University, Carbondale

Abbreviations

assn.	association
CNR	Consiglio Nazionale delle Ricerche
CNRS	Centre National de la Recherche Scientifique
comp.	compiler
cont.	continued
CSIC	Consejo Superior de Investigaciones Científicas
dept.	department, departamento
diss.	dissertation
ed(s).	editor(s), edited by
EDUCA	Editorial Universitaria Centroamericana
enl.	enlarged
EU	Editorial Universitaria
Excmo(a).	Excelentísimo(a)
fwd.	foreword
inst.	institut, institute, instituto
ist.	istituto
ns	new series
pref.	preface
PU	Presse universitaire
rev.	revised
SALALM	Seminar on the Acquisition of Latin American Library Materials
sec.	section
ser.	serie, series
SEREC	Servicio de Extensión de la Cultura Chilena al Mundo (Santiago, Chile)
soc.	society, sociedad
supp.	supplement
trans.	translator, translated by
UNAM	Universidad Nacional Autónoma de México
UNAN	Universidad Nacional Autónoma de Nicaragua
UNL	Universidad Nacional del Litoral
UP	University Press
vol(s).	volume(s)

Bibliographies of
Both Literature and Language

1. "Bibliografía." *Revista de filología española* 1– (1914–).
    Classified section on the Spanish language as well as a section on Spanish literature arranged by chronological periods.

2. "Bibliografía." *Revista de filología hispánica* 1–8 (1936–46); cont. in *Nueva revista de filología hispánica* 1– (1947–).
    The coverage has varied over the years. Volumes 1–33 exclude references to Spanish America and Brazil. With Volume 34 (1985–86), material on Spanish American literature has been added. Volumes 35–38 contain no bibliography, while volume 39 (1991) tries to catch up with a highly classified, 655-page bibliography for Spanish language and literature as well as Spanish American literature.

3. *Bibliographische Berichte*. 30 vols. Frankfurt: Klostermann, 1958–88.
    This semiannual bibliography of bibliographies includes sections on national bibliographies, language, and literature. There are also sections on philosophy, the sciences, social sciences, and so forth.

4. *Bulletin signalétique: Histoire et sciences de la littérature*. Sec. C23. Paris: CNRS; Centre de Documentation Sciences Humaines, 1947–68. Sec. 523, 1969–85.
    Until it dropped Spanish with volume 42.1 (1988), this quarterly review annotated each year more than 300 items appearing in journals on Hispanic literatures. Each number has an author index and a subject index; each volume has "Tables annuelles; Revues, concepts, auteurs."

5. Golden, Herbert H., and Seymour O. Simches. *Modern Iberian Language and Literature: A Bibliography of Homage Studies*. Cambridge: Harvard UP, 1958. x + 184 pp.
    Of value are the sections on Spanish (including Spanish America), entries 531–796; Spanish literature, 1024–1721; and Latin American literature, 1722–1917. The fourth section, "Literary and Intellectual Relations," is smaller.

6. Heydenreich, Titus, and Christoph Strosetski, eds. *Bibliographie der Hispanistik in der Bundesrepublik Deutschland, Österreich und der deutschprachigen Schweiz*. 3 vols. Iberoamericana. Reiche 2. Bibliographische Reihe 4–5. Frankfurt: Vervuert, 1988–90.
    Volume 1 covers 1978–81; volume 2, 1982–86; volume 3, 1987–89. Highly classified bibliography of materials published in these areas on the Spanish language in both Spain and Spanish America, Spanish and Spanish American literature, Catalan, Portuguese in both Portugal and Brazil, and Portuguese and Brazilian literature.

7. Koch, Hans-Albrecht, and Uta Koch, eds. *Internationale Germanistische Bibliographie (1980–)*. New York: Saur, 1981– .
    Has 2 sections of interest: "Konstrastive Linguistik" and "Komparatistik, Weltliteratur, Literaturbeziehungen."

8.   Modern Language Association of America. *MLA International Bibliography of Books and Articles on the Modern Languages and Literature*. New York: MLA, 1956– .

The MLA bibliography became international in scope in 1956. From 1921 to 1955 it was limited to publications of the United States. Since 1969, the material on the Spanish language and American Spanish has appeared in the linguistics volume. Available on compact disk from 1981 to the present.

9.   *Romanische Bibliographie*. Tübingen: Niemeyer, 1965– .

Contains a classified bibliography of Spanish linguistics and literature of the Spanish-speaking world. It includes books, articles, book reviews, dissertations, and contributions to Festschriften. It formerly appeared as a supplement to the *Zeitschrift für romanische Philologie*, 1875/6–1879– (no volumes appeared for 1914–23). There are volumes for 1940–50, 1951–55, 1956–60, 1961–62, and 1963–64; volumes since 1956–60 have covered a 2-year period.

10.   *The Year's Work in Modern Language Studies*. London: Modern Humanities Research Assn., 1931–39, 1950– .

Especially valuable for its indexing of over 1,200 serials. Includes a classified listing of material on the Spanish language in both Spain and Spanish America as well as the literature of these two areas. Notable for its pithy commentary on the items it includes. The material is signed, and each volume has an author and subject index. Annual volumes for 1931–39 and 1950– (vol. 11 covers 1940–49).

The Spanish of Spain

Bibliographies

11. Bach, Kathryn F., and Glanville Price. *Romance Linguistics and the Romance Languages: A Bibliography of Bibliographies*. Research Bibliographies and Check Lists 22. London: Grant, 1977.

Items 116–34 (67–73) are a classified, annotated bibliography of Ibero-Romance, while items 148–215 (78–98) are a classified, annotated bibliography of Spanish. Book reviews are often cited in the extremely useful annotations.

12. Báez San José, Valerio, dir. *Bibliografía de lingüística general y española (1964–1990)*. Vol 1. Alcalá: Servicio de Publicaciones, U de Alcalá, 1995. 582 pp. 1 vol. to date.

The first volume of this multivolume set contains 13,320 entries divided into "0. Repertorios bibliográficos e informes de investigación," "1. El devenir del pensamiento lingüístico," and "2. Conceptos teóricos y metodológicos." Parts 1 and 2 have numerous subdivisions. The work attempts to be international in scope. When completed, it should be an outstanding source for material published during these years on Spanish linguistics. There is also an 118-page separately published "Tomo de índices y abreviaturas."

13. "Bibliografía." *Revista de filología española*. See no. 1.

14. "Bibliografía." *Revista de filología hispánica*. See no. 2.

15. Comité International Permanent des Linguistes. *Bibliographie linguistique des années, 1939–47*. 2 vols. Utrecht: Spectrum, 1949–50.

16. ———. *Bibliographie linguistique de l'année*. Annual vols. for 1948–75. Utrecht: Spectrum, 1951–78.

17. ———. *Bibliographie linguistique de l'année*. Annual vols. for 1976– . The Hague: Nijhoff, 1980– .

The fullest current bibliography of the Spanish language, regardless of where it is spoken. Material on American Spanish is scattered throughout the 14 parts of recent volumes. Of special interest are the sections on dialectology and sociolinguistics. Includes material published as books and in Festschriften, journals, book reviews, and dissertations if there exists a published extract.

18.   *Comparative Romance Language Newsletter* 1– (1950–   ).
The annual bibliography number of this publication, issued by the MLA's Comparative Romance Linguistics Discussion Group, devotes a section to Spanish.

19.   Golden, Herbert H., and Seymour O. Simches. See no. 5.

20.   *MLA International Bibliography*. See no. 8.

21.   Nuessel, Frank. *Theoretical Studies in Hispanic Linguistics, 1960–   : A Selected, Annotated Research Bibliography*. Bloomington: Indiana U Linguistics Club, 1988. 355 pp.
This volume brings together, with excellent critical annotations, bibliographical studies published from 1974 to 1986 in such places as *Lenguaje y ciencias*, *Bilingual Review/Revista bilingüe*, *Hispanic Linguistics*, and *Revista argentina de lingüística*.

22.   ———. "A Supplementary Annotated Bibliography of Generative-Based Grammatical Analyses of Spanish, 1984–85: Phonology and Morphology; Syntax and Semantics." *Hispanic Linguistics* 2.2 (1989): 335–56.
Gives 40 extremely full annotations for material published on this subject during this period.

23.   ———. "A Supplementary Annotated Bibliography of Generative-Based Grammatical Analyses of Spanish, 1985–86: Phonology and Morphology; Syntax and Semantics." *Hispanic Linguistics* 3.1–2 (1989): 239–70.
Lists 51 well-annotated entries.

24.   ———. "A Supplementary Annotated Bibliography of Generative-Based Grammatical Analyses of Spanish, 1987–1988: Phonology and Morphology; Syntax and Semantics." *Hispanic Linguistics* 4.1 (1990): 185–223.
Lists 72 well-annotated entries.

25.   ———. "A Supplementary Annotated Bibliography of Generative-Based Grammatical Analyses of Spanish, 1989–90: Phonology and Morphology; Syntax and Semantics." *Hispanic Linguistics* 4.2 (1991): 411–56.
Lists 78 well-annotated entries.

26.   ———. "A Supplementary Annotated Bibliography of Generative-Based Grammatical Analyses of Spanish, 1991–92: Phonology and Morphology; Syntax and Semantics." *Hispanic Linguistics* 5.1 (1992): 353–91.
Lists 86 well-annotated items.

These bibliographies (nos. 22–26) include dissertations, articles, books, and book reviews. Nuessel is a recognized authority on Spanish generative-based grammatical analyses, and his critical comments are especially valuable.

27.   Rohlfs, Gerhard. "Filología española." *Manual de filología hispánica: Guía bibliográfica, crítica y metódica.* Trans. Carlos Patiño Rosselli. Publicaciones del Inst. Caro y Cuervo 12. Bogotá: Inst. Caro y Cuervo, 1957. 47–227.
Classified and annotated, often critically.

28.   *Romanische Bibliographie.* See no. 9.

29.   Serís, Homero. *Bibliografía de la lingüística española.* Publicaciones del Inst. Caro y Cuervo 19. Bogotá: Inst. Caro y Cuervo, 1964. lviii + 981 pp.
The fullest bibliography of the Spanish language for the scholar. Includes books, book reviews, and articles, with many entries annotated, and provides an elaborate table of contents as well as an author-subject index. The principal parts are "Lingüística general," "Lingüística románica," "Lingüística española," "Lenguas peninsulares (catalán, valenciano, balear, gallego)," "Dialectos hispánicos," "El español en América," and "Enseñanza del español."

30.   Troike, Rudolph C. *General and Indo-European Languages of Europe.* Philadelphia: Benjamins, 1990. 192–216. Vol. 1 of *Bibliography of Bibliographies of the Languages of the World.*
All items (1187–1396) that deal with Spanish are briefly annotated.

31.   *The Year's Work in Modern Language Studies.* See no. 10.

32.   Zubatsky, David S. "Hispanic Linguistic Studies in Festschriften: An Annotated Bibliography (1957–73)." *Hispania* 60 (1977): 655–717.
Updates Golden and Simches's *Modern Iberian Language and Literature.* See no. 5.

DICTIONARIES

Bibliographies and Guides

33.   Alvar Ezquerra, Manuel. *Lexicología y lexicografía: Guía bibliográfica.* Colección guías bibliográficas 1. Salamanca: Almar, 1983. 283 pp.
"La intención perseguida es la de poner un instrumento de trabajo en manos de los estudiantes universitarios y del profesorado de enseñanza media y superior" (7). "[E]n la segunda parte . . . presento los diccionarios . . . pero mi propósito no era el de enumerar cuantos diccionarios recogen nuestra lengua, sino el de dar cuenta de los diccionarios generales del idioma, realizados con unas bases científicas suficientes" (9). The many critical evaluations make this bibliography a useful guide to the available dictionaries.

34.   *Diccionarios españoles.* Madrid: Inst. Nacional del Libro Español, 1980.
       207 pp.
A useful and interesting classified bibliography of 975 items. Based on the catalog of a bibliographical exposition organized by its publisher, it makes no attempt to be comprehensive.

35.   Fabbri, Mauricio. *A Bibliography of Hispanic Dictionaries: Catalan, Galician, Spanish, Spanish in Latin America and the Philippines.* Impola: Galeati, 1979. xiv + 381 pp.
The section containing data on dictionaries of American Spanish is probably the weakest of this volume, which is one of the first of its kind. Many bilingual Spanish-Indian language dictionaries are missing. Appendix includes a bibliography of Basque dictionaries.

36.   Haensch, Günther, and Elizabeth Lederer. "Bibliografía de diccionarios especializados bilingües y multilingües." *Español actual* 8 (Sept. 1966): 24–26; 9 (Mar. 1967): 43–46; 10 (Nov. 1967): 24–27; 11 (Feb. 1968): 26–30.
Has 82 sections. "Se han tenido en cuenta los diccionarios en los que aparece el español en combinación con otras lenguas" (24).

Etymological Dictionaries

37.   Corominas, Joan, and José A. Pascual. *Diccionario crítico etimológico castellano e hispánico.* 6 vols. Biblioteca Románica Hispánica, Diccionarios 7. Madrid: Gredos, 1980–91.
Vol. 1: A–Ca, 1980, lxxv + 938 pp.; vol. 2: Ce–F, 1980, 985 pp.; vol. 3: G–Ma, 1980, 903 pp.; vol. 4: Me–Re, 1981, 907 pp.; vol. 5: Ri–X, 1983, 850 pp.; vol. 6: Y–Z + Indices, 1991, 1,047 pp. The best and most scholarly dictionary of its kind, this work is essentially a much enlarged and revised version of Coromina's *Diccionario crítico etimológico de la lengua castellana,* 4 vols. (Berna: Francke, 1954–57). Corominas writes "Al añadir una palabra al título se hace porque se hizo objetivamente preciso. Las nuevas aportaciones al estudio del léxico gallego, y del gallego-portugués en general, lo convierten en un diccionario, crítico y completo en el aspecto etimológico, de la lengua del Oeste; sus contribuciones nuevas al análisis de lo mozárabe y de lo romance vasconizado no son de inferior entidad ni de amplitud menor" (1: xii).

38.   Gómez de Silva, Guido. *Elsevier's Concise Spanish Etymological Dictionary.* New York: Elsevier, 1985. xii + 559 pp.
The only Spanish etymological dictionary in English, it rests on much of the latest research on the subject and includes material not usually found in such dictionaries (e.g., etymologies of personal and place names, endings, and prefixes).

39.   Tibón, Gutierre. *Diccionario etimológico comparado de los apellidos españoles, hispanoamericanos y filipinos*. México: Diana, 1988. 433 pp.

40.   Romera-Navarro, Miguel. *Registro de lexicografía hispánica*. Revista de filología española, Anejo 54. Madrid: CSIC, 1951. 1,013 pp.
       Gives 80,000 references in 3,134 sources to a listing of about 50,000 words.

Historical Dictionary

41.   Real Academia Española. *Diccionario histórico de la lengua española*. Madrid: Real Acad. Española, 1960–   .
       The 16 fascicles (through fascicle 1 of vol. 3) that appeared from 1960 to 1993 cover A–Aonio. According to the prologue, "El . . . tendrá 25 volúmenes de unas 1.400 páginas a tres columnas. Su disposición será alfabética" (vii). The prologue deserves a careful reading. The parts published to date have been compiled with great erudition, and the set shows that the work, when completed, should be extremely useful to students of the history of the Spanish vocabulary.

Medieval Spanish

42.   Alonso, Martín. *Diccionario medieval español desde las Glosas Emilianenses y Silenses (siglo X hasta el siglo XV)*. 2 vols. Salamanca: U Pontificia de Salamanca, 1986.
       Vol. 1: A–C; vol. 2: Ch–Z. The "Introducción a la lexicografía medieval" (ix–lvii) should be of great interest to the user of this set. The bibliography (lix–lxxvii) is divided into "I. Autores y obras que se citan como autoridades" and "II. Obras de consulta y diccionarios utilizados." This set is the fullest attempt yet at a dictionary of medieval Spanish. One might occasionally question the text cited. Citations from *El libro de buen amor* are from the 1901 edition of Ducamin. Parts of speech, etymology, earliest century found, definition, and quotations in which the term is used are provided.

43.   Dworkin, Steven N., and David J. Billick. *Lexical Studies of Medieval Spanish: A Bibliography of Concordances, Glossaries, Vocabularies, and Selected Word Studies*. Madison: Hispanic Seminary of Medieval Studies, 1993. xiii + 207 pp.
       An enlarged version of a series of articles with a similar title that was published in *La Corónica* 13.1 (1984): 109–29; 13.2 (1985): 262–83; 14.1 (1985): 131–65. The 802 entries are arranged by the centuries in which the medieval Spanish texts were written. Since no dictionary of medieval Spanish thoroughly covers the period, this bibliography should be particularly helpful to those who wish to study the vocabulary of an individual author or work.

44.   Niederehe, Hans-Josef. *Bibliografía cronológica de lingüística, la gramática y la lexicografía del español desde los principios hasta el año 1600*. Studies in the History of Language Sciences 76. Philadelphia: Benjamins, 1994. 457 pp.
Items 1–849 describe, comment on, and locate copies of works on linguistics, grammar, and lexicography. Items 850–985 deal with reprints published between 1737 and 1993. The bibliography (291–337) is quite useful. The 5 indexes should assist the scholar in making the maximum use of this work.

45.   Chikematsu, Horo. *Diccionario del español medieval*. Tokyo: Shoko, 1980. 587 pp.
Mistitled, since it is a glossary based on Torres Naharro's *Propalladia*.

46.   Galmes de Fuentes, A., et al. *Glosario de voces Aljamiado-Moriscas*. Biblioteca Arabo-Románica 1. Oviedo: U de Oviedo, 1994. xxv + 762 pp.
". . . hemos establecido en la obra tres secciones: 1) VOCES COMUNES, donde se recogen las palabras romances que difieren gráfica, fónica, morfolólogica y semánticamente del español actual y que no aparecen generalmente, en el *Diccionario de la Lengua Española* de la Real Academia . . . 2) NOMBRES PROPIOS . . . y 3) FRASES Y EXPRESIONES ARABES . . ." (ix–x).

47.   Müller, Bodo. *Diccionario del español medieval.* Sammlung Romanischer Elementar- und Handbücher. Dritte Reihe: Wörterbücher. Band 12. Heidelberg: Universitätsverlag C. Winter, 1987– .
The 13 fascicles through early 1966 include A–Afer. The "Introducción" (v–vi) notes that "*El Diccionario del español medieval (DEM)* pretende recolectar el caudal léxico de la lengua escrita desde los primeros documentos hasta aproximadamente el año 1400. La base material en que se apoya está constituida por unos 500 textos, colecciones de textos y obras de dicho período así como también por vocabularios, glosarios, concordancias, etc. referentes al español de la Edad Media" (v).
Page vii is "Estructura de los artículos," while pages viii–xliv are a 3-part "Bibliografía provisional," divided into "Fuentes," "Diccionarios, vocabularios, concordancias, y estudios léxicos," and "Revistas." "Abreviaturas y siglas" occupy pages xlv–xlvi.
The dictionary provides definitions and citations from medieval works; cites previous etymologies sometimes with approval and sometimes in disagreement; and lists previous dictionaries that have dealt with the term. Constantly makes bibliographical references to studies found in the "Bibliografía provisional." When and if completed, it will probably become the fullest medieval dictionary of a modern European language.

48.   Riesco Terrero, Angel. *Diccionario de abreviaturas hispanas de los siglos XIII al XVIII: Con un apéndice de expresiones y fórmulas jurídico-diplomáticas de uso corriente.* [Salamanca]: [Varona], 1983. 607 pp.
Should greatly interest those who work with Spanish manuscripts of this period. "Con el fin de facilitar la lectura y desciframiento de nuestros textos hispanos de los siglos XIII–XVIII, escritos en distintos y con variadísimas grafías—modificadas éstas por el uso frecuente de nexos, ligados, abreviaturas y rasgueos envol-

ventes—confeccioné, a modo de ensayo, un pequeño diccionario de nexos, abreviaturas y alfabetos que sirviese de ayuda a nuestro alumnado" (10).

49. Villaverde Amieva, Juan C. *Mozárabe. Elementos de bibliografía.* Oviedo: Facultad de Filología, U de Oviedo, 1984. 62 pp.

Golden Age

50. Alonso Hernández, José Luis. *Léxico del marginalismo del Siglo de Oro.* Acta Salmanticensia, Filosofía y Letras 99. Salamanca: U de Salamanca, 1976. xxxv + 801 pp.
     "El objeto de este léxico es doble: Por una parte, aclarar, o tratar de hacerlo, una gran cantidad de términos generalmente no registrados en las obras de lexicografía conocidas, o registrados con un significado diferente, y que aparecen, sin embargo, con relativa frecuencia en los textos literarios del Siglo de Oro español. Por otra parte, reunir en un trabajo coherente una serie de vocabularios parciales empleados por las clases marginales de la sociedad española clásica en relación con ellas" (xi). Deals with the speech of "Prostitutas, Rufianes, Valentones, Tahures y Fulleros, Ladrones, Estafadores y Embusteros" (xii). Defines words and illustrates their use with quotations from literary works of the period.

51. Covarrubias Orozco, Sebastián de. *Tesoro de la lengua castellana o española.* Edición de Felipe C. R. Maldonado. Revisada por Manuel Camarero. Nueva biblioteca de erudición y crítica 7. Madrid: Castalia, 1994. xviii + 1,047 pp.
     "Características de la presente edición" (xvii–xviii) notes that "I. Se han modernizado las grafías y la puntuación, adecuándolas a la norma de uso en nuestros días. II. Se han respetado, en cambio, peculiaridades lingüísticas de la época. . . . III. Se ha regularizado el orden alfabético de acuerdo con la modernización gráfica, solventando de esta manera la necesidad de índices auxiliares" (xvii).

52. Fontecha, Carmen. *Glosario de voces comentadas en ediciones de textos clásicos.* Madrid: CSIC, 1941. viii + 409 pp.
     The definitions come from critical editions of Golden Age authors.

53. Gili Gaya, Samuel. *Tesoro lexicográfico (1492–1726).* Madrid: CSIC, 1947–56.
     The 4 completed fascicles cover the letters A–E. Regrettably, the work was discontinued with the death of Gili Gaya. It combines the data found in 70 published and manuscript dictionaries that appeared during the period researched. Since many of these volumes are extremely rare, it is a valuable source for the study of the Spanish vocabulary of the sixteenth and seventeenth centuries. One can only hope that a way will someday be found to resume its compilation and publication.

For glossaries on individual authors of the period see those on Cervantes (no. 354), Lope de Rueda (no. 364), Santa Teresa de Jesús (no. 380), and Lope de Vega (no. 369).

Eighteenth Century

54.   Real Academia Española. *Diccionario de la lengua castellana*. 5 vols. Madrid: Gredos, 1979.

A facsimile edition of the first dictionary of the Academia Española, it is often referred to as the "Diccionario de autoridades," for its vocabulary is based on that of the authors the academy considers the best. The first edition was published in 6 volumes between 1726 and 1729.

Twentieth Century

55.   Alonso, Martín. *Enciclopedia del idioma. Diccionario histórico y moderno de la lengua española (siglos XII al XX) etimológico, tecnológico, regional e hispanoamericano*. 3 vols. Madrid: Aguilar, 1958.

"La mayoría de los artículos . . . llevan el siguiente orden en su estructura interna: a) la etimología . . . b) la morfología lexicográfica . . . c) la cronología . . . d) definición y localización del vocablo . . . e) orden de las acepciones . . . f) agrupación alfabética . . . g) comprobación de fechas y acepciones . . . h) notación fonética . . ." (1: xxii–xx).

56.   Casares, Julio. *Diccionario ideológico de la lengua española desde la idea a la palabra, desde la palabra a la idea*. Barcelona: Gili, 1951. lxxi + 1,124 pp.

Divided into "Parte sinóptica," "Parte analógica," and "Parte alfabética." The "plan de la obra e instrucciones para su manejo" (ix–xxiv) should be read carefully.

57.   Alvar Ezquerra, Manuel, ed. *Diccionario de voces de uso actual*. Madrid: Arco Libros, 1994. 632 pp.

A dictionary of words currently used in Spain but which do not appear in the academy dictionary. "Es el fruto de un atento examen realizado durante varios años de periódicos de ámbito nacional, de revistas de información general y de divulgación científica." Provides quotations that show the word's use.

58.   *Diccionario de uso. Gran diccionario de la lengua española*. Ed. Aquilino Sánchez. Alcobendas (Madrid): Soc. General Española de Librería, 1985. 1,983 pp.

Defines more than 60,000 words and illustrates their meaning and use with examples from current, rather than literary, language. Shows syllabification, indicates pronunciation with the International Phonetic Alphabet adapted for Spanish, notes what prepositions go with verbs and adjectives, gives synonyms and antonyms, includes Americanisms and the most used technical terms, and concludes with "Gentilicios" (1978–83).

59. Moliner, María. *Diccionario de uso del español*. 2 vols. Madrid: Gredos, 1966–67, 1984.

Moliner's introduction to this work, one of the most important of twentieth-century Spanish dictionaries, should be carefully read (i–xxx). "La denominación 'de uso' aplicada a este diccionario significa que constituye un instrumento para guiar en el uso del español tanto a los que lo tienen como idioma propio como a aquellos que lo aprenden y han llegado en el conocimiento de él a ese punto en que el diccionario bilingüe puede y debe ser substituido por un diccionario en el propio idioma que se aprende. Y ello, en primer lugar, trayendo a la mano del usuario todos los recursos de que el idioma dispone para nombrar una cosa, para expresar una idea con la máxima precisión o para realizar verbalmente cualquier acto expresivo. Y, en segundo lugar, resolviendo sus dudas acerca de la legitimidad e ilegitimidad de una expresión, de la manera correcta de resolver cierto caso de construcción, etc. Estos objetivos se persiguen con dos de las características del diccionario: 1. Con un sistema de sinónimos, palabras afines y referencias que constituye una clave superpuesta al diccionario de definiciones para conducir al lector desde la palabra que conoce al modo de decir que desconoce o que no acude a su mente en el momento preciso: de la idea a la expresión. 2. Con ciertas indicaciones gramaticales en cada artículo y el desarrollo de los que son propiamente gramaticales, que resuelven las dudas sobre construcción; así como con los ejemplos que acompañan a las definiciones, los cuales ponen ante el lector el valor 'de uso' de las palabras, no siempre claro aun conociendo exactamente su valor lógico" (ii).

60. *Pequeño Larousse ilustrado: 1996*. México: Larousse, 1995. 1,792 pp.

Handy recent monolingual dictionary with sections "Frases célebres" (1057–62) and "Refranes" (1063–72) and a dictionary of places and persons (1073–1785).

61. Real Academia Española. *Diccionario de la lengua española*. 21st ed. Madrid: Real Acad. Española, 1992 [colophon gives 1993]. 1,513 pp.

The most recent edition of the Spanish Academy dictionary is much more comprehensive than earlier editions were. The "Preámbulo" notes the improved etymologies, due to the use of Corominas's studies, and the addition of many technical and scientific terms. Earlier editions generally contained only the vocabulary of leading authors, thus precluding scientific and technical terms, slang, and colloquial expressions. The newer editions of the dictionary also have more *americanismos*. Available on CD-ROM.

Reverse Dictionaries

62. Mighetto, David, and Per Rosengren. *Proyecto DR: Diccionario reverso*. In collaboration with Sprakdata and Christian Sjögreen. Göteborg: Göteborgs U Inst. för Romanska Sprak, 1985. x + 206 pp.

The vocabulary, that of daily and weekly newspapers, derives from the compilers' *Banco de datos de prensa española: Concordancia lingüística y texto fuente* (1982).

63.   Stahl, Fred A., and Gary E. A. Scavnicky. *A Reverse Dictionary of the Spanish Language.* Urbana: U of Illinois P, 1973. 181 pp.
The vocabulary is taken from the academy dictionary.

Slang

64.   Hernández Castanedo, Francisco. *Glosario de la mala palabra (De los mil y pico nombres con que atienden las del más viejo oficio).* Madrid: Avapiés, 1994. 281 pp.
Pages 269–71 contain a "Glosario de voces jergales que acaso precisen explicación." Terms for *prostitute* are taken from texts as far back as Alfonso el Sabio through contemporary authors and slang.

65.   León, Víctor. *Diccionario de argot español y lenguaje popular.* Madrid: Alianza, 1980. 157 pp.
Based on the speech of Barcelona, Zaragoza, Bilbao, and Sevilla, as well as on the slang in 130 novels by contemporary authors. Includes a useful bibliography of recent studies on Spanish slang (25–27).

66.   Martín, Jaime. *Diccionario de expresiones malsonantes del español: Léxico descriptivo.* [2nd ed.] Colección fundamentos 44. Madrid: Istmo, 1974. lxxx + 368 pp.
Based on the speech of Madrid. The "Nota preliminar" discusses the types of words included. "Distribución por campos semánticos" (277–368), a kind of thesaurus, has the following subdivisions: "Partes anatómicas del cuerpo," "Sexo y órganos sexuales," "Vida y actividades humanas," "El entendimiento y la voluntad," "La afectividad," and "El lenguaje y la comunicación humana."

67.   Martínez Márquez, José Ramón Julio (Ramoncín). *El tocho cheli. Diccionario de jergas, germanías y jerigonzas.* Madrid: Temas de Hoy, 1993. 392 pp.
Slang dictionary of the mid-1990s with an emphasis on drug culture, sex, prostitution, and so on. Pages 279–392 contain a Castellano-jergas glossary in which the standard Spanish term is followed by the slang terms for the word. Back cover states, "Se trata, sin duda, del mejor compendio de toda clase de jergas jamás publicado, fresco, desenfadado y vivo, las formas en la que realmente se expresan jóvenes, rockeros, profesionales, delincuentes, recogidas en todos los puntos de España." Martínez Márquez is also the compiler of *El nuevo tocho cheli. Diccionario de jergas* (Diccionarios de hoy. Madrid: Temas de Hoy, 1996. 333 pp.)

Synonyms

68.   Batchelor, R. E. *Using Spanish Synonyms.* Cambridge: Cambridge UP, 1994. 721 pp.
An extremely useful synonym dictionary for speakers of English.

69. Corripio, Fernando. *Gran diccionario de sinónimos, voces afines e incorrecciones.* Barcelona: Bruguera, 1971. 1,128 pp.
Provides synonyms and related words.

70. Sáinz de Robles, Federico Carlos. *Ensayo de un diccionario español de sinónimos y antónimos.* 8th ed. Madrid: Aguilar, 1985. 1,149 pp.

71. Gili Gaya, Samuel. *Vox: Diccionario de sinónimos.* 9th ed. Barcelona: Bibliograf, 1983. xvi + 357 pp.
Not only lists synonyms but provides, for many of the entries, "explicaciones, de extensión y precisión variables, sobre todos o algunos de los vocablos enumerados" (xii). The prologue, "Concepto y historia de la sinonimia," (v–xiii), evaluates a handful of synonym dictionaries from the eighteenth through the twentieth centuries.

Bilingual Dictionaries

72. *The Duden Pictorial Encyclopedia, in Five Languages: English, French, German, Italian, Spanish.* New York: Murray Printing for Ungar, [1943]. 2,588 pp.
Subtitled *30,000 Words Explained by Pictures.* Lists many technical terms grouped by subject, such as particular industries.

73. *The Oxford-Duden Pictorial Spanish-English Dictionary.* Oxford: Clarendon, 1985. 885 pp., incl. 112 pp., index of Spanish words; 96 pp., index of English words.
Translation of a German pictorial dictionary. Lists terms relating to grouped images (e.g., herbs, painters, camping, motorcycles). Provides many technical terms relating to specialized occupations.

74. *The Oxford Spanish Dictionary: Spanish-English/English-Spanish.* Ed. Beatriz Galimberti Jarman and Roy Russell, et al. Oxford: Oxford UP, 1994. li + 1,829 pp.
Emphasizes coverage of Latin American Spanish and provides up-to-date coverage of new terms, extensive treatment of specialist and scientific vocabulary, and a guide to personal and business correspondence. Claims more than 275,000 words and phrases and 450,000 translations and offers detailed usage labels.

75. Smith, Colin, in collaboration with Manuel Bermejo Marcos and Eugenio Chang-Rodríguez. *Collins Spanish-English, English-Spanish Dictionary.* Unabridged 4th ed. London: HarperCollins, 1996. xxv + 1,688 pp.
Usage-level, extensive coverage of Latin American Spanish and a 72-page thematic guide to self-expression. Emphasis is on current Spanish and English languages.

76. *Vox New College Spanish and English Dictionary: English-Spanish/Spanish-English.* Comp. Carlos F. McHale and the editors of Bibliograf, S.A. North

American ed. prepared by eds. of the National Textbook Co. Lincolnwood: Natl. Textbook, 1984. xix + 1,455 pp.

Grammatical data for each language are scattered throughout the volume. The appendixes have sections on the most commonly used abbreviations of the two languages, false cognates and "part-time cognates, business correspondence in Spanish, monetary units, weights and measures, numbers, temperature, etc." The preface, by Theodore V. Higgs, further notes that both "American and British spellings are given at the head of a single article . . ." and "when British and American usage differs . . . this difference is clearly shown. In addition, irregular verbs are generally conjugated as part of each article . . ." (vii). Although the editors attempt to indicate the areas in which Americanisms are used, they could have placed more emphasis on American English. Under *to knock up*, for example, they ignore the American English slang usage and give Spanish equivalents for only the British English usage.

SPECIAL TOPICS

Anglicisms

77.   Teschner, Richard Vincent. "A Critical Annotated Bibliography of Anglicisms in Spanish." *Hispania* 57 (1974): 631–78.

Covers studies of all kinds in this field published between 1850 and 1971. The section "Regional and National Studies" deals with anglicisms in American Spanish. This excellent scholarly bibliography provides quotations from reviews.

78.   Lorenzo, Emilio. *Anglicismos hispánicos*. Biblioteca Románica Hispánica. Estudios y ensayos 396. Madrid: Gredos, 1996. 710 pp.

The fullest treatment of anglicisms in Spanish.

Computers and Spanish Linguistics

79.   Sáez-Godoy, Leopoldo. "Las computadoras en el estudio del español: Bibliografía." *Thesaurus* 38 (1983): 340–75.

Divided into "Bibliografía clasificada" (342–62) and "Indice alfabético" (362–75). "Esta bibliografía intenta abarcar las publicaciones sobre lengua y literaturas españolas en las que de algún modo se han utilizado computadoras electrónicas o sus predecesoras mecánicas" (341).

Gestures

80.   Meo-Zilio, Giovanni, and Silvia Mejía. *Diccionario de gestos: España e His-panoamérica.* 2 vols. Bogotá: Inst. Caro y Cuervo, 1980–83.
    This dictionary describes each gesture in detail, often with an illustrative photograph, and indicates countries in which each is used. A model dictionary for the study of gestures.

Grammar Bibliography

81.   McKay, John C. "Spanish." *A Guide to Romance Reference Grammars: The Modern Standard Languages.* Amsterdam Studies in the Theory and History of Linguistic Science 5; Library and Information Sources in Linguistics 6. Amsterdam: Benjamins, 1979. 93–110.
    McKay evaluates 12 recent reference grammars in Spanish, English, and Russian, emphasizing their good and bad points (93–106), and performs the same service for 4 volumes devoted to the study of Spanish syntax (107–10). His critical comments should prove quite useful. Just as scholars and students often use a number of dictionaries, they will probably find themselves consulting several grammars, or sometimes even full-length studies on individual parts of speech, before they find the answer to a given grammatical or syntactical problem.

Historical Syntax

82.   Davies, Mark. "A Bibliography of Historical Spanish Syntax." *Hispanic Linguistics* 5.1–2 (1992): 279–351.
    Classified, unannotated bibliography of 601 items divided into 50 sections.

Language Acquisition

83.   Rodríguez, Oralia, and Ma[ría]. Paz Berruecos. *La adquisición del español como lengua materna: Bibliografía descriptiva.* México: Colegio de México, 1993. xiii + 172 pp.
    The majority of the 232 items are annotated with material from *Dissertation Abstracts International* translated into Spanish.

Morphology and Morphosyntax

84.   García Medall, Joaquín. "Ensayo bibliográfico sobre la morfología no flexiva del español (1950–1992)." *Boletín de filología* [Santiago de Chile] 34 (1993–94): 111–85.
    Mostly unannotated, classified bibliography of 706 entries.

85.   Stevenson, J. "Morfosintaxis del moderno español peninsular: Ensayo bibliográfico de estudios descriptivos (1950–1972)." *Español actual* 31 (1976): 1–32; 33 (1977): 29–53.

Lists 1,791 items. "Me refiero sólo al español de España. . . . El criterio seguido para establecer las categorías es puramente práctico, teniendo por objeto facilitar la consulta: (1) Nombre, pronombre, adjetivo, artículo; (2) Adverbio, conjunción y elementos de relación; interjección; partícula, preposición y régimen; verbo (primera parte); (3) Verbo (segunda parte); otros estudios específicos; (4) Estudios generales" (1).

Onomastics

86.   Ariza, Manuel. *Intento de bibliografía de la onomástica hispánica.* Supp. to *Anuario de estudios filológicos.* Cáceres: U de Extremadura, 1981 [copyright 1982]. 116 pp.

This bibliography, apparently the first on this topic, lists 2,066 items divided into 2 parts. "La primera es una clasificación temática en la que aparece la numeración que cada título lleva en la segunda parte. Esta consiste en una lista alfabética de autores" (11). The thematic classification is divided into 3 large sections: "Generalidades y temas monográficos," "Elementos constitutivos," and "Clasificación geográfica." Bibliographical data are incomplete for many items.

Phonetics and Phonology

87.   Quilis, Antonio. *Bibliografía de fonética y fonología españolas.* Collectanea phonetica 9. Madrid: CSIC, 1984. 481 pp.

This highly classified bibliography of 2,823 items could have been greatly improved with better proofreading and the completion of the many entries in which bibliographical data are missing. Provides a subject index, an author index, and an index of geographical names and languages.

Proverbs (Dichos and Refranes)

88.   Jaime Gómez, José de, and José María de Jaime Lorén. *Catálogo de bibliografía paremiológica española.* Valencia: ECV, SA, 1992. 234 pp.

This bibliography lists 1,627 manuscripts, books, and articles on this subject. "Historiografía de la paremiología española" (12–20) is a brief but interesting, century-by-century discussion of this topic.

89.   Diez Barrio, Germán. *Dichos populares castellanos.* Colección Nueva Castilla 11. Valladolid: Castilla, 1993. 131 pp.

Origin and meaning of 300 *dichos.* It is a pity that the "Introducción" (9–15) is not longer, since it is extremely interesting in what it says; it could be further developed. It is divided into "El dicho," "Origen de los dichos," "Estructura," and "Tradición y vigencia."

90. Iribarren, José María. *El porqué de los dichos: Sentido, origen y anécdota de los dichos, modismos y frases proverbiales de España con otras muchas curiosidades.* 6th ed. Introd. and index by José María Romera. Pamplona: Dept. de Educación y Cultura, Gobierno Navarra, 1994. xxxi + 421 pp.

The volume's 6 parts are "Dichos proverbiales y modismos de uso corriente," "Comparaciones populares," "Expresiones afortunadas y frases históricas," "Origen de algunas palabras," "Notas sobre proverbios, sentencias y aforismos," and "Curiosidades diversas." Extremely useful bibliography (363–79) and "Indice alfabético."

Sociolinguistics

91. Wood, Richard E. "Current Sociolinguistics in Latin America." *Latin American Research Review* 16.1 (1981): 240–51.

Subjunctive

92. Navas Ruiz, Ricardo. "Bibliografía crítica sobre el subjuntivo español." *Actas del XI Congreso Internacional de Lingüística y Filología Románicas.* Vol. 4. Madrid: CSIC, 1968. 1823–38.

This annotated bibliography contains a section entitled "El subjuntivo en Hispanoamérica."

Syntax

93. González Pérez, Rosario, and Ana M. Rodríguez Fernández. *Bibliografía de sintaxis española (1960–1984).* Verbo, Anexo 31. Santiago de Compostela: U de Santiago de Compostela, 1989. 245 pp.

Highly classified bibliography of 3,271 unannotated entries.

Word Formation

94. Bosque, Ignacio, and José Antonio Mayoral. "Formación de palabras. Ensayo bibliográfico." *Cuadernos bibliográficos* 38 (1979): 245–75.

Lists 445 items. The fifth section, "Formación de palabras en español" (257–75), is divided into "Estudios de carácter general," "Estudios particulares," "Derivación," "Prefijos," "Interfijos e infijos," "Sufijos," "Nominales," "Adjetivales," "Verbales," "Adverbiales," and "Composición y parasíntesis."

95. García Medall, Joaquín. *Casi un siglo de formación de palabras del español (1900–1994). Guía bibliográfica.* Anejo 13. Valencia: U de Valencia, 1995. 166 pp.

Classified, unannotated bibliography of 1,265 entries divided into "Panorama de la formación de palabras en español," "Bibliografías, revisiones generales y diccionarios," "Estudios de morfología no flexiva," "El español y otras lenguas,"

"Neología, estilística, lenguajes especiales, productividad," "Indice de autores," and "Indice de revistas, actas y congresos."

SPANISH DIALECTS

96.   Alvar [Ezquerra], Manuel. *Dialectología española.* Cuadernos bibliográficos 7. Madrid: CSIC, 1962. 93 pp.

Divides 1,037 items into 2 sections, each with subdivisions: "Dialectos españoles: leonés, extremeño, riojano, aragonés, murciano, andaluz y canario" and "Complementos bibliográficos: español de América, papiamento, español de Filipinas y judeo-español."

97.   Luzón, María Angustias. *Indices léxicos de los atlas lingüísticos españoles.* Spec. issue of *Español actual* 47 (1987): 1–181 pp.

This index should be extraordinarily useful for individuals who have access to *Atlas lingüístico de Andorra, Atlas lingüístico de Cataluña, Atlas lingüístico-etnográfico de Andalucía; Atlas lingüístico-etnográfico de Aragón, Navarra y Rioja; Atlas lingüístico-etnográfico de las Islas Canarias; Atlas lingüístico-etnográfico de Santander; Atlas lingüístico de los Marineros Peninsulares; Atlas lingüístico de la Península Ibérica;* and *Atlas lingüístico del Valle de Arán.* The volume also contains "Nombres científicos de animales y plantas" (169–81).

98.   Viudas Camarasa, Antonio. *Dialectología hispánica y geografía lingüística en los estudios locales (1920–1984). Bibliografía crítica y comentada.* Colección "Plenos de la Confederación española del centro de estudios/locales" 4. Cáceres: Inst. Cultural "El Brocense." Excma. Diputación Provincial de Cáceres, 1986. 347 pp.

Judeo-español

99.   Studemund, Michael. *Bibliographie zum Judenspanischen.* Romanistik in Geschichte und Gegenwart 2. Hamburg: Buske, 1975. 148 pp.

American Spanish

General Bibliographies

100. Bach, Kathryn F., and Glanville Price. See no. 11.

101. Comité International Permanent des Linguistes. See nos. 15–17.

102. Dabbs, Jack Autrey. "Namelore in Latin America." *Names* 1.3 (1953): 77–87; 2.4 (1954): 234–48; 4.1 (1956): 18–36.
A bibliography of personal and place name studies. The 496 items are arranged by country.

103. Fontanella de Weinberg, María Beatriz. "Spanish outside of Spain." *Language and Philology in Romance*. Ed. Rebecca Posner and John N. Green. The Hague: Mouton, 1982. 319–411. Vol. 3 of *Trends in Romance Linguistics and Philology*. Trends in Linguistics, Studies and Monographs 14.
A bibliographical essay divided as follows: "1. Introduction," "2. American Spanish," "2.1. Historical Studies," "2.1.1. General Surveys," "2.1.2. The Substratum Question," "2.1.3. The Debate on 'andalucismo,' " "2.1.4. Evolution of the Main Phonological and Syntactic Features," "2.2. Descriptive Studies," "2.2.1. General Surveys," "2.2.2. Dialectal Classification and Linguistic Geography," "2.2.3. Studies of General Scope," "2.2.4. General Studies on the Speech of Countries or Regions," "2.2.5. Phonological Descriptions," "2.2.6. Morphosyntactic Descriptions," "2.2.7. Linguistic Contact and Contact Languages," "2.3. Conclusions," "3. The Speech of the Canary Islands," "3.1. General Characters: Canary as Part of Atlantic Spanish," "3.2. Descriptive Studies," "4. Judeo-Spanish," "4.1. General," "4.2. Description of Different Judeo-Spanish Dialects in the Old World," "4.3. Judeo-Spanish in the New World," "4.4. Consequences of Linguistic Contact in Judeo-Spanish Dialects," "4.5. Obsolescence of Judeo-Spanish," "5. The Spanish of the Philippines," "5.1. The Place of Spanish in the Philippines," and "5.2. Spanish Based Creoles."

104. *Handbook of Latin American Studies*. Vols. 1–13 (1935–47). Cambridge: Harvard UP, 1936–51. Vols. 14–40 (1948–74). Gainesville: U of Florida P, 1951–78. Vols. 41– . Austin: U of Texas P, 1979– .
Each of the first 25 annual volumes is a selective annotated bibliography of works on both the humanities and the social sciences. Each section is by an expert in the field. Since volume 26, the sections dedicated to Spanish American literature and to the Spanish language in the New World have appeared in the volume

devoted to the humanities, which alternates with one on the social sciences. In every volume there is a section on general works that includes both national and subject bibliographies. For many years the *HLAS* has been an important current source for the study of Latin American culture. Vols. 1–3 (1936–94) are available on a CD-ROM that "provides full-text searches in addition to field searches of each bibliographic record's author, title, subject headings, annotation, publisher, and year of publication, as well as the record's corresponding HLAS volume and item number" (Fall 1996 catalog).

105.   Malkiel, Yakov. "Hispanic Philology." *Ibero-American and Caribbean Linguistics.* The Hague: Mouton, 1968. 158–228. Vol. 4 of *Current Trends in Linguistics.* Ed. Thomas A. Sebeok.
    Bibliographical essay divided into 10 parts. The notes are an extraordinarily valuable bibliographical source.

106.   ———. *Linguistics and Philology in Spanish America: A Survey (1925–1970).* Janus Linguarum, Series Minor, 97. The Hague: Mouton, 1972. 179 pp.

107.   Nichols, Madaline Walls, ed. *A Bibliographical Guide to Materials on American Spanish.* ACLS, Committee on Latin American Studies, Miscellaneous Publications 2. Cambridge: Harvard UP, 1941. xii + 114 pp.
    Arranged by country and then subdivided. This volume is the most important bibliography on the subject through 1940. Its 1,072 books and articles are usually briefly annotated. Updated by Woodbridge in *Kentucky Foreign Language Quarterly* (no. 132) and *Revista interamericana de bibliografía* (no. 136).

108.   *Romanische Bibliographie.* See no. 9.

109.   Serís, Homero. See no. 29.

110.   Solé, Carlos Alberto. *Bibliografía sobre el español en América 1920–1967.* Washington: Georgetown UP, 1970. vi + 175 pp.
    The majority of the 1,500 items of this classified bibliography are not annotated. There is an author index.

111.   ———. *Bibliografía sobre el español en América (1920–1986).* Publicaciones del Inst. Caro y Cuervo 88. Bogotá: [Inst. Caro y Cuervo] 1990. 348 pp.
    The volume's 3,558 entries include and supplement the material in no. 110 and its update through 1971 in *Anuario de letras* [10 (1972): 253–88]. The major sections for each country are "Bibliografía," "Estudios generales," "Fonología y fonética," "Morfología y sintaxis," "Estudios de lexicología," "Estudios regionales," "Fauna y flora," "Indigenismos," and "Toponimia y onomástica." Some

entries have lengthy annotations, others none. Many reviews are missing and at least an author index would have been helpful. Entries within sections are arranged in chronological order.

112.   *The Year's Work in Modern Language Studies.* See no. 10.

Dictionaries and Lexicons
of Americanisms

113.   Bowman, Peter Boyd. *Léxico hispanoamericano del siglo XVI.* London: Támesis, 1971. 1,004 pp.

114.   ———. *Léxico hispanoamericano del siglo XVII.* Madison: Hispanic Seminary of Medieval Studies, 1982. 3,125 pp. Microfiche.

115.   ———. *Léxico hispanoamericano del siglo XVIII.* Madison: Hispanic Seminary of Medieval Studies, 1983. 2,493 pp. Microfiche.

116.   ———. *Léxico hispanoamericano del siglo XIX.* Madison: Hispanic Seminary of Medieval Studies, 1984. 3,968 pp. Microfiche.

These volumes (nos. 113–16) are based on representative documentary sources for each region. They give no definitions but report American usage and cite short texts that illustrate the form, meaning, and grammatical function of each word or phrase included.

117.   Malaret, Augusto. *Diccionario de americanismos.* 3rd ed. Biblioteca Emecé de obras universales, referencia y varios. Buenos Aires: Emecé, 1946. 835 pp.
Defines words and indicates regions where they are used.

118.   ———. *Lexicón de fauna y flora.* Madrid: Comisión Permanente de la Asociación de Academias de Lengua Española, 1970. vii + 569 pp.
Each entry gives the gender of the word, the countries in which it is found, and its scientific name and indicates whether the word appears in the dictionary of the Spanish Academy (1927–35). The scientific names are provided first, followed by the common names for the plant or animal (463–569).

119.   Morínigo, Marcos A. *Diccionario manual de americanismos.* 2nd ed. Barcelona: Muchnik, 1985. 738 pp.

120.   Neves, Alfredo N. *Diccionario de americanismos.* Buenos Aires: Sopena Argentina, 1975. 591 pp.
Defines words and indicates countries where they are used.

121.   Santamaría, Francisco J. *Diccionario general de americanismos.* 2nd ed. 3 vols. Villahermosa: Gobierno Estado Tabasco, 1988.
The fullest general dictionary of its kind. Gives the word's meaning and often its etymology as well as the area in which it is used. Provides the scientific name for fauna and flora.

122.   Trejo, Arnulfo D. *Diccionario etimológico latinoamericano del léxico de la delincuencia.* México: UTEHA, [1968]. 226 pp.
The fullest dictionary of American Spanish slang. Has a classified arrangement and a word index and includes one of the few bibliographies of Spanish American slang (197–210).

Argentina

123.   Davis, Jack Emory. *The Spanish of Argentina and Uruguay. An Annotated Bibliography for 1940–1978.* Janus Linguarum, Series Major 105. Berlin: Mouton, 1982. ix + 360 pp.
Contains more than 1,200 items: books, dissertations, book reviews, articles, and material published in newspapers. Some of the annotations are book-review length. This excellent bibliography is an update of a series by the same title that appeared in *Orbis* in volumes 15 (1966), 17 (1968), and 19–20 (1970–71).

124.   Donni de Mirande, Nélida, et al. *Argentina — Paraguay — Uruguay.* El español de América, Cuadernos bibliográficos 4. Madrid: Arco Libros, 1994. 150 pp.
Classified, unannotated bibliography of almost 1,600 items. Few reviews are provided.

125.   Valle, Enrique Ricardo del. "Bibliografía fundamental del lunfardo." *Boletín de la Academia Porteña del lunfardo* 1.1 (1968–).

126.   Abad de Santillán, Diego. *Diccionario de argentinismos de ayer y de hoy.* Buenos Aires: Tipográfica, 1976. 1,000 pp.
Includes many Americanisms among its 11,000 words and phrases.

127.   Coluccio, Félix. *Diccionario de voces y expresiones argentinas.* 2nd ed. Buenos Aires: Plus Ultra, 1985. 334 pp.
Provides a definition and often gives the word in context from a newspaper or book.

128.   Gobello, José. *Diccionario lunfardo y de otros términos antiguos y modernos usuales en Buenos Aires.* 5th ed. Buenos Aires: Peña Lillo, 1985. 234 pp.
Defines 3,000 terms with quotations from literary sources. Following the dictionary is an unnumbered appendix that lists the author's sources.

129. Haensch, Günther, and Reinhold Werner, eds. *Nuevo diccionario de argentinismos.* Nuevo diccionario de americanismos 2. Bogotá: Inst. Caro y Cuervo, 1993. lxvii + 708 pp.

The "Introducción" (xix–xlvii) should be carefully read. Page xx states that "Como diccionario sincrónico, el NDArg registra elementos léxicos del español usados en Argentina en la segunda mitad del siglo XX."

"Como diccionario descriptivo, el NDArg pretende informar sobre el inventario léxico y el uso de los diferentes elementos léxicos y no establece o postula criterios normativos. Por lo tanto, no se excluyen, en él, préstamos de otras lenguas, neologismos, ni las llamadas voces malsonantes."

"Como diccionario diferencial con elementos contrastivos, el NDArg registra los elementos léxicos usuales en Argentina . . . que presentan una diferencia de uso frente al español de la Península Ibérica . . . . El que la variante peninsular sea la variante de referencia . . . se justifica por el hecho de ser el español de España, en la actualidad, el mejor conocido y mejor descrito."

This dictionary seems to be based on the extensive bibliography (xlix–lxvii). It contains "Indice español, peninsular-español, argentino" (635–94), "Indice de nomenclatura botánica" (695–700), and "Indice de nomenclatura zoológica" (701–06).

It appears to be the fullest and most scientifically compiled dictionary of Argentine Spanish yet published.

130. Peña, Martín Rodolfo de la. *Diccionario de nombres vulgares de la fauna argentina.* Santa Fe: Facultad de Agronomía y Veteriniara, U Nacional del Litoral, [1986]. 206 pp.

131. Saubidet Gache, Tito. *Vocabulario y refranero criollo.* 7th ed. Buenos Aires: Sainte-Claire, 1978. 421 pp.

Bolivia

132. Woodbridge, Hensley C. "An Annotated Bibliography of Publications concerning the Spanish of Bolivia, Cuba, Ecuador, Paraguay and Peru for the Years 1940–1957." *Kentucky Foreign Language Quarterly* 7 (1960): 37–54.

Updates Nichols's *Bibliographical Guide to Materials on American Spanish* (no. 107).

133. Fernández Naranjo, Nicolás. *Diccionario de bolivianismos.* 4th ed. La Paz: Amigos de Libro, 1980. 247 pp.

Besides the dictionary, the volume contains 8 supplements that deal with Bolivian idioms, Aymara and Quechua words found in common speech and in the Spanish of other Latin American countries, and Bolivianisms in the dictionary of the Spanish Academy. Originally published in 1964.

Caribbean

134.   López Morales, Humberto. *Las Antillas. El español de América,* Cuadernos bibliográficos 3. Madrid: Arco Libros, 1994. 205 pp.

An unannotated, classified bibliography of Cuban, Dominican, and Puerto Rican Spanish that also lists material on the Spanish of Curaçao, the Virgin Islands, Jamaica, and Trinidad. It contains between 2,000 and 2,500 items.

135.   Rivas Dugarte, Rafael Angel, et al. *Bibliografía sobre el español del Caribe hispánico.* Caracas: Inst. Universitario Pedagógico de Caracas, 1985. 294 pp.

Lists 2,406 items classified by country or area. It covers Cuba, the Dominican Republic, Puerto Rico, Colombia, Venezuela, each of the 5 Central American countries, and Panama, with a concluding section on the Spanish of Trinidad, Curaçao, Belize, and the Dutch Antilles. There is a broad classified index by country.

Central America

136.   Woodbridge, Hensley C. "Central American Spanish: A Bibliography (1940–1953)." *Revista interamericana de bibliografía* 6 (1956): 103–15.

Supplements Nichols's *Bibliographical Guide to Materials on American Spanish* (no. 107) for Central America and Panama. Annotated.

Chile

137.   González Parra, José Raúl. *Manual de proverbios en Chile, frases, dichos y refranes de uso muy corriente en Chile. Incluye: Más de cinco mil trescientas expresiones.* 3rd ed. Santiago: Perfex, n.d. 208 pp.

Often misalphabetizes items. Useful for giving the meaning of the proverb or expression. Makes attempt to cross-reference terms with those of other areas of the Spanish-speaking world.

138.   Rojas Carrasco, Guillermo. *Filología chilena: Guía bibliográfica crítica.* Santiago: U de Chile, 1940. 300 pp.

139.   Sáez Godoy, Leopoldo. "La lingüística en Chile: Artículos sobre temas lingüísticos publicados en revistas chilenas 1843–1972." *Boletín de filología* [Chile] 25–26 (1974–75): 151–287; 27 (1976): 163–280.

Most of the articles deal with Spanish or Chilean Spanish. There is a useful keyword index.

140.   Zenteno, Carlos. "La psicolingüística en Chile: Bibliografía." *Lenguas modernas* 6 (1979): 111–13.

141.   Morales Pettorino, Félix. *Diccionario ejemplificado de chilenismos.* 4 vols. Valparaíso: Academia Superior de Ciencias Pedagógicas, 1985–87.

This dictionary is the fullest yet published for the Spanish of any Latin American country. Supplies etymologies, as well as quotations from newspapers, periodicals, and books. It completely supersedes the Academia Chilena's *Diccionario del habla chilena* (Santiago: Universitaria, 1978) and Miguel Subercaseaux's *Diccionario de chilenismos* (Santiago: Juvenil, 1986).

Colombia

142. Montes, José Joaquín. "Contribución a una bibliografía de los estudios sobre el español de Colombia." *Thesaurus* 20.3 (1965): 425–65.
Classified bibliography of 342 items with an author index and an index for subjects, words, and expressions.

143. Pluto, Joseph A. "Contribución a una bibliografía anotada de los estudios sobre el español de Colombia, 1965–1975." *Thesaurus* 35.2 (1980): 288–358.
Updates Montes (no. 142). 216 items.

144. *Atlas lingüístico-etnográfico de Colombia*. 6 vols. Bogotá: Inst. Caro y Cuervo, 1981–83.
Vol. 1: "Tiempo y espacio," "Campos, cultivos, otros vegetales; algunas industrias relacionadas con la agricultura" (1981); vol. 2: "Ganadería," "Animales domésticos," "Reptiles, insectos, pájaros, animales salvajes" (1982); vol. 3: "Familia, ciclo de vida," "Instituciones, vida religiosa," "Festividades y distracciones" (1982): vol. 4: "Vestido, vivienda" (1983); vol. 5: "Cuerpo humano," "Alimentación" (1983); and vol. 6: "Oficios y empleos," "Transportes," "Embarcaciones y pesca," "Fonética," "Gramática" (1983).

145. Alariodi Filipo, Mario. *Léxico de colombianismos*. 2nd ed. 2 vols. Bogotá: Biblioteca Luis-Angel Arango, 1983.
One of the most comprehensive dictionaries of Colombianisms.

146. Haensch, Günther, and Reinhold Werner, eds. *Nuevo diccionario de colombianismos*. Nuevo diccionario de americanismos 1. Bogotá: Inst. Caro y Cuervo, 1993. lv + 496 pp.
For a description of the type of material found in this volume see the discussion of the *Nuevo diccionario de argentinismos* (no. 129). The material seems to be based on the extensive bibliography of previous Colombian lexical studies (xli–lv).

Costa Rica

147. López Martín, Alfonso. "Estudios filológicos y gramaticales costarricenses: Bibliografía analítica." *Revista de la Universidad de Costa Rica* 32 (1971): 201–13.

148. Woodbridge, Hensley C. See no. 136.

149.   Gagini, Carlos. *Diccionario de costarriqueñismos.* 3rd ed. San José: Costa Rica, 1975. 243 pp.
First edition was entitled *Diccionario de barbarismos y provincialismos de Costa Rica* (1892). Contains valuable comments on the country's lexicographical features as well as several lists of place names.

150.   Quesada Pacheco, Miguel A. *El español colonial de Costa Rica.* San José: U de Costa Rica, 1990. 287 pp.
Chapter 3, "Nivel léxico-semántico" (127–249), is divided into inactive and active vocabulary and then further subdivided. The volume includes an extensive bibliography and a word index. It is one of the few volumes to study the colonial Spanish of a Spanish American area.

151.   ———. *El español de Guanacaste.* San José: U de Costa Rica, 1991. 235 pp.
Of special interest is chapter 7, "Glosario" (109–83). The volume concludes with a bibliography, linguistic maps, and texts.

Cuba

152.   García González, José. "Para una bibliografía de los estudios sobre el español de Cuba." *Islas* 64.152 (1979): 185–202.
Lists 193 unannotated items.

153.   López-Iñiguez, Iraida. "Bibliografía de estudios lingüísticos publicados en Cuba (1959–1980)." *Cuban Studies. Estudios cubanos* 13.1 (1981): 41–68.
Of the 207 items, numbers 130–207 deal with the Spanish of Cuba. The majority of the items are annotated.

154.   López Morales, Humberto. "El español de Cuba: Situación bibliográfica." *Revista de filología española* 51 (1968): 111–37. Rpt. in *Estudios sobre el español de Cuba.* New York: Américas, 1971. 142–88.
This bibliographical essay concludes with a bibliography of 188 items (131–36).

155.   Noroña, María Teresa. "Bibliografía lingüística, 1966–1978." *Anuario L/L* 9 (1978): 220–26.
Classified, annotated bibliography.

156.   Rodríguez Herrera, Esteban. *Léxico mayor de Cuba.* 2 vols. La Habana: Lex, 1958.
A purist dictionary whose aim is to help the average Cuban speak and write better Spanish.

157.   Sánchez-Boudy, José. *Diccionario de cubanismos más usuales: Como habla el cubano.* 5 vols. Miami: Universal, 1978–1989.

Volume 1 contains a valuable introduction, "Sobre los cubanismos" (7–14), that discusses previous dictionaries of Cubanisms.

Dominican Republic

158.   Cruz Brache, José Antonio. *5600 refranes y frases de uso común entre los dominicanos.* 2nd ed. Santo Domingo: Galaxia, 1992. xiv + 311 pp.

Proverbs and colloquial expressions in common use are often cross-referenced to collections in other parts of the Spanish-speaking world. Entries are sometimes not in strictly alphabetical order.

159.   Patín Maceo, Manuel A. *Dominicanismos.* 2nd ed. Ciudad Trujillo: Librería Dominicana, 1947. 206 pp. Rpt. in *Obras lexicográficas.* Santo Domingo: Soc. Dominicana de Bibliófilos, 1989. 23–212.

Gives parts of speech, definitions, and often illustrations of usage. *Obras lexicográficas* also contains "Americanismos en el lenguaje dominicano" (213–355).

160.   ———. *Del vocabulario dominicano.* Fundación Rodríguez Demorizi 17. Santo Domingo: Taller, 1983. 297 pp.

The word, idiom, or proverbial expression is provided along with a meaning. Etymologies and parts of speech are not given. Occasionally, the work of others who have written on the subject is cited or a quotation may be provided. Includes a bibliography of studies on Dominican Spanish.

161.   ———. *Obras lexicográficas.* Santo Domingo: Soc. Dominicana de Bibliófilos, 1989. 355 pp.

Pages 23–212 contain the third edition of *Dominicanismos* (earlier editions in 1940, 1947), while pages 213–355 provide "Americanismos en el lenguaje dominicano," published for the first time. This volume appears to be the fullest treatment of the vocabulary of the Dominican Republic.

162.   Rodríguez Demorizi, Emilio. *Enciclopedia dominicana del caballo.* Ciudad Trujillo: Montalbo, 1960. 303 pp.

A rather specialized dictionary concerning the vocabulary of horses, their breeding, diseases, colors, and so on. Examples of the word's use are cited from Dominican authors. There is a person and place index.

Ecuador

163.   Córdova Malo, Carlos Joaquín. *El habla del Ecuador. Diccionario de ecuatorianismos. Contribución a la lexicografía ecuatoriana.* 2 vols. Cuenca: U de Azuay, 1995.

Fullest and most recent dictionary of the Spanish of Ecuador.

164.   Rodríguez Castelo, Hernán. *Léxico sexual ecuatoriano y latino-americano.*
        Quito: Libri Mundi, 1979. 399 pp.
        This dictionary of sexual terminology is divided into 11 sections. Emphasis is
on the Spanish of Ecuador, though synonyms from the Spanish of other countries
are given.

El Salvador

165.   Woodbridge, Hensley C. See no. 136.

Guatemala

166.   Armas, Daniel. *Diccionario de la expresión popular guatemalteca.* 2nd ed.
        [Guatemala]: Piedra Santa, 1982. vi + 438 pp.
        The first part of this dictionary is based on the speech of the area around the
capital. The second part, "Modismos, adagios y refranes," is helpful in explaining
local proverbs and idioms. After defining the word and giving its part of speech,
the entries often provide a sentence illustrating the word's use.

167.   Arriola, Jorge Luis. *Pequeño diccionario etimolólogico de voces guatemaltecas.*
        2nd ed. Biblioteca de cultura popular 50. Guatemala: Ministerio de Edu-
        cación Pública, [1954]. 199 pp.
        The author seems particularly interested in the etymological origins from the
Mayan and Nahuatl of many Guatemalan place names. Gives definitions and etymologies for other types of words.

168.   Carlos, Juan (Wonka), and Mark Brazaitis. *¿Que onda vos? Expresiones popu-*
        lares. Dichos. Palabras vulgares. El pronombre vos. [Antigua]: privately
        printed, 1996. 296 pp.
        Spanish-English dictionary of Guatemalan Spanish.

169.   Rubio, J. Francisco. *Diccionario de voces usadas en Guatemala.* Guatemala:
        Piedra Santa, 1982. 392 pp.
        Includes words, phrases, and place names.

170.   Sandoval, Lisandro. *Semántica guatemalense: O diccionario de guatemaltequis-*
        mos. 2 vols. Guatemala: [Tipografía Nacional], 1941–42.
        Fullest dictionary of the regional words of the country.

Honduras

171.   Herranz, A. "El español de Honduras a través de su bibliografía." *Nueva*
        revista de filología hispánica 38 (1990): 15–61. Rpt. in *El español hablado en*
        Honduras. Tegucigalpa: Guaymuras, 1990. 61–86.

172.   ————. "Bibliografía comentada del español de Honduras." *El español hablado en Honduras.* Tegucigalpa: Guaymuras, 1990. 272–98.
Annotated bibliography of close to 170 entries by 113 authors.

173.   Woodbridge, Hensley C. See no. 136.

174.   Membreño, Alberto. *Hondureñismos.* 3rd ed. Tegucigalpa: Guaymuras, 1982. xiii + 232 pp.
Seems to be the only important lexicographical study of the area. The first edition was published in 1895 and a second in 1897. The edition of 1982 follows that of 1897. Lacks vocabulary to describe fauna and flora and omits many twentieth-century words.

Mexico

175.   Davis, Jack Emory. "The Spanish of Mexico: An Annotated Bibliography for 1940–1969." *Hispania* 54 (1971): 624–56.
Supplements Nichols's *Bibliographical Guide to Materials on American Spanish* (no. 107) with 302 critically annotated items.

176.   Fulk, Randal C. "The Spanish of Mexico: A Partially Annotated Bibliography of 1970–1990." *Hispania* 76 (1993): 245–70, 446–68.
This classified, often critically annotated bibliography of 346 items includes books, articles, book reviews, material in Festschriften, and dissertations.

177.   Guzmán Betancourt, Ignacio. *Toponimia mexicana: Bibliografía general.* Cuadernos de trabajo 2. México: Dirección de Lingüística, Inst. Nacional de Antropología e Historia, 1989. 75 pp.
Useful bibliography of Mexican place name studies that sometimes lacks certain bibliographical details such as pagination. It has 319 entries and "Indice lingüístico," "Indice geopolítico y regional," "Indice temático," and "Estudios sobre nombres particulares."

178.   Islas Escárcega, Leovigildo, and Rodolfo García Bravo y Olivera. *Diccionario y refranero charro.* México: Edamex, 1992. 179 pp.
Dictionary of *charro* terms that sometimes notes the Mexican region in which they are found. There are numerous illustrations as well as a "Refranero charro" (135–79).

179.   Martínez Caraza, Leopoldo. *Léxico histórico militar.* Colección textos básicos y manuales. México: Inst. Nacional de Antropología e Historia, 1990. 107 pp.
This illustrated lexicon should be of interest both to the linguist and to the historian. The emphasis is on terms of the Mexican Revolution.

180.   Santamaría, Francisco J. *Diccionario de mejicanismos.* 2nd ed. México: Porrúa, 1978. xxiv + 1,207 pp.
Besides providing a definition of the word or phrase, the entries give uses of the word from published sources. Especially valuable for words derived from the Indian languages of Mexico.

181.   *Acronyms Commonly Used in Mexico.* Borderlands Research Monograph Series 4. Las Cruces: Joint Border Research Inst., New Mexico State U, 1987. 26 pp.
Lists Mexican acronyms, the Spanish for them, and English translations.

182.   *Atlas lingüístico de México.* Dir. Juan M. Lope Blanch. México: Colegio de México, UNAM, and Fondo de Cultura Económica, 1990– .
The "Prólogo," "Introducción," and "Metodología" should be read carefully. Tomo 1, volumen 1. *Fonética* contains maps 1–119. Tomo 1, volumen 2 contains maps 129–276. This work, which surveys 193 localities, should be an outstanding source for the study of Mexican dialectology when completed.

Nicaragua

183.   Woodbridge, Hensley C. See no. 136.

184.   Arellano, Jorge Eduardo. "El español en Nicaragua: Bibliografía fundamental (1837–1977)." *Boletín nicaragüense de bibliografía y documentación* 19 (Sept.-Oct. 1977): 92–124. Rpt. with 10-item app. Managua: n.p., 1978. 40 pp. Rev. and rpt. as *El español en Nicaragua: Bibliografía fundamental y analítica (1837–1980).* Managua: Dept. de Español, UNAN, 1980. 46 pp. 79 entries. Rev. and rpt. as "Bibliografía del español en Nicaragua." *El español de Nicaragua y Palabras . . .* [1874]. Managua: Inst. Nicaragüense de Cultura Hispánica, 1992. 126–34. 120 entries.
Arellano provides data on more than 200 studies on the Spanish of Nicaragua.

185.   Berendt, C. H. "Palabras y modismos de la lengua castellana, según se habla en Nicaragua [1874]." *El español de Nicaragua y Palabras . . .* [1874]. Ed. Jorge Eduardo Arellano. Managua: Inst. Nicaragüense de Cultura Hispánica, 1992. 135–200.
Arellano (see no. 184) transcribed this early glossary of Nicaraguan words and idioms.

186.   Gómez, Orlando. *Diccionario de siglas e inicialismos nicaragüenses.* Managua: Banco Central de Nicaragua, 1980. xxxvi + 66 pp.
Compiled by Gómez for the degree of "Licenciado en humanidades," this work is valuable for those interested in acronyms and abbreviations for all kinds of Nicaraguan institutions, both governmental and private. Contains approximately 750 acronyms and abbreviations.

187.   Incer Barquero, Jaime. *Toponimias indígenas de Nicaragua*. San José: Asociación Libro Libre, 1985. 481 pp.
Dictionary of place names arranged by ethnic group.

188.   Mantica, Carlos. *El habla nicaragüense: Estudio morfológico y semántico*. [San José]: EDUCA, [1973]. 429 pp.
The 2 most important parts are "Diccionario de nahuatlismos nicaragüenses" (89–178) and "Toponomias nahuatl de Nicaragua" (179–273).

189.   Matus Lazo, Roger. *Léxico de la ganadería en el habla popular en Chontales*. Managua: Ministerio de Educación, 1982. 142 pp.
Specialized dictionary of those who raise cattle in this particular area of Nicaragua. Pages 35–77 and addenda (105–08) are a "Léxico de la ganadería" that gives the part of speech, the word's meaning, and a sentence to illustrate its use. Chapter 3 studies the material collected.

190.   Van der Gulden, Cristina María. *Vocabulario nicaragüense*. Serie habla nicargüense 1. Managua: Editorial Universidad Centro Americana Colección Alternativa, [1995] 408 pp.
The fullest dictionary of the Spanish of any Central American country. Provides etymologies, definitions, quotations from Nicaraguan authors, and previous dictionaries of Nicaraguan Spanish. A work of considerable scholarship, should be of great value to all interested in Nicaraguan language, folklore, and culture.

Panama

191.   Isaza Calderón, Baltasar, and Ricardo J. Alfaro. *Panameñismos*. 2nd ed. Panamá: Impresora Panamá, 1968. 117 pp.
The first edition appeared in 1964. In 1968 Alfaro published "Panameñismos" in the *Boletín de la Academia Panameña de la Lengua* [3rd ser. 3 (Mar. 1968): 73–94], which included about 200 words and expressions not found in the first edition of Isaza Calderón's dictionary. The 1968 edition adds Alfaro's data to the data found in the earlier edition. This dictionary provides parts of speech, definitions, and sometimes examples of usage. If the word is considered an anglicism or a gallicism, the word's etymology is provided.

192.   Higuero Morales, Arnoldo. *Diccionario de términos panameños*. Chicago: Allied, 1993. 97 pp.
The entry is defined in Spanish; sometimes an etymology is given. Pages 96–97 contain "Algunos términos usados en Panamá que sí se encuentran en el Diccionario de la Real Academia."

Paraguay

193.   Woodbridge, Hensley C. See no. 132.

Peru

194.   Woodbridge, Hensley C. See no. 132.

195.   Carrión Ordóñez, Enrique, and Tilbert Diego Stegmann. *Bibliografía del español en el Perú.* Tübingen: Niemeyer, 1973. xiii + 274 pp.
Classified, annotated bibliography of almost 500 items, with 8 indexes.

196.   Bendezú Neyra, Guillermo E. *Argot limeño: O jerga criolla del Perú: Teoría del argot, argot, jerga y replana, vocabulario y fraseología.* Lima: Librería, Importadora, Editora y Distribuidora Lima, [1977]. 348 pp.
Chiefly a dictionary of the slang used in Lima.

197.   Foley Gambetta, Enrique. *Léxico del Perú: Peruanismos, replana criolla, jerga del hampa, regionalismos, provincialismos, locuciones, modismos, etc. usuales en el Perú.* Lima: Privately printed, 1983– .
The compiler has not been able to publish monthly installments of 90 pages as planned. He has collected 25,000 words with 50,000 meanings. When and if the work is completed, it will become the fullest and most comprehensive dictionary of Peruvian Spanish. The 8 parts to date cover A–Ch.

Pidgins

198.   Reinecke, John E., in collaboration with David DeCamp, Ian F. Hancock, Stanley M. Tusuraki, and Richard E. Wood. "Spanish-Based Creoles and Pidgins." *A Bibliography of Pidgin and Creole Languages.* Oceanic Linguistics Special Publication 14. Honolulu: UP of Hawaii, 1975. 125–216.
A bibliography on Planequero, Papiamento, and the pidgin languages found in Colombia and neighboring areas, Nicaragua, Cuba, Puerto Rico, and the Dominican Republic. Each item is critically annotated.

199.   *Carrier Pidgin.* Stanford: Dept. of Linguistics, Stanford U, 1973– .
This periodical, issued 3 times each year, publishes a current nonclassified bibliography of pidgin studies. A classified arrangement would make the bibliography much more useful.

Puerto Rico

200.   "El español en Puerto Rico: Bibliografía." *Revista de estudios hispánicos* [Puerto Rico] 1 (1971): 111–24.
Collects 318 unannotated items.

201.   Malaret, Augusto. *Vocabulario de Puerto Rico.* 2nd ed. New York: Américas, 1967. 293 pp.

Includes Puerto Rican Spanish and vocabulary. Notes other areas where the word is used, provides part of speech and definition, and cites examples of the word's use by Puerto Rican authors. Gives the scientific names of plants and animals. Etymologies are generally not provided except, occasionally, when other studies have indicated a word's origin. Malaret notes whether the word is of English or French origin or whether it has become archaic in standard Spanish but is found in Puerto Rico.

202.   Maura, Gabriel Vicente. *Diccionario de voces coloquiales de Puerto Rico.* San Juan: Zemi, 1984. xxx + 567 pp.

Usually provides little more than part of speech and definition. Occasionally the word's origin is given. Includes lists of archaic words, as well as a list of proverbial expressions (544–67), which would have been useful had some brief explanation been given of the meaning of these expressions.

United States

203.   Becker, Kristin R. "Spanish/English Codeswitching: A Synthetic Model." MA thesis. Southern Illinois U, 1994. 97 leaves.

Leaves 87–97 are an extremely useful list of references on codeswitching through 1993. The thesis is an excellent summary of the research on the subject.

204.   Bills, Garland D., Jerry C. Craddock, and Richard V. Teschner. "Current Research on the Language(s) of U.S. Hispanos." *Hispania* 60 (1977): 347–58.

The 253 unnanotated items update no. 205, below.

205.   Teschner, Richard V., Garland D. Bills, and Jerry C. Craddock. *Spanish and English of United States Hispanos: A Critical Annotated Linguistic Bibliography.* Arlington: Center for Applied Linguistics, 1975. xxii +352 pp.

Three scholars have produced this excellent classified, critically annotated, comprehensive bibliographical study on all phases of the Spanish of the United States.

206.   Galván, Roberto A. *The Dictionary of Chicano Spanish. El diccionario del español chicano.* 2nd ed. Lincolnwood: Nat. Textbook, 1995. xii + 244 pp.

Originally compiled by Galván and Richard V. Teschner. Galván revised and augmented this edition. The dictionary "features words and expressions not usually found in standard references. . . . Many terms . . . have been labeled according to their current usage in Chicano speech . . ." (vii). The three appendixes are "Proverbs and Sayings," "Verbs in-ear/-iar," and "Bibliography," which includes no references after 1975. With more than 9,000 entries this dictionary is the standard in its field.

Uruguay

207.   Davis, Jack Emory. See no. 123.

208.   Guarnieri, Juan Carlos. *Diccionario del lenguaje campesino rioplatense. Contiene alrededor de tres mil voces y locuciones, aclaradas y comentadas.* Montevideo: Florensa, 1968. 144 pp.

This revision of the author's *Nuevo diccionario campesino rioplatensel* (1957) has been enlarged by the addition of many words and idioms. Coverage of the nomenclature of Uruguay's flora and fauna has been greatly increased.

209.   Kuhl de Mones, Ursula. *Nuevo diccionario de uruguayismos.* Nuevo diccionario de americanismos 3. Bogotá: Inst. Caro y Cuervo, 1993. 499 pp.

For a description of the type of material found in this volume see *Nuevo diccionario de argentinismos* (no. 129).

Venezuela

210.   García Riera, Gladys. "Bibliografía sobre el español de Venezuela." *Letras* [Caracas] 43 (1985): 255–318.

Lists 562 books, reviews, articles, papers delivered at conferences, and unpublished theses. Systematic index.

211.   Obregón Múñoz, Hugo, and Sergio Serrón Martínez. *La investigación lingüística dialectológica en Venezuela.* Maracay: Inst. Universitario Pedagógico de Maracay, 1983. 314 pp.

Cover title: *Estudios lingüísticos y dialectológicos.*

212.   Serrón Martínez, Sergio. *Aporte para una ficha bibliográfica de la dialectología venezolana hasta 1975.* Caracas: Dept. de Castellano, Literatura y Latín, Inst. Universitario Pedagógico de Caracas, 1978. 66 pp.

Items 86–334 (23–53) are a classified bibliography of Venezuelan Spanish. Includes an author index and a 62-item bibliography of Papiamento (59–64).

213.   Armas Chitty, José Antonio de. *Vocabulario del hato.* Colección Avance 13. [Caracas]: U Central de Venezuela, [1966]. 209 pp.

This glossary is based on the speech of certain areas of the Venezuelan states of Anzoátegui and Guárico. Usually the entries give little more than the meaning of the term. The scientific names of flora and descriptions are included.

214.   Cáceres, Julio. *Malas y peores palabras: Diccionario del argot caraqueño.* 2nd ed. Caracas: Nueva Cádiz, 1977. 91 pp.

The vocabulary in this dictionary of Caracas slang was gathered off the streets of Caracas. The entries do not provide data on part of speech but do provide definitions and sometimes synonyms and often a sentence using the word.

215. Fraíno Cordero, Francisco. *Glosario folklórico y paremiológico: Recopilación de dichos, frases hechas, refranes, glosados y comentados.* 2 vols. Valencia: Dirección de Cultura, U de Carabobo, 1977.
Arranged by keyword. Identifies the kind of expression and defines it. Sometimes gives its origin and often gives its use in literature or in other dictionaries and encyclopedias. One of the larger national collections of proverbial materials.

216. Ocampo Marin, Jaime, and Luis Quiroga Torealba. *Diccionario de andinismos.* Mérida: Facultad de Humanidades y Educación, Centro de Investigaciones Literarias, U de los Andes, 1969. 142 pp.
Based on the speech of 200 informants in 30 localities of the states of Mérida, Táchira, and Trujillo. The dictionary provides data on the part of speech and a definition of each entry. Includes a lexical thematic index.

217. Tejera, María Josefina, ed. *Diccionario de venezolanismos.* 3 vols. Caracas: Academia Venezolana de la Lengua, U Central, 1983–93.
One of the most scholarly of the dictionaries of American Spanish. It is unfortunate that this dictionary follows historical principles and makes no attempt to provide etymologies. The material on each word is divided into "el lema, la definición, las abreviaturas de las partes de la oración y de la localización geográfica, la sinonimia, la documentación, los testimonios, y expresiones idiomáticas y refranes."

Spanish Literature of Europe

CURRENT LITERATURE
BIBLIOGRAPHIES

218. "Bibliografía." *Revista de filología española*. See no. 1.

219. "Bibliografía." *Revista de filología hispánica*. See no. 2.

220. "Bibliographie." *Revue d'histoire du théâtre* 1– (1948–).
With few exceptions each volume devotes an entire issue to a useful classified theater bibliography. Bibliographical data are not as full as in other current bibliographies. Some of the journals indexed are not in other bibliographies listed in this section.

221. *Bibliographische Berichte*. See no. 3.

222. *Bulletin signalétique*. . . . See no. 4.

223. *Indice español de humanidades*. Serie C: Lingüística y literatura. Madrid: Inst. de Información y Docu-mentación en Ciencias Sociales y Humanidades (ISOC); Centro Nacional de Información y Documentación, CSIC, Jan.–June 1978– .
The first issue reproduces the list of articles and reviews in 171 journals published in 1976. A keyword index allows scholars to locate material on a given author or subject. Volume 12 was published in 1995.

224. *International Bibliography of Theatre*. New York: Theatre Research Data Center, 1980– .
The volume for 1990–91 was published in 1995. The subject index allows items not indexed elsewhere to be located through this highly classified bibliography.

225. *MLA International Bibliography*. See no. 8.

226. *Romanische Bibliographie*. See no. 9.

227. Simón Díaz, José. "Información bibliográfica: Literatura castellana." *Revista de literatura* 6–43(1954–81).

228. Simón Palmer, María del Carmen. "Información bibliográfica: Literatura castellana." *Revista de literatura* 44– (1982–).
Classified chiefly by literary periods. Lists books, articles, reviews, and material in collections such as *homenaje* volumes. Colonial Spanish American authors are included, but Rubén Darío is the only Spanish American from the period after the New World countries became independent.

229. *The Year's Work in Modern Language Studies*. See no. 10.

MANUALS

230.   Arata, Stefano, ed. *Letterature iberiche (spagnola, catalana, ispanoamericana, portoghese, brasiliana)*. Strumenti di studi. Guide bibliografiche. Milano: Garzanti, 1992. 457 pp.
A bibliographical guide to Catalan, Portuguese, Spanish, Brazilian, and Spanish American literature. The Spanish literature section is arranged by chronological periods. The coverage is sometimes erratic.

231.   Bleznick, Donald W. *A Sourcebook for Hispanic Literature and Language: A Selected Annotated Guide to Spanish, Spanish-American and United States Hispanic Bibliography, Literature, Linguistics, Journals and Other Source Materials*. 3rd ed. Lanham: Scarecrow, 1995. x + 310 pp.
Scholarly, well-annotated, classified bibliography of 1,518 entries. The 15 chapters are as follows: (1) "Aims and Methods of Literary Research," (2) "Style Guides," (3) "General, Bibliographic Guides and References," (4) "Bibliographies of Hispanic Literature," (5) "Literary Bio-bibliographies, Dictionaries, and Encyclopedias," (6) "Histories of Hispanic Literatures," (7) "Hispanic Literature in the United States: Chicano and Cuban," (8) "Books on Metrics," (9) "Literature in Translation: Bibliographies," (10) "Hispanic Linguistics," (11) "Scholarly Periodicals," (12) "Libraries," (13) "Guides to Dissertations," (14) "Other Useful References in the Hispanic Field," and (15) "Selected Book Dealers." An author index completes the volume.

232.   Foster, David William, and Virginia Ramos Foster. *Manual of Hispanic Bibliography*. 2nd ed., rev. and enl. Garland Reference Library of the Humanities 851. New York: Garland, 1977. 329 pp.
Lists general bibliographies and period bibliographies on the literature of each country, including bibliographies appearing in journals.

233.   Jauralde Pou, Pablo. *Manual de investigación literaria (Guía bibliográfica para el estudio de la literatura española)*. Biblioteca Románica Hispánica, Manuales 48. Madrid: Gredos, 1981. 416 pp.
Contents: (1) "Bibliografía general," (2) "Bibliografía general española," (3) "Documentación," (4) "Grandes manuales," (5) "Enciclopedias. Diccionarios. Grandes manuales," (6) "Estudios y obras lingüísticas," (7) "Imprenta. Libros. Bibliotecas," (8) "Paleografía," (9) "Bibliotecas," (10) "Archivos," (11) "Crítica textual," (12) "Bibliografías de la literatura española," (13) "Diccionarios: Historias y manuales de literatura," (14) "Historias de la literatura española," (15) "Antologías de la literatura española," (16) "Edad media," (17) "El Siglo de Oro," (18) "El siglo XVIII," (19) "El siglo XIX," (20) "El siglo XX," (21) "Métrica," and (22) "Revistas profesionales." Many of the 1,996 items are annotated. Some deal only incidentally with literature. Several sections seem much fuller than necessary for such a manual, while others—"Revistas profesionales," for example, with only 13 items—could have been greatly expanded. Various *excursos* found in neither Bleznick

(no. 231) nor Foster and Foster (no. 232) should be useful to students of Spanish literature. There is an author index.

The 8-page table of contents is the closest the *Manual* comes to a subject index.

GENERAL WORKS

Dictionaries

234.   Bleiberg, Germán, Maureen Ihrie, and Janet Pérez. *Dictionary of the Literature of the Iberian Peninsula*. 2 vols. Westport: Greenwood, 1993.

Extraordinarily useful dictionary that includes Spanish, Catalan, Galician, Portuguese, and Basque authors. After the author's biographical-critical sketch are a bibliography of primary texts, translations of the author's works into English, and critical studies.

235.   *Diccionario de literatura española*. Ed. Germán Bleiberg and Julián Marías. 4th ed., rev. and enl. Madrid: Revista de Occidente, 1972. 1,191 pp.

Produced by a team of 17 scholars, this dictionary is one of the best of its kind in Spanish. It includes the literature of Spain and Spanish America, providing data on authors, Hispanists, literary movements, and terms. Each article is signed with the initials of its author.

236.   Gullón, Ricardo, et al. *Diccionario de literatura española e hispanoamericana*. 2 vols. Madrid: Alianza, 1993.

This work of many experts not only provides data about Spanish and Spanish American authors but also contains articles on literary genres and other types of material. "Este *Diccionario* pretende ofrecer un panorama completo de las diversas manifestaciones literarias en lengua castellana. Tal delimitación lingüística justifica la importancia concedida a autores y obras de literaturas sefardí, filipina o chicana, habitual e injustamente ausente en este tipo de compilaciones, y a la vez explica la ausencia de los escritores que han usado exclusivamente las otras lenguas peninsulares . . ." (1- ix).

237.   *Oxford Companion to Spanish Literature*. Ed. Philip Ward. Oxford: Clarendon, 1978. 629 pp. Spanish translation: *Diccionario Oxford de literatura española e hispanoamericana*. Barcelona: Crítica, 1984. 864 pp.

Includes authors who write in Catalan, Galician, and Spanish from both parts of the Spanish-speaking world. For many authors the brief bibliographies could be greatly improved.

General Bibliographies

238.   Serís, Homero. *Manual de bibliografía de la literatura española*. 1 vol. in 2 pts. Syracuse: Centro de Estudios Hispánicos, 1948, 1954. xliii + 1,086 + xiii pp.

This classified, often critically annotated bibliography of 8,779 items is divided into "Obras generales," "Obras bio-bibliográficas," "Géneros literarios," and "Cultura."

239.   Simón Díaz, José. *Bibliografía de la literatura hispánica*. 16 vols. to date. Madrid: CSIC, 1950– .

Vol. 1, 3rd ed., rev. and updated, 1983, xxxii + 916 pp. The section "Literatura castellana" is divided into "Historia de la literatura," "Colección de textos," "Antologías," "Monografías," "Relaciones con otras literaturas," and "Bibliografías literarias." "Literatura catalana" has the same divisions, as do "Literatura gallega," except for the omission of "Bibliografías literarias," and "Literatura vasca," except for the omission of "Relaciones con otras literaturas." The sections have many subdivisions. The volume has 6,206 entries, not counting reviews, which are not numbered. There are 3 indexes.

Vol. 2, 3rd ed., rev. and updated, 1986, 610 pp. Of interest are "Bibliografías de bibliografías," "Biografías y bio-bibliografías," "Bibliografías generales," "Catálogos de bibliotecas," "Catálogos de hemerotecas," "Catálogos de archivos," "Indices de publicaciones periódicas," "Bibliografías literarias," and "Bibliografías de otras materias."

Vol. 3, pt. 1, 2nd ed., 1963, viii + 623 pp., and pt. 2, 2nd ed., 1965, 626 pp. Covers the Middle Ages.

Vol. 4, 2nd ed., 1972, 834 pp.; vol. 5, 2nd ed., 1973, 937 pp.; vol. 6, 2nd ed., 1973, 1,062 pp.; vol. 7, 1968, 954 pp.; vol. 8, 1970, 808 pp.; vol. 9, 1971, 916 pp.; vol. 10, 1972, 890 pp.; vol. 11, 1976, 876 pp.; vol. 12, 1982, xii + 895 pp.; vol. 13, 1984, xiv + 928 pp.; vol. 14, 1984, xv + 895 pp.; vol. 15, 1992, xiii + 785 pp.; vol. 16, 1994, xiii + 805 pp. These volumes cover Renaissance and Golden Age authors. (A–Francisco Pacheco). Simón Díaz attempts to provide a comprehensive bibliography of Castilian, Basque, Galician, and Catalan literature and the literature of the Spanish American countries until they became independent. Reviews are listed. For important authors the many subdivisions make the bibliography easy to use. Indicates a library (usually Spanish) that has at least one copy of each book. The multiple indexes should make material readily accessible. For the periods and authors covered, the set is indispensable. Proofreading in early volumes allowed many typographical errors in non-Spanish titles.

240.   ———. *Manual de bibliografía de la literatura española*. 3rd ed., reorg., rev., and enl. Biblioteca Románica Hispánica, Manuales 47. Madrid: Gredos, 1980. 1,156 pp.

Selective bibliography of more than 27,000 items. Rubén Darío is the only postcolonial Spanish American writer included.

Regional Bibliographies

There are a great variety of biobibliographical dictionaries for Spanish cities, regions, and provinces. Volume 2 of the *Bibliografía de la literatura hispánica* (no. 239) has a "Biografías y bio-bibliografías" section, and each number of the "Bibliografía" of the *Revista de literatura* lists such dictionaries. Because of these guides, only a few of the type need be listed here.

241. Martínez Añibarro y Rives, M. *Intento de un diccionario biográfico y bibliográfico de autores de la provincia de Burgos.* Salamanca: Europe Artes Gráficas for Junta de Castilla y León, Consejería de Cultura y Turismo, 1993. 547 pp.
Facsimile reprint of a volume first published in 1889. In a new 53-page preface, M. Esteban Piñeiro finds that this volume "constituye una tentativa de elaboración de un catálogo, presentado por orden alfabético, de noticias biográficas y bibliográficas, a veces excesivamente breves, sobre aquellos que habiendo nacido en tierras burgalesas fueron autores de algún texto, manuscrito o impreso en cualquier momento de la historia" (9).

242. Rios Ruiz, Manuel. *Diccionario de escritores gaditanos.* Cádiz: Inst. de Estudios Gaditanos, 1973. 217 pp.
Emphasis on Cádiz authors who were alive when the volume was written. Not as scholarly as certain other biobibliographical dictionaries.

243. Millares Carlo, Agustín, and Manuel Hernández Suárez. *Biobibliografía de escritores canarios (siglos XVI, XVII, y XVIII).* 2nd ed. 5 vols. to date. Las Palmas: Museo Canario, 1975– .
Vol. 1: A, 1975, xvi + 276 pp.; vol. 2: B–C, 1977, 318 pp.; vol. 3: D–H, 1979, 288 pp.; vol. 4: Iriarte, 1981, 335 pp; vol. 5: J–P, 1987, 406 pp. According to Martínez de la Fe (no. 244) this dictionary, when completed, will be in 8 volumes. Millares Carlo compiled the first edition (1932).

244. Martínez de la Fe, Juan A. "Bibliografía de escritores canarios (tomos iii a iv). Indices sistemáticos y de órdenes religiosas." *Boletín Millares Carlo 2* (1981): 217–72.
The index is divided into "Indice sistemático" (218–71) and "Indice de autores religiosos, ordenados por instituciones" (272–73).

245. Rodríguez Padrón, Jorge. *Primer ensayo para un diccionario de la literatura en Canarias.* Colección Clafijo y Fajardo 14. Madrid: Mariar, 1992. 337 pp.
Presents data on writers from the Canary Islands as well as on newspapers, journals, and literary collections.

246. "Bibliografía atlántica y especialmente canaria." *Anuario de estudios atlánticos 1–* (1955–).
This bibliography, which appears in each issue of the yearbook, has a section on the literature of the Canary Islands.

247. Ortega, José, and Celia del Moral. *Diccionario de escritores granadinos (siglos VIII–XX).* Granada: U de Granada, 1991. 223 pp.
Biobibliographical dictionary of writers from Granada. Page 11 contains "Glosario de términos técnicos árabes." Especially useful for authors who wrote in Arabic and for lesser-known Spanish authors.

248.   Caballero Venzalá, Manuel. *Diccionario bio-bibliográfico del Santo Reino*. Vol. 1. Jaén: Inst. de Estudios Giennenses, Excma. Diputación Provincial, 1979. xx + 403 pp.

The first volume of this outstanding biobibliographical dictionary, the only one published to date, covers A–B and provides 8 indexes.

"Los diversos artículos de que consta esta obra, se enumeran por orden alfabético de apellidos y pretenden constar de tres partes bien definidas: datos biográficos del autor, fichas de su producción con su consiguiente localización y bibliografía acerca del mismo.

"En su correspondiente lugar irán apareciendo los artículos dedicados a revistas y periódicos, bibliografía particular de nuestros pueblos y ciudades, y obras anónimas cuya inclusión se hará atendiendo a los respectivos títulos de las mismas" (xv).

Pseudonyms

249.   Rogers, Paul P., and Felipe Antonio Lapuente. *Diccionario de seudónimos literarios españoles, con algunas iniciales*. Biblioteca Románica Hispánica, Diccionarios 6. Madrid: Gredos, 1977. 608 pp.

Identifies 11,500 pseudonyms and includes 475 that the authors cannot identify.

MIDDLE AGES

Dictionary

250.   *Dictionary of the Middle Ages*. Ed. Joseph R. Strayer. 13 vols. New York: Scribner's, 1982–89.

According to an early announcement of the set:

"The Dictionary covers every aspect of medieval life in western Europe, Islam, Byzantium and the Slavic World from A.D. 300 to 1500.

"The twelve alphabetically arranged volumes contain over 5,000 articles—all specially commissioned and written by distinguished medievalists. The articles, which range in length from 5-word definitions to 10,000-word essays, are the work of over 1,000 scholars. . . .

"Each article ends with a selective bibliography. . . ."

Volume 11 has the following sections that deal with medieval Spain: "Spain" (historical subjects), 347–89; "Spanish Language," 390–405; and "Spanish Literature," 405–60. Volume 13 is an index to the set.

Current Bibliography and Surveys

251.   *La Corónica: Spanish Medieval Language and Literature Newsletter* 1– (1972–).

Volumes 1–15 contain a "Bibliography of Medieval Spanish Literature," compiled by Oliver T. Myers. Volumes 5–17 (1976–88) usually have a "Book Review Bibliography," compiled by Harold G. Jones.

252. Burke, James F. "Spanish Literature." *The Present State of Scholarship in Fourteenth-Century Literature*. Ed. Thomas D. Cooke. Columbia: U of Missouri P, 1982. 259–304.
Deals with research published between 1960 and 1980. Includes a critical essay (259–87) divided into a general section followed by subdivisions on historical background, thematic studies, drama, romances, prose, Arthurian legends, Juan Manuel, Juan Ruiz, and other studies. There is also a classified bibliography of 202 entries (288–304).

General Bibliographies

253. *Bibliography of Old Spanish Texts*. Comp. Charles F. Faulhaber, Angel Gómez Moreno, David Mackenzie, John J. Nitti, and Brian Dutton (with the assistance of Jean Lentz). 3rd ed. Bibliographic Series 4. Madison: Hispanic Seminary of Medieval Studies, 1984. xxxii + 341 pp.
" . . . la BOOST incorpora las características de tres tipos diferentes de obras de consulta: 1. Sirve como censo de manuscritos españoles. . . . 2. Sirve como catálogo colectivo de incunables españoles y aspira a localizar cada ejemplar conocido. . . . 3. Finalmente, la BOOST está llamada a ser el repertorio que se necesita de MSS españoles que ofrezcan indicaciones sobre su fecha, origen geográfico y copista" (xxi). The bibliography provides data on 3,378 manuscripts and works published before 1501 and has 11 indexes.

254. Sáez, Emilio, and Mercé Rossell. *Repertorio de medievalismo hispánico (1955–1975)*. 4 vols. Barcelona: "El Albir," 1976–85.
Vol. 1: A–F, 1976, 658 pp.; vol. 2: G–M, 1978, 786 pp.; vol. 3: N–R, 1983, 512 pp.; vol. 4: S–Z, 1985, 570 pp. Arranged by author. Lists not only works in print but also those *en prensa* and *en preparación*.

255. Simón Díaz, José. *La Edad Media*. 2nd ed. 2 pts. Madrid: CSIC, 1962–65.
Vol. 3 of *Bibliografía de la literatura hispánica*.
The fullest bibliography of the period. See no. 239.

256. Snow, Joseph T. "Spain." *The Current State of Research in Fifteenth-Century Literature: Germania-Romania*. Ed. William C. McDonald. Göppinger: Kümmerlie, 1986. 153–76.
Half of this article is a running commentary on important publications in the field; the other half is a bibliography.

Aljamiado Literature

257. Bernabé Pons, Luis F. *Bibliografía de la literatura aljamiado-morisca*. Colección Xarc Al-andalus 5. Alicante: U de Alicante, 1992. 152 pp.
Pages 38–124 feature a "Bibliografía de la literatura aljamiada y morisca" of 498 items. Pages 10–17 discuss the various approaches to this literature. There are 3 indexes.

258.   López-Morillas, Consuelo. "Aljamiado Studies since 1970." *La Corónica* 4 (1975): 30–34.
Divided into background, library resources, and an unannotated list of recent and forthcoming publications.

Arthurian Legends

259.   *Bulletin bibliographique de la Société Internationale Arthurienne* 1– (1949–).
A comprehensive current bibliography that arranges material by country of publication and provides appropriate indexes.

260.   Sharrer, Harvey L. *Texts: The Prose Romance Cycles*. Research Bibliographies and Check Lists 3. London: Grant, 1977. 55 pp. Vol. 1 of *A Critical Bibliography of Hispanic Arthurian Material*. 1 vol. to date.
"Included in this volume are the prose romances of the Vulgate, Post-Vulgate and Tristan cycles; that is, the surviving manuscripts and early printed editions, together with modern editions and reviews thereof" (10). Includes 4 indexes.

Ballads

261.   Armistead, Samuel G. "A Critical Bibliography of the Hispanic Ballad in Oral Tradition (1971–1979)." *El romancero hoy: Historia, comparatismo, bibliografía crítica*. Ed. Armistead, Diego Catalán, and Antonio Sánchez Romeralo. Vol. 3. Madrid: Gredos; Cátedra Seminario Menéndez Pidal, 1979. 199–310. 3 vols.
"I have listed, with brief commentary, every publication on the Hispanic ballad which has come to my attention for the years 1971–1978. Books and articles published prior to this period, but reviewed after 1971, have also been listed, but without critical commentary" (199). An excellent annotated bibliography by a leading expert on the subject.

262.   ———. "*Romancero*: Studies, 1977–79." *La Corónica* 8 (1979): 57–66.
Armistead lists "all publications on Hispanic balladry" and notes an emphasis on "*romancero viejo romance* in modern oral tradition" (57).

263.   Benmayor, Rina. "Current Work in the Romancero Viejo Tradicional, Modern Oral Tradition." *La Corónica* 4 (1975): 49–53.
Divided into "Field Collections," "Catalogues and Archive Collections," and "Critical Studies."

Cancioneros

264.   Dutton, Brian. *Catálogo-índice de la poesía cancioneril del siglo XV*. With the collaboration of Stephen Fleming, Jineen Krogstad, Francisco Santoyo

Vázquez, and Joaquín González Cuenca. 2 vols. Bibliographic Series 3. Madison: Seminary of Medieval Studies, 1982.

Vol. 1: "Prefacio," "Introducción," "Catálogo de fuentes manuscritas e impresas," "Indice de primeros versos." Vol. 2: "Indice de autores," "Indice de destinatarios," "Indice de títulos," "Indice de géneros," "Indice de lenguas," "Indice de relaciones," "Indice de fuentes manuscritas," "Indice de fuentes impresas," "Indice de los poemas publicados por Foulché-Delbosc," "Bibliografía selecta," "Apéndice I. Descripción técnica," "Apéndice II. La música y los cancioneros, 1480–1520, con un catálogo de los compositores," "Errata y adiciones," "Indice general."

265. Steunou, Jacqueline, and Lothar Knapp. *Bibliografía de los cancioneros castellanos del siglo XV y repertorio de sus géneros poéticos.* 2 vols. to date. Documents, Etudes et Répertoires Publiés par l'Institut de Recherche et d'Histoire des Textes 22. Paris: CNRS, 1976– .

An excellent descriptive bibliography. The "Nota preliminar" states that this will be a 3-volume set (5). "La primera parte, que ocupa el tomo I, ofrece la *Bibliografía de los cancioneros colectivos castellanos del siglo XV*, tanto de los manuscritos como de las antiguas ediciones. . . . La segunda parte, que ocupa los tomos II y III, está intitulada *Repertorio de los géneros literarios* y ofrece un detallado sistema de información sobre los géneros literarios de la poesía cancioneril . . . " (5).

Dissertations

266. Chatham, James R., and Carmen C. McClendon. "Dissertations in Medieval Hispanic Languages and Literatures Accepted in the United States and Canada, 1967–1976." *La Corónica* 6 (1978): 97–103; 7 (1978): 43–50.

267. Tate, R. Brian, et al. "Bibliography of Doctoral Dissertations and Theses of Medieval Peninsular Literature." *La Corónica* 6 (1977): 26–37.

Arranged alphabetically by authors.

Festschriften Index

268. Williams, Harry Franklin. *An Index of Medieval Studies Published in Festschriften, 1865–1946, with Special Reference to Romanic Material.* Berkeley: U of California P, 1951. 115–22.

The Spanish section includes items 4507–85 on language and items 4586–687 on literature.

Kharjas

269. Hitchcock, Richard. *The Kharjas: A Critical Bibliography.* Research Bibliographies and Check Lists 20. London: Grant, 1977. 68 pp.

"The object of this bibliography has been to compile a list which includes all items concerned directly with the interpretation and significance of the kharjas, together with a representative selection of items dealing with their context, the problems they raise and less central issues" (8).

270.   Armistead, Samuel G. "Some Recent Developments in Kharja Scholarship." *La Corónica* 8 (1980): 197–203.
Supplements Hitchcock (no. 269) with a critical assessment of 24 items.

Law

271.   Seniff, Dennis P. "Hispanic." *Literature and Law in the Middle Ages: An Annotated Bibliography of Scholarship*. By Seniff and John A. Alford. Garland Reference Library of the Humanities 378. New York: Garland, 1984. 227–63.
Entries 801–915 are well classified and annotated. "The annotations . . . are intended not as summaries of the works but as guides to the legal content there of" (xii).

Lost Literature

272.   Deyermond, Alan. *La literatura perdida de la Edad Media castellana. Catálogo y estudio*. 1 vol. to date. Salamanca: U de Salamanca, 1995– .
Vol. 1, *Epica y romances*; vol. 2 (in collaboration with Jane Whetnall), *Lírica y teatro*; vol. 3, *Ficción y historiografía*; vol. 4, *Literaturas religiosa, didáctica y técnica*.
"En el presente tomo y en los siguientes ofrezco un catálogo de las obras literarias castellanas de la Edad Media hoy perdidas, acompañado de una serie de estudios" (13). "Problemas y métodos de la investigación de la literatura perdida" is a discussion of this catalog and the reasons for lost literature. This first volume, which has 7 indexes, is divided into "Epica" and "Romances."

Trojan War

273.   Rey, Agapito, and Antonio García Solalinde. *Ensayo de una bibliografía de las leyendas troyanas en la literatura española*. Indiana University Publications, Humanities Series 6. Bloomington: Indiana UP, 1942. 103 pp.
Deals with the manuscripts and books that use the theme of the Trojan War in the literature of the Middle Ages and the Golden Age.

Authors

274.   *Noticiero Alfonsí* 1–7 (1982–88).
Indispensable for students of the life and works of Alfonso el Sabio. The bibliography in each issue is usually divided into "Miscelánea," "Libros," "Reseñas," "Artículos y capítulos de libro," "Ponencias," "Conferencias/sesiones celebradas," "Conferencias/sesiones venideras," "Tesis doctorales," "Estudios en preparación,"

and "Trabajos terminados o en prensa." According to Anthony J. Cárdenas, Terry R. Craddock, and Barbara de Marco ("A Decade of Alfonsine Studies: Working Notes and Bibliography." *Romance Philology* 49 [1995]: 192–244), this "newsletter has been temporarily halted; it will resume in the near future" (192).

275. Snow, Joseph T. *The Poetry of Alfonso X, the Sabio: A Critical Bibliography*. Research Bibliographies and Check Lists 19. London: Grant, 1977. 140 pp.
Excellent critical annotations on 383 items arranged chronologically.

276. ———. "Trends in Scholarship in Alfonsine Poetry." *La Corónica* 11 (1983): 248–57.
Supplements no. 275 to a certain extent. Includes a chronological list of 38 items published between 1972 and 1983 (254–57).

277. Sas, Louis F. *Vocabulario de* Libro de Alexandre. Supp. to *Anejos del Boletín de la Real Academia Española* 34. Madrid: Real Acad. Española, 1976. 686 pp.
"El plan de este diccionario es el de catalogar cada palabra en O y P, usando P como la primera fuente, puesto que es más larga que la O. . . . Un segundo programa de computadora me proporcionó la frecuencia de cada palabra o forma verbal en O y P" (10).

278. Alvar [Ezquerra], Manuel, ed. Libro de Apolonio: *Estudios, ediciones, concordancias.* . . . Vol. 3. Valencia: Fundación Juan March; Madrid: Castalia, 1976. 3 vols.
Volume 3 (498 pp.) is divided into "Concordancias," "Indice de rimas," and "Indice de frecuencia."

279. Carrión Gútiez, Manuel. *Bibliografía de Jorge Manrique (1479–1979): Homenaje al poeta en el V centenario de su muerte*. Palencia: Inst. Tello Téllez de Meneses, 1979. 96 pp.
A classified bibliography of 422 items by and about Manrique, some of which are annotated. The bibliography of Manrique's works has sections on manuscripts, records, and translations.

280. Devoto, Daniel. *Introducción al estudio de Don Juan Manuel y en particular de* El Conde Lucanor: *Una bibliografía*. Madrid: Castalia, 1972. 505 pp.
A classified and annotated bibliography of books, articles, dissertations, and reviews. Includes a general index.

281. Gorog, Ralph de, and Lisa S. de Gorog. *Concordancias del "Arcipreste de Talavera."* Madrid: Gredos, 1978. 430 pp.
Based on the 1949 Riquer edition of the "Arcipreste de Talavera" (Alfonso Martínez de Toledo).

282.   Baro, José. *Glosario completo de* Los Milagros de Nuestra Señora *de Gonzalo de Berceo*. Denver: Soc. of Spanish and Spanish-American Studies, 1987. 249 pp.
A glossary of this work based on Antonio Solalinde's edition (Madrid: Espasa-Calpe, 1968).

283.   López Estrada, Francisco. *Panorama crítico sobre el* Poema del Cid. Madrid: Castalia, 1982. 337 pp.
This bibliographical work in essay form is divided into an introduction and the following sections: "El códice del *Poema del Cid*," "Unidad y composición del contenido . . . ," "Los personajes . . . y su caracterización literaria," "Configuración literaria . . . ," and "Posteridad. . . ." The bibliography (299–322) is followed by an index of authors, characters, and subjects.

284.   Magnotta, Miguel. *Historia y bibliografía de la crítica sobre el* Poema de mío Cid *(1750–1971)*. North Carolina Studies in the Romance Languages and Literatures 145. Chapel Hill: Dept. of Romance Languages, U of North Carolina, 1976. 300 pp.
Classified bibliography in essay form divided into "El problema de la fecha," "Problema en torno al autor," "El problema de los orígenes," "Las influencias en el Cantar," "Relación entre el Cantar y las crónicas," "Relaciones entre el Cantar y los romances," "El problema de la versificación," "El Cantar como obra de arte," "Apéndices," "Conclusiones," "Bibliografía," and "Indice general de autores y materiales."

285.   Jurado, José. *Diccionario de concordancias del* Poema de mío Cid. Ottawa: Carleton UP, 1982. iii + 274 pp.
Based on Menéndez Pidal's critical edition of this poem.

286.   Waltman, Franklin M. *Concordance to* Poema de mío Cid. University Park: Pennsylvania State UP, 1972. xiii + 465 pp.
"This concordance listing is based on the paleographic edition of the poem by Menéndez Pidal" (x).

287.   *Celestinesca* 1– (1977–).
In each issue Joseph Snow publishes an annotated bibliography listing editions of and studies on this work.

288.   Mandel, A. S. La Celestina *Studies: A Thematic Survey and Bibliography 1824–1970*. Metuchen: Scarecrow, 1971. 261 pp.
Annotated bibliography divided into "Author, Authorship, and Date of Composition," "Editions," "Sources and Tradition," "The Influence of *La Celestina*," "*La Celestina* as a Work of Art," "Ethical Values," and "The Historic Moment in *La Celestina*."

289.   Snow, Joseph T. Celestina *by Fernando de Rojas: An Annotated Bibliography of World Interest*. Madison: Hispanic Seminary of Medieval Studies, 1985. iii + 123 pp.

Annotates more than 1,240 entries, including books, articles, book reviews, theses, and dissertations, as well as translations of this work into 17 languages. It also includes data on theatrical, musical, dance, and verse adaptations. The final section provides complete coverage of editions: facsimile, critical, popular, and student editions. Contains a complete subject guide to the entries and annotations, as well as an index of names of authors, editors, directors, translators, and actors who have performed in stage versions of the work.

290. Kasten, Lloyd, and Jean Anderson. *Concordance to the* Celestina (*1499*). Spanish Series 1. Madison: Hispanic Seminary of Medieval Studies and the Hispanic Soc. of America, 1976. viii + 337 pp.
Based on the edition of 1499(?). Includes a "Keyword Frequency Count" (261–91) and a detailed description of the 1499(?) edition (295, 297, 299).

291. Jurado, José. *Bibliografía sobre Juan Ruiz y su* Libro de buen amor. Madrid: CSIC, 1993. 228 pp.
Excellent partially annotated bibliography that lacks author and subject indexes.

292. Vetterling, Mary-Anne. *A Computerized Bibliography for Juan Ruiz'* Libro de buen amor. Cambridge: Privately printed, 5 Nov. 1982 (date of copy examined).
"Continually updated and revised." Includes an index of keywords of 9 leaves and a bibliography of 88 leaves with close to 1,300 entries.

293. García-Antezana, Jorge. Libro de buen amor: *Concordancia completa de los códices de Salamanca, Toledo y Gayoso.* Toronto: U of Toronto P, 1981. 11 microfiches.

294. Mignani, Rigo, Mario A. DiCesare, and George F. Jones. *Concordance to Juan Ruiz:* Libro de buen amor. Albany: State U of New York P, 1977. xiii + 328 pp.
"We decided therefore to concord a complete 'text' of the poem as it now exists, and to use as our base the most complete of the three manuscripts, S, complemented by the G manuscript and appropriate fragments (T has no unique passages)" (viii).
The volume has an introduction, the concordance, and 3 appendixes: prose and fragments, word frequency alphabetically, and word frequency by frequency.

295. Alvar Ezquerra, Manuel. *Concordancias e índices léxicos de la* Vida de San Ildefonso. Málaga: U de Málaga, 1980. 448 pp.
Contents: "Textos," "Concordancias de la transcripción del manuscrito," "Indice alfabético de frecuencias de la transcripción del manuscrito," "Indice numérico decreciente de frecuencias de la transcripción del manuscrito," "Concordancias lematizadas de la edición reconstruida," "Indice alfabético de frecuencias de formas de la edición reconstruida," "Indice numérico decreciente de frecuencias de formas de la edición reconstruida," "Indice alfabético inverso de formas de la edición reconstruida," and "Indice de rimas."

296.   Olsen, Marilyn A., ed. *Libro del Cauallero Cifar*. Madison: Hispanic Seminary of Medieval Studies, 1984.
Contains a concordance to this edition on 4 microfiches.

RENAISSANCE AND GOLDEN AGE

Current Bibliographies and Surveys

297.   Beardsley, Theodore S. "Spanish Literature." *The Present State of Scholarship in Sixteenth-Century Literature*. Ed. William M. Jones. Columbia: U of Missouri P, 1978. 71–100.
Extremely useful survey that updates Green's article (no. 299) through 1974. The bibliography is divided into "Bibliographies," "Surveys of Scholarship," "Catalogs and Surveys of Renaissance Texts," "General and Comprehensive Studies," "Specialized Studies," and "Linguistics."

298.   Fédération Internationale des Sociétés et Instituts pour l'Etude de la Renaissance. *Bibliographie internationale de l'humanisme et de la Renaissance*. Genève: Droz, 1966– .
Volumes 1 to 6 (for 1965–70) are arranged alphabetically by author with a subject index. Later volumes (for 1971–) have 2 parts, "Personages et œuvres anonymes" and "Matières," and include author indexes. Unlike the *MLA International Bibliography* (no. 8), this one also provides data on new editions of authors and translations of their works. It would be even more useful if it could be published with a shorter time lag. The volume for 1991 was published in 1995. It is the fullest current bibliography of European culture of the sixteenth and seventeenth centuries.

299.   Green, Otis H. "A Critical Survey of Scholarship in the Field of Spanish Renaissance Literature, 1914–1944." *Studies in Philology* 44 (1947): 228–62.
"This article is written from the standpoint of the history of ideas, sacrificing to this purpose an account of scholarship on the literature of the period, genre by genre, or author by author. . . . Renaissance is understood to cover the period from 1473 . . . to 1600" (228).

300.   "Literature of the Renaissance." *Studies in Philology* 36–66 (1939–69).
For three decades the standard bibliography in its field. Includes book reviews and material on phases of culture other than literature.

General Bibliographies

301. Delgado Casado, Juan, and Julián Martín Abad. *Repertorios bibliográficos de impresos del siglo XVI (españoles, portugueses e iberoamericanos). Con su fórmula abreviada de referencia.* Madrid: Arco Libros, 1993. 166 pp.
Contains 933 items that deal with printing in sixteenth-century Spain, Portugal, and Iberoamerica. Some are bibliographies of literary genres and authors of the century.

302. Moseley, William M., Glenroy Emmons, and Marilyn C. Emmons. *Spanish Literature, 1500–1700: A Bibliography of Golden Age Studies in Spanish and English, 1925–80.* Westport: Greenwood, 1984. 765 pp.
An extremely useful bibliography listing 11,191 studies published in English and Spanish. The first part is a classified bibliography of general works on the literature of the period; the second provides bibliographies of individual authors. The subject index could have been more detailed.

303. Simón Díaz, José. *Bibliografía de la literatura hispánica.* Vols. 4– . Madrid: CSIC, 1972– .
For the part of the alphabet covered, the fullest bibliography of period yet published. See no. 239.

304. ———. *Impresos del siglo XVII: Bibliografía selectiva por materias de 3,500 ediciones príncipes en lengua castellana.* Madrid: CSIC, 1972. xv + 926 pp.
Classified arrangement with author and subject indexes.

305. ———. *Impresos del siglo XVI: Novela y teatro.* Cuadernos bibliográficos 19. Madrid: CSIC, 1966. 20 pp.
Lists 125 items. ". . . ha parecido oportuno desglosar las primeras ediciones de obras novelescas y dramáticas" (3).

306. Strosetzki, Christoph. "Neuere Literatur zu Humanismus und Gelehrsamkeit im Spanien des 16. Jahrhunderts." *Romanistisches Jahrbuch* 32 (1981): 260–85.
Critical classified bibliographical essay divided into "Vorstufen im 15. Jahrhundert," "Antiker Einfluss," "Wirkung und Verbreitung des Humanismus," "Erasmus," "Buchdruck," "Zensur," "Inquisition," "Staat," "Gesellschaft," "Comunidades," "Armas y letras," "Laudres litterarum," "Poetik und Rhetorik," "Kommentare," "Ubersetzungen," "Bibelausgaben," "Sprachreflexion," "Humanisten und Medizener," "Villalón," "Mexía," "Servet," "Huarte," "Guevara," "Valdés," and "Vives."

307. Totok, Wilhem. "Renaissance in Spanien." *Handbuch der Geschichte der Philosophie.* Vol. 3, pt. 2. Frankfurt: Klostermann, 1980. 485–565. 5 vols. to date. 1964– .

Selective bibliography of the humanists, mystics, and philosphers of the period. Volume 5, published in 1986, deals with the eighteenth and nineteenth centuries.

Ballads and Poetry

308.   Bergmann, Emilie L. "Estudios sobre poesía lírica en los siglos de oro en los Estados Unidos." *Arbor* 116 (1983): 89–103.
Useful annotated and classified survey of contributions in the United States to the study of the lyric poetry of this period.

309.   Mauleón, Judith H. "Recent Work in the *Romancero nuevo*: Editions and Studies since 1950." *La Corónica* 5 (1976): 26–30.
Deals with Hispanic *romances* of 1580–1650.

310.   Piacentini, Giuliana. "Los pliegos sueltos." Fascicle 1 of *Ensayo de una bibliografía analítica del romancero antiguo. Los textos (siglos XV y XVI)*. Collana di testi e studi ispanici 4. Richerche bibliografiche 2: Investigaciones sobre el romancero antiguo. Pisa: Giardini, 1981. 151 pp.
"Concebido y preparado dentro de un programa de investigación y edición del Romancero antiguo, este Catálogo cumple por un lado su función de ir organizando una bibliografía razonada de los textos objeto del programa y que son los que se suelen considerar como la base más antigua y autorizada del género; por otro lado, incluyendo buen número de romances que caen fuera de la investigación antedicha, el Catálogo se propone como instrumento de consulta más general, en vista también de una fijación del corpus del Romancero antiguo que una reciente encuesta internacional ha propuesto a los especialistas de tal materia" (9). Includes 7 indexes.

311.   ———. *Ensayo de una bibliografía analítica del romancero antiguo. Los textos (siglos XV y XVI)*. Supp. to Collana di testi e studi ispanici 4. Ricerche bibliografiche 2. Pisa: Giardini, 1982. 39 pp.
Continues no. 310. Includes a list of errata (37–39).

312.   Rodríguez-Moñino, Antonio. *Diccionario bibliográfico de pliegos sueltos poéticos (siglo XVI)*. Madrid: Castalia, 1970. 735 pp.
Has 1,179 items. After a very valuable introduction, the work is divided into "I. Autores," "II. Anónimos," "III. Las series Valencianas del Romancero Nuevo," "IV. Pliegos poéticos fragmentarios," and "V. Apéndice." It has the following indexes: "Indice de procedencia," "Indice tipográfico," "Indice de autores," "Indice general de primeros versos," "Indice de tomos para cantar y bailes," and "Indice de personas y lugares."

313.   Simón Díaz, José. *Impresos del siglo XVI: Poesía*. Cuadernos bibliográficos 12. Madrid: CSIC, 1964. 55 pp.

314.   Aguilar Piñal, Francisco. *Impresos del siglo XVI: Poesía (adiciones)*. Cuadernos bibliográficos 12a. Madrid: CSIC, 1965. 16 pp.

These two bibliographies, no. 313 and the supplementary no. 314, provide data on 327 separately published works on sixteenth-century poetry.

Cancioneros

315.   Rodríguez-Moñino, Antonio. *Manual bibliográfico de cancioneros y romanceros. Impresos durante el siglo XVI.* Ed. Arthur L.-F. Askins. 2 vols. Madrid: Castalia, 1973.
Describes 250 items. Has the following indexes: "Indice alfabético de libros descritos," "Indice tipográfico," "Indice de procedencias," "Indice de primeros versos," and "Indice de nombres y lugares."

316.   ———. *Manual bibliográfico de cancioneros y romanceros. Impresos durante el siglo XVII.* Ed. Arthur L.-F. Askins. 2 vols. Madrid: Castalia, 1977–78.

Nos. 315 and 316 were published posthumously under the direction of Arthur L.-F. Askins. The publishers have treated them as a 4-volume set. No. 315 includes volumes 1 and 2; no. 316 includes volumes 3 and 4. Volume 3 describes fully 256 seventeenth-century cancioneros and romanceros. Volume 4 contains the following indexes: "Indice alfabético de libros descritos, autores y compiladores," "Indice tipográfico," "Indice de procedencias," "Indice de primeros versos," "Indice de nombres y lugares," and "Indice general."

Directory of Golden Age Specialists

317.   *Anuario áureo*. Criticón 57. Toulouse: France-Ibérie Recherche, 1993. 343 pp.
The most important sections are "Lista de investigadores (por orden alfabético)," "Lista de centros especializados (por países)," "Indice de investigadores (por países)," and "Indice de temas." Attempts to provide each scholar's date of birth, home and academic addresses, published works and works in progress on the Golden Age, and special interests in the period. Scholars are listed from Germany, the United States, Algeria, Argentina, Austria, Belgium, Canada, Spain, France, Great Britain, Ireland, Northern Ireland, Italy, Puerto Rico, and Switzerland.

Don Juan Theme

318.   Singer, Armand Edwards. *The Don Juan Theme, Versions and Criticisms: A Bibliography. West Virginia University Bulletin* ser. 54 (1965): 1–370. Cont. with 5 supps: *West Virginia University Bulletin Philological Papers* 15 (1966): 76–88; 17 (1970): 102–78; 20 (1973): 66–106; 22 (1975): 70–140; supp. to 26 (1980): 1–112.

The fullest bibliographies yet compiled on the Don Juan theme in all its ramifications in drama, fiction, movies, opera, ballet, and so on. Coverage is international. The main volume and the supplements contain more than 7,000 items, including creative works based on the theme. Critical studies are included.

319. ———. *The Don Juan Theme: An Annotated Bibliography of Versions, Analogues, Uses, and Adaptations.* Morgantown: West Virginia UP, 1993. xiii + 415 pp.

Classified bibliography of more than 3,000 items, divided into origins, versions, and a chronological list of versions. Singer has devoted a lifetime to the study of the Don Juan theme; to those interested in it, this series of bibliographies should be of inestimable value. Continues no. 318.

Drama

320. *Bulletin of the Comediantes* 3– (1951–).

A classified bibliography of studies on Golden Age dramatists appears in each volume with varying titles and compilers.

321. Reichenberger, Kurt, and Roswith Reichenberger, eds. *Das spanische Drama in Golden Zeitalter: Ein bibliographisches Handbuch* (title also in Spanish). Teatro del Siglo de Oro. Bibliografías y catálogos 2. Kassel: Reichenberger, 1989. xiv + 319 pp.

This bibliographical handbook for Spanish Golden Age drama is divided into "1. Generalidades," "2. El teatro de los siglos de oro," "3. Bibliografías de orientación temática," "4. Los autores y sus obras dramáticas," "5. El escenario y las representaciones," "6. La impresión de textos dramáticos," and "7. Catálogos." There is an "Indice temático" as well as an "Indice de autores modernos" and a "Registro de bibliotecas." Many of the entries are annotated and reviews are given.

322. Casa, Frank P., José M. Ruano, and Henry W. Sullivan. "Cincuenta años de investigación sobre el teatro español del Siglo de Oro en Norteamérica (1933–1983)." *Arbor* 116 (1983): 71–87.

Annotated, classified survey of the research done in the United States on the theater of this period.

323. Cilveti, Angel L., and Ignacio Arellano. *Bibliografía crítica para estudio del auto sacramental con especial atención a Calderón.* Teatro del Siglo de Oro. Bibliografías y catálogos 13. Pamplona: U de Navarra; Kassel: Reichenberger, 1994. 473 pp.

The 1,365 entries are well and critically annotated with special emphasis on the *autos sacramentales* of Calderón; however, other studies by other authors are included. Eva Reichenberger produced the 4 indexes: "Indice de obras," "Indice onomástico," "Indice toponímico," and "Indice temático."

324.   McCready, Warren T. *Bibliografía temática de estudios sobre el teatro español antiguo*. Toronto: U of Toronto P, 1966. xix + 445 pp.
Contains 3,957 entries. "La obra consta de los estudios (artículos, libros y reseñas) que se publicaron desde 1850 hasta 1950 inclusive, y que tratan del teatro español desde sus orígenes en la Edad Media hasta el fin del Siglo de Oro y principios del Neo-clasicismo, a mediados del siglo XVIII" (ix). Part 1, "Período formativo," covers the period from the beginning until Juan de la Cueva; part 2, "Período aureosecular," from Lope de Vega until José de Cañizares.

325.   Sumner, Gordon H. "Una bibliografía anotada de las comedias de santos del siglo diez y siete." Diss. Florida State U, 1980. 117 pp.
"Esta tesis doctoral es una bibliografía anotada de las comedias de santos del siglo diez y siete. Presentará más de doscientas cincuenta obras con documentación bibliográfica, amplificada donde posible por un resumen del drama" (1).
"La bibliografía anotada que sigue está ordenada por el nombre del autor. Incluye la información a continuación: 1. el autor. 2. el título de la comedia. 3. referencia bibliográfica de la primera edición o anotación que justifica la apariencia de la comedia en esta bibliografía. 4. ediciones modernas, si existen. 5. el protagonista o santos principales de la comedia. 6. un resumen de la comedia, donde ha sido posible" (17). Includes indexes of saints and titles.

326.   Madrigal, José A. *Bibliografía sobre el pundonor: Teatro del Siglo de Oro*. Miami: Universal, 1977. 56 pp.
Divides 569 unannotated items into general studies and sections on Lope de Vega, Calderón de la Barca, and Rojas Zorrilla. An author index would have been useful because items are arranged chronologically. "Se ha tratado de ofrecer una guía al estudioso de la temática del honor, no sólo en cuanto a lo que se ha escrito sobre las obras de teatro que dramatizan dicho tema, sino también en cuanto se ha opinado en estudios en España, al igual que en otros países, que se pueden considerar como fuentes, comentarios o disquisiciones ideológicos pertinentes a la cuestión del pundonor en el teatro del Siglo de Oro" (9).

327.   Wynne, Charles Edward. "An Annotated Bibliography of the Biblical Theater of the *Siglo de Oro*." Diss. U of Cincinnati, 1983. 284 pp.
"Chapter I deals with Old Testament drama of the *Siglo de Oro*. It is divided (as are all the chapters) into the following sections: manuscripts and editions, articles and doctoral dissertations. Chapter II deals with the New Testament drama of the *Siglo de Oro*, and the last chapter treats the *Autos sacramentales* exclusively. Our study concludes with an alphabetical index of the authors and a general bibliography" (*DAI* 44 [1983]: 1811A). Wynne's bibliography, the first on the topic, is marred by inconsistencies.

Fiction

328.   Eisenberg, Daniel. *Castilian Romances of Chivalry in the Sixteenth Century: A Bibliography*. Research Bibliographies and Check Lists 23. London: Grant, 1979. 112 pp.

The volume's main divisions are "General Works," "Individual Romances," "Texts and Studies on Chivalry," and "Chivalric Elements in Early and Golden Age Drama." It catalogs "the manuscripts and editions of the Castilian romances of chivalry published during the period 1508–1602, together with a number of works published later or still in manuscript, which were written during this period or shortly before it" (7). It also includes "secondary material . . . and some items dealing with their translations." The author's "intent has been to be as comprehensive as possible" (8).

329.   El Saffar, Ruth. "El hispanismo norteamericano frente a la novelística del Siglo de Oro." *Arbor* 116 (1983): 55–59.

Annotated, classified survey of important research done in the United States on the novels of the period.

330.   Fernández, Angel-Raimundo. "Situación actual de los estudios sobre novela corta del siglo XVII." *Actas del Séptimo Congreso de la Asociación Internacional de Hispanistas*. Roma: Bulzoni, 1982. 437–43.

Lists the few studies that exist on the short novel of the seventeenth century.

331.   Formichi, Giovanna de Gregori. "Saggio sulla bibliografia critica della novella spagnuola seicentesca." *Lavori ispanistici*. 3rd ser. Messina: D'Anna, 1973. 1–105.

332.   Greene, Vinson Fleming. "A Critical Bibliography of the Spanish Pastoral Novel (1559–1633)." Diss. U of North Carolina, 1969. 120 pp.

Contains 403 items concerning 20 pastoral novels. "With the exception of those entries that could not be located in time for inclusion in this bibliography, each entry contains a summary of that material dealing with the pastoral. The majority of the entries are followed by comments evaluating the works or articles in question . . ." (2).

333.   López Estrada, Francisco, Javier Huerta Calvo, and Víctor Infantes de Miguel. *Bibliografía de los libros de pastores en la literatura española*. Supp. 1 of *Dicenda*. Madrid: U Complutense, 1984. 205 pp.

Classified and partially annotated. Has "Indice de nombres," "Indice de títulos de las obras," and "Indice general."

334.   Laurenti, J. L. *Catálogo bibliográfico de la literatura picaresca (siglos XVI–XX)*. Kassel: Reichenberger, 1988. xi + 605 pp.

This bibliography of 4,509 items is an outstanding guide to studies on all phases of the picaresque novel. Few of the entries are annotated. There are name and subject indexes.

335.   Ricapito, Joseph V. *Bibliografía razonada y anotada de las obras maestras de la picaresca española*. Madrid: Castalia, 1980. 613 pp.
A fine bibliography on this genre by a scholar in the field. "La novela picaresca española" and the sections on *La vida de Lazarillo de Tormes, Guzmán de Alfarache*, and *Vida del Buscón* are the most important. There is an elaborate table of contents (607–13), and numerous cross-references throughout the bibliography replace a subject index. Biographical and critical material published before 1970 is almost always well annotated. The 2 appendixes list but do not annotate material published in the 1970s.

336.   Ripoll, Begoña. *La novela barroca. Catálogo biobibliográfico (1620–1700)*. Salamanca: U de Salamanca, 1991. 193 pp.
The author notes that "De cada autor . . . elaboramos un perfil biográfico, un listado de obras (primeras ediciones, reimpresiones, adaptaciones, traducciones . . . y, si los hubiere, mencionamos trabajos sobre ellos . . ." (13). Title pages of first editions are reproduced. "Recopilaciones y colecciones" is followed by 3 indexes. Of value for its survey of recent studies on the novel of this period is "Estado actual de los estudios sobre la novela del S. XVII." (14–21).

337.   Whinom, Keith. *The Spanish Sentimental Romance 1440–1550: A Critical Bibliography*. Research Bibliographies and Check Lists 41. London: Grant, 1983. 85 pp.
An annotated and critical bibliography by an outstanding scholar of the sentimental novel. Divided into 18 sections with 2 indexes. Includes manuscripts and printed works as well as critical studies.

Library Catalogs and Union Lists

338.   Laurenti, Joseph L., and Alberto Porqueras-Mayo. *The Spanish Golden Age (1472–1700): A Catalog of Rare Books Held in the Library of the University of Illinois and in Selected North American Libraries*. Fwd. N. Frederick Nash. Reference Publications in Latin American Studies. Boston: Hall, 1979. 593 pp.
This volume supersedes the series of articles, scattered in various journals, that the compilers wrote about this library's collection in the field. Items are alphabetized by author and elaborately described. There is an index of printers. "Printers' names and places of publications have been somewhat modernized in spelling. The titles of books are reproduced as they appear in the original imprints" (523).

339.   Biblioteca Nacional de Madrid. *Catálogo colectivo de obras impresas en los siglos XVI al XVII existentes en las bibliotecas españolas*. Provisional ed. 15 vols. Madrid: Biblioteca Nacional, 1972–85.
This union list should be extremely helpful to students of sixteenth-century literature and printing. It consists of photographic reproductions of library catalog cards and indicates which libraries have the books. It is hoped that later a much revised printed version of this set will become available. Despite the title there will

apparentely be a separate series for each century. No part for the seventeenth century has yet been published.

340.   Penny, Clara L. *Printed Books 1468–1700 in the Hispanic Society of America: A Listing.* New York: Hispanic Soc. of America, 1965. xliii + 614 pp.
A short-title catalog of the books the society's library has for this period.

Authors

341.   Parker, Jack H., and Arthur M. Fox, gen. eds. *Calderón de la Barca Studies 1951–1969: A Critical Survey and Annotated Bibliography.* [Toronto]: U of Toronto P, 1971. xiii + 274 pp.
The critical survey for these years (3–23) is followed by an annotated bibliography divided into editions and studies of Calderón's works.

342.   Reichenberger, Kurt, and Roswitha Reichenberger. *Bibliographischen Handbuch der Calderón-Forschung. Manual bibliográfico calderoniano.* 3 vols. Würzburger romanische Arbeiten 1. Kassel: Thiele 1979– .
"La presente bibliografía incluirá en el primer tomo las obras de Calderón, en el segundo los trabajos sobre el mencionado autor; el tercer tomo, además de los registros y de los cuadros sinópticos del material publicado, comprenderá descripciones de *sueltas*, en particular de los volúmenes del *Pseudo*-Vera Tassis" (1: 9).
Vol. 1: *Die Calderón-Texte und ihre Uberlieferung. Los textos de Calderón y su transmisión*, 1979, xiii + 832 pp. Divided into "Introducción: Observaciones críticas en torno a la investigación calderoniana. Los textos de Calderón y su transmisión: Observaciones preliminares" (also in German); "1. Comedias"; "2. Autos sacramentales"; "3. Obras cortas"; "4. Poesías menores"; "5. Textos en prosa"; "6. Antologías"; "7. Piezas desaparecidas"; "8. Obras supuestas"; "Indice de abreviaturas"; and "Addenda & corrigenda y epílogo." Cites libraries that have copies of the editions. Contains more than 3,352 items and a variety of tables, such as the second, "Vera Tassis-Bände in europäischen und Nordamerikanischen Bibliotheken" (30–31).
Vol. 2: Not published as of 1995.
Vol. 3: 1981, xiii + 838 pp. Contents: "Introducción: Calderón y el comercio español del libro" (by Don W. Cruickshank); "1. Listas contemporáneas de la obras de Calderón"; "2. Descripciones bibliográficas de obras sueltas"; "2.0. Advertencia preliminar, con tabla sinóptica de las sueltas hasta ahora descritas"; "2.1. Las sueltas de Calderón en la Biblioteca Universitaria de Friburgo de la Birsgovia" (by Edwin Stark); "2.2. Las sueltas de Calderón existentes en bibliotecas alemanas y austríacas" (by Roswitha Reichenberger); "2.3. Las sueltas de Calderón de la Universidad de Texas, Austin" (by Mildred V. Boyer); "2.4. Las sueltas de Calderón conservadas en bibliotecas inglesas e irlandesas" (by Edward M. Wilson and Don W. Cruickshank); "2.5. Indicaciones sobre partes y sueltas perdidas, especialmente de la antigua Biblioteca Estatal Alemana (Deutsche Staatsbibliothek)"; "2.6. Glosario de términos técnicos"; "3. Calderón: Vida y obra"; "4. La época de Calderón"; "Addenda & corrigenda al tomo I"; "Indice de títulos para los tomos I y III "; "Indice de abreviaturas."

343.   Flasche, Hans, and Gerard Hofmann. *Konkordanz zu Calderón. . . . Computerized Concordance to Calderón*. Autos sacramentales. 5 vols. Hildesheim: Olms, 1980–83.
Based on Angel Valbuena Prat's 1952 edition of *Autos sacramentales*.

344.   Cherchi, Paolo. *Capitoli di critica cervantina (1605–1789)*. Biblioteca di cultura 96. Roma: Bulzoni, 1977. 213 pp.

345.   Drake, Dana B. *Cervantes'* Novelas ejemplares: *A Selective Annotated Bibliography*. 2nd ed., rev. and exp. Vol. 1. Garland Reference Library of Humanities 243. New York: Garland, 1981. xxiv + 218 pp.
A classified, well-annotated bibliography of 554 items on the *Novelas ejemplares*, with an index of authors and one of subjects. Continued in nos. 346 and 347.

346.   ———. Don Quijote *(1894–1970): A Selected Annotated Bibliography*. Vol. 2. North Carolina Studies in the Romance Languages and Literatures 138. Chapel Hill: Dept. of Romance Languages, U of North Carolina, 1974. 267 pp.
Lists 321 items that are limited to "leading works dealing extensively with the Quijote, its meaning, its composition, style and structures, its principal characters, or its overall criticism over the years" (12).

347.   ———. Don Quijote *(1894–1975): A Selective Annotated Bibliography*. Vol. 3. Miami: Universal, 1978. 269 pp.
The 359 items include "leading indexes, bibliographies and studies on Cervantes vocabulary and grammar." As Drake notes, "Many of the works presented here seek to examine the related questions: 1. The true purpose of Cervantes in writing the Quijote and 2. The general attitude of the author" (6).

348.   Drake, Dana B., and Dominick L. Finello. *An Analytical and Bibliographical Guide to Criticism on* Don Quijote *(1790–1893)*. Newark: Juan de la Cuesta, 1987. x + 248 pp.
"In this main body of our study we have included all major publications of Spain, the rest of Europe and America, and to round out the picture, we have added many brief but interesting items" (ix). Excellent annotated critical evaluations of 536 references published between 1790 and 1893.

349.   Drake, Dana B., and Frederick Viña. Don Quijote *(1894–1970): A Selective Annotated Bibliography*. Vol. 4 extended to 1979. Lincoln: Soc. of Spanish and Spanish-American Studies, 1984. 214 pp.
Includes 562 well-annotated items divided into 18 sections, with an index of authors and one of subjects.

350.   Fernández, Jaime. *Bibliografía del* Quijote *por unidades narrativas y materiales de la novela*. Alcalá de Henares: Centro de Estudios Cervantinos, 1995. xvi + 1,343 pp.

This bibliography lists material in English, Spanish, French, German, Catalan, Italian, and Portuguese. Its emphasis is on twentieth-century publications. The 100 sections are classified bibliographies on each chapter or episode within a chapter. Indexes would have been helpful. While there is at least one reference to Graham Greene's *Monsignor Quijote*, there is no way to locate it. Pages 913–1343 are "Títulos y siglas. Referencia completa."

351.   Sánchez, Alberto. "Bibliografía cervantina." *Anales cervantinos* 1– (1951–).
A current annual classified bibliography of Cervantine studies with some annotations the length of short reviews. It is the best current bibliography of Cervantes.

352.   ———. *Cervantes: Bibliografía fundamental (1900–1959)*. Cuadernos bibliográficos 1. Madrid: CSIC, 1961. 16 pp.
A classified bibliography of 242 items.

353.   Simón Díaz, José. "Cervantes, Miguel de." *Bibliografía de literatura hispánica*. Vol. 8. Madrid: CSIC, 1970. 3–422.
Almost this entire classified bibliography of 3,767 items is devoted to Cervantes. Items 1–103 are a bibliography of Cervantine bibliographies.

354.   Fernández Gómez, Carlos. *Vocabulario de Cervantes*. Madrid: Real Acad. Española, 1962. x + 1,136 pp.
Based on the *Obras completas* de Cervantes (1917, 1923).

355.   Lacarta, Manuel. *Diccionario del* Quijote. Madrid: Alderabán, 1994. 237 pp.
A useful dictionary of proper names and of obsolete words and phrases found in *Don Quijote de la Mancha*.

356.   Torbert, Eugene Charles. *Cervantes' Place-Names: A Lexicon*. Metuchen: Scarecrow, 1978. xix + 181 pp.
"This work lists and explains the origins and meanings of toponyms in the complete works of Miguel de Cervantes Saavedra and indicates their possible significance to Cervantes and his works" (vii).

357.   Ruiz-Fornells, Enrique. *Las concordancias de* El ingenioso hidalgo Don Quijote de la Mancha. 2 vols. to date. Madrid: Cultura Hispánica, 1976– .
Vol. 1: A, 1976, vi + 321 pp.; vol. 2: B–Ch, 1980, 663 pp. Based on Martín de Riquer's edition of *Don Quijote* (Barcelona: Planeta, 1967). "La primera [parte] contiene la concordancia completa del Quijote cervantino, y la segunda la del Quijote de Alonso Fernández de Avellaneda" (12).

358.   ———. *Concordancias del* Quijote *de Avellaneda*. 2 vols.
Monografías 28. Madrid: Fundación Universitaria Española, 1984.
Based on the edition by Martín de Riquer (Barcelona: Planeta, 1967). Vol. 1: A–Manus. Vol. 2: Manzanares–Zutano; appendix A: Orden alfabético de palabras; appendix B: Orden numérico de palabras.

359.   Aquila, A. J. *Alonso de Ercilla y Zúñiga: A Basic Bibliography*. Research Bibliographies and Check Lists 11. London: Grant, 1975. 96 pp.
Divided into sections on editions and translations of *La Araucana*, other works by Ercilla, critical studies, and related material on *La Araucana*. Includes an index.

360.   Sarmiento, Edward. *Concordancias de las obras poéticas en castellano de Garcilaso de la Vega*. Madrid: Castalia; Columbus: Ohio State UP, 1970. 583 pp.
Based on Elias L. Rivera's edition of Garcilaso de la Vega's *Obras completas* (1964, 1968). Contents: "Lista de las palabras excluidas de las concordancias en orden alfabético" (13), "Concordancia" (15–541), "Palabras de la concordancia en orden alfabético con su frecuencia y el número de poemas en que aparecen" (543–78), "Lista de palabras incluidas en la concordancia en orden de su frecuencia excluidas las que aparecen menos de diez veces" (579–81), "Análisis numérico de los vocablos incluidos en las concordancias" (583).

361.   Richards, Ruth M. *Concordance to the Sonnets of Góngora*. Madison: Hispanic Seminary of Medieval Studies, 1982. 183 pp.
Based on Biruté Ciplijauskaite's edition of *Los Sonetos*.

362.   Hanke, Lewis, and Manuel Giménez Fernández. *Bartolomé de las Casas, 1474–1566. Bibliografía crítica y cuerpo de materiales para el estudio de su vida, escritos, actuación y polémica que suscitaron durante cuatro siglos*. Santiago de Chile: Fondo Histórico y Bibliográfico José Toribio Medina, Universitaria, 1954. xxxvii + 394 pp.
The 849 items are arranged chronologically and are fully annotated. The authors' purpose is "hacer fácilmente asequible la información relativa a todos los documentos de significación que se relacionan con la vida y las obras de Las Casas" (xxvii).

363.   Lazcano, Rafael. *Fray Luis de León: Bibliografía*. 2nd ed. Madrid: Revista Agustiniana, 1994. 679 pp.
This greatly revised version of the 1990 edition has the following parts: "Prólogo," by Cristóbal Cuevas, "Presentación," "Cronología de Fray Luis de León," "Siglas y abreviaturas," "Fuentes bibliográficas," "Manuscritos," "Ediciones de las obras," "Estudios," and "Fray Luis de León en los medios de comunicación social." There are 3 indexes: "Cronológico," "Onomástico," and "General." Items 787–2626 list critical studies and videocassettes that deal with Luis de León.

364.   Sabido, Vicente. *Concordancias de la poesía original de Fray Luis de León*. Granada: U de Granada, 1992. 485 pp.
This concordance is based on the edition by José Manuel Blecua, *Fray Luis de León. Poesía completa* (157–257). The "Indice de lemas" is followed by "Concordancias."

365.   Chiari, Maria Paola Miazzi, and Blanca Luca de Tena. *Don Agustín Moreto y Cavanna: Bibliografía crítica*. Biblioteca de teatro raro del barroco español 1. Milano: Ricci, 1979. 64 pp.

Lists Moreto's works in the Biblioteca Palatina of Parma. Fully describes the individual works, locating them in the libraries of Europe and the United States. Includes translations.

366.   Profeti, Maria Grazia. *Per una bibliografia di J. Pérez de Montalbán.* Verona: Inst. di Lingue e Letterature Straniere, 1976. xxxii + 547 pp.
Divided into "I. Opere non drammatiche o miscellanee"; "II. Commedie certe o attribuite pubblicate in raccolta"; "III. a) Rassegna analitica delle commedie certe" and "b) Rassegna analitica delle commedie di discussa attribuzione"; and "IV. Poesie sciolte, versi laudatori, varia." There are 6 indexes.

367.   ———. *Per una bibliografia di J. Pérez de Montalbán: Addenda e corrigenda.* Verona: Facoltà di Economia e Commercio, U degli Studi di Padova, 1982. 72 pp.
Supplements no. 366.

368.   Crosby, J. O. *Guía bibliográfica para el estudio crítico de Quevedo.* Research Bibliographies and Check Lists 13. London: Grant, 1976. 140 pp.
Most of the 1,005 items are not annotated; a few are known secondhand. Includes 3 indexes.

369.   Fernández Mosquera, Santiago, and Antonio Azaústre Galiana. *Indices de la poesía de Quevedo.* Barcelona: Promociones y Publicaciones Universitarias, 1993. 1,053 pp.
The concordance is divided into "Indice de las palabras de los textos base en la edición de Blecua," "Indice de las palabras de los textos considerados variante," "Indice de las palabras de los epigrafes," and "Diccionario inverso."

370.   Jauralde Pou, Pablo. "Addenda Crosby 'Guía . . . Quevedo.' " *Cuadernos bibliográficos* 38 (1979): 153–58.
A 70-item supplement to no. 368.

371.   MacCurdy, Raymond R. *Francisco de Rojas Zorrilla: Bibliografía crítica.* Cuadernos bibliográficos 18. Madrid: CSIC, 1975. 43 pp.
Divided into "Catálogo general de las obras de Rojas," "Manuscritos," "Colecciones especiales de comedias . . . ," "Comedias de Rojas en colecciones generales," "Ediciones y . . . sueltas," "Influencias," and "Estudios."

372.   Tusón, Vicente. *Lope de Rueda: Bibliografía crítica.* Cuadernos bibliográficos 16. Madrid: CSIC, 1965. 85 pp.
The first part is "Ediciones"; the second part is "Estudios, notas y juicios sobre Lope de Rueda."

373.   Sáez–Godoy, Leopoldo. *El léxico de Lope de Rueda. Clasificaciones conceptual y estadística.* Inaug. Diss. Bonn, 1968. 415 pp.
"Pretendemos aportar a un estudio lingüístico de la obra de Rueda: A.—Una clasificación del léxico en campos conceptuales. B.—Una ordenación alfabética

con indicación de variantes y sus frecuencias. C.—Una ordenación según niveles de lenguaje con indicación de las frecuencias de distribución" (10).

374.   Jiménez Salas, María. *Santa Teresa de Jesús: Bibliografía fundamental.* Cuadernos bibliográficos 6. Madrid: CSIC, 1962. 86 pp.
A classified bibliography of 1,924 items. Lacks author and subject indexes.

375.   Poitrey, Jeannine. *Vocabulario de Santa Teresa.* Colección "Espirituales españoles," Serie C: Monografías 15. Madrid: Fundación Universitaria Española, U Pontificia de Salamanca, 1983. 727 pp.
The introduction is divided into "El objetivo," "El fichaje," "Análisis y clasificación," "Criterios de transcripción," "Siglas y lecturas del vocabulario," and "Sentido y destino." "El blanco de nuestro trabajo ha sido constituir un vocabulario teresiano; voces y acepciones, modismos, tomados de los libros *Vida* y *Camino de perfección*, códice de El Escorial . . ." (7). Defines words with examples of their usage in these two works and lists the places where they are used.

376.   San José, Luis de. *Concordancias de las obras y escritos de Santa Teresa de Jesús.* Archivo silveriano de historia y espiritualidad carmelitana 9. Concordancias. Burgos: "El Monte Carmelo," 1965. 1,440 pp.
The author attempts to provide "un índice lo más completo que nos ha sido posible, de todas las materias, personajes y aun palabras o seudónimos empleados por la Santa, que ofrezcan algún interés." He notes that "para las citas hemos empleado la edición brevario del R. P. Silverio de Santa Teresa . . . " (8).

377.   Williamsen, Vern G., gen. ed., and Walter Poesse, comp. *An Annotated, Analytical Bibliography of Tirso de Molina Studies, 1627–1977.* Columbia: U of Missouri P, 1979. xv + 239 pp.
Besides the general editor, 12 contributors helped to annotate these 1,372 items. Each annotation is signed with the writer's initials. Includes an index of book reviewers and an index of subjects.

378.   Parker, Jack H., and Arthur M. Fox. *Lope de Vega Studies 1937–1962: A Critical Survey and Annotated Bibliography.* Toronto: U of Toronto P, 1964. xi + 201 pp.
A classified and annotated bibliography divided into editions and critical studies.

379.   Pérez y Pérez, María Cruz. *Bibliografía del teatro de Lope de Vega.* Cuadernos bibliográficos 29. Madrid: CSIC, 1973. 128 pp.
Divided into manuscripts; general editions; special editions; "Teatro menor"; an index of titles, "autos," and "comedias"; and an index of dances, "entremeses," and "loas."

380.   Simón Díaz, José, and Juana de José Prades. *Ensayo de una bibliografía de las obras y artículos de Lope de Vega Carpio.* Madrid: Centro de Estudios sobre Lope de Vega, 1955. ix + 233 pp.
A classified bibliography of 2,437 items.

381.   ———. *Lope de Vega: Nuevos estudios (adiciones . . .)*. Cuadernos bibliográficos 4. Madrid: CSIC, 1961. 16 pp.
Lists 221 items.

382.   Fernández Gómez, Carlos. *Vocabulario completo de Lope de Vega*. 3 vols.
Madrid: Real Acad. Española, 1971.
Vol. 1: A–D, cxx + 978 pp. Vol. 2: E–O, 979–1991. Vol. 3: P–Z, 1993–2968;
"Vocabulario de obras dudosas," 2971–3028. "Pretende ser una recopilación de
todos los vocablos y de sus acepciones utilizados por el escritor en verso más prolí-
fico español en todas las producciones que de él han llegado hasta nosotros" (iii).
The author also notes, "Cada voz va seguida de los textos donde aparece, según
sus distintas acepciones que están agrupadas según el orden establecido en el Diccionario de la Real Academia" (v).
The 4 appendixes are "I) Extensión de la producción de Lope, dividida en tres
apartados: a) Teatro, b) Prosa, c) Verso. II) Estadística . . . de las voces diferentes.
III) Resúmenes estadísticos, extensión total del conjunto de los escritos de Lope,
porcentajes y datos diversos. IV) 'Los muncos de Lope' (Recopilación de las palabras usadas por éste en diversas materias)" (1: vii–viii).

383.   Hauer, Mary G. "Critical Bibliography." *Luis Vélez de Guevara: A Critical
Bibliography*. North Carolina Studies in the Romance Languages and Lit-
eratures; Texts, Textual Studies and Translations 5. Chapel Hill: U of
North Carolina, 1975. 37–167.
Contains 295 well-annotated items, a subject index, and an index of comedies.

384.   ———. "An Addendum to *Luis Vélez de Guevara: A Critical Bibliography*."
Antigüedad y actualidad de Luis Vélez de Guevara. Amsterdam: Benjamins,
1983. 254–98.
Supplements no. 383 with 97 annotated items.

385.   Rozas, Juan Manuel. *El Conde Villamediana: Bibliografía y contribución al estudio de sus textos*. Cuadernos bibliográficos 11. Madrid: CSIC, 1964. 108 pp.
Divided into works and studies of the works.

Women in Golden Age Literature

386.   Salstad, M. Louise. *The Presentation of Women in Spanish Golden Age Literature: An Annotated Bibliography*. Boston: Hall, 1980. xix + 129 pp.
"The present work includes published studies on women as they appear in sixteenth and seventeenth century Castilian literature" (ix). Almost all the 372 items
are well annotated. Includes neither dissertations nor their published abstracts.

Eighteenth Century

Current Bibliographies

387. "Bibliografía dieciochista." *Boletín del Centro de Estudios del Siglo XVIII* 1–(1973–).
This bibliography deals with all phases of eighteenth-century Spain. The sections on "literatura" include "Bibliografía general," "Poesía," "Teatro," "Prosa," "Prensa," and "Bibliografía específica de personas." Many of the annotations are the equivalent of short reviews but are not signed.

388. *The Eighteenth Century: A Current Bibliography of 1970–1974*. Iowa City: U of Iowa, 1971–75, cont. for 1975– in ns 1– . Philadelphia: American Soc. of Eighteenth-Century Studies, 1978– .
This annual, now several years behind in publication, has sections on printing and bibliographical studies; historical, social, and economic studies; philosophy, science, and religion; the fine arts; literary studies; and individual authors. Spanish culture appears to be slighted in favor of English and French cultures. The excellence of the critical annotations, some almost review-length, makes this work an important bibliographical guide for the period.

General Bibliographies

389. Aguilar Piñal, Francisco. *Bibliografía fundamental de la literatura española: Siglo XVIII*. Colección temas 7. Madrid: Soc. General de Librería, 1976. 304 pp.
Divided into "Bibliografía," "Historias generales," "Monografías," "Géneros literarios," "Textos y antologías," "Relaciones con otras literaturas," and "Autores." Provides brief biographies, followed by biographical and critical studies, for each author.

390. ———. *Bibliografía de autores españoles del siglo XVIII*. 8 vols. to date. Madrid: CSIC, 1981– .
Vol. 1: A–B, 1981, 862 pp.; vol. 2: C–Ch, 1983, 836 pp.; vol. 3: D–F, 1984, 688 pp.; vol. 4: G–K, 1986, 936 pp.; vol. 5: L–M, 1989, 1,007 pp.; vol. 6: N–Q, 1991, 688 pp.; vol. 7: R–S, 1993, 926 pp.; vol. 8: T–Z, 1995, 706 pp. Vol. 9: Anónimas, and vol. 10: Estudios generales, have not yet been published.
This work is the fullest bibliography of eighteenth-century Spanish literature. Each entry provides a one- or two-word identification along with data on manuscripts, works by the author, critical studies, and the location of the works in at least one library. There are a variety of indexes: "Onomástico," "Materias," "Tipográfico," "Títulos de obras teatrales," and "Impresores," as well as "Bibliotecas consultades" and "Repertorios citados."
Belén Tejerina published in *Dieciocho* this series of additions to the first 2 volumes of this set: "Añadidos del catálogo de libros impresos de la Biblioteca Apostólica Vaticana a la *Bibliografía de autores españoles del siglo XVIII*. Tomo II (C–Ch)

de Francisco Aguilar Piñal, Comentario, notas, lista de obras" [8 (1985): 99–127];
"Añadidos . . . lista de obras" [10 (1987): 63–88]; "Añadidos . . . Piñal" [6 (1983):
138–46]; and "Lista de obras existentes en la Biblioteca Apostólica Vaticana que
faltan en la *Bibliografía* de Aguilar Piñal" [6 (1983): 147–64].

391.   Gies, David T. "El hispanismo norteamericano y el siglo XVIII español:
        Avances y contribuciones de los últimos cincuenta años." *Arbor* 116 (1983):
        105–15.
    Useful annotated list of contributions of United States scholars to studies of
the period.

392.   Tietz, Manfred. "La ilustración española y la investigación alemana."
        Dieciocho 4 (1981): 34–50.
    A bibliographical essay on publications by German scholars that appeared be-
tween 1929 and 1980. Includes a bibliography of 101 items (42–50).

Ballads and Poetry

393.   Aguilar Piñal, Francisco. *Romancero popular del siglo XVIII.* Cuadernos bi-
        bliográficos 27. Madrid: CSIC, 1972. xix + 311 pp.
    A listing of 2,104 *romanceros*, divided into "históricos, novelescos, festivos, reli-
giosos, teatrales," and 6 indexes.

394.   ———. *Indice de las poesías publicadas en los periódicos españoles del siglo XVIII.*
        Cuadernos bibliográficos 43. Madrid: CSIC, 1981. xv + 342 pp.
    Contains 5,422 poems indexed by first line that were found in 25 "periódicos
del siglo XVIII" (xiv). Provides an author index and an index of types of poems.

395.   Sánchez Romeralo, Antonio, Samuel G. Armistead, and Suzanne H.
        Petersen, with the collaboration of Diego Catalán, Soledad Martínez de
        Pinilla, and Karen L. Olson. *Bibliografía del romancero oral.* Vol. 1. Madrid:
        Cátedra Seminario Menéndez Pidal, 1980. xxv + 227 pp. 1 vol. to date.
    "The volume constitutes only a first edition—relatively complete, but not ex-
haustive—of bibliographical references to primary sources and studies of the Romancero in modern oral tradition, from 1700 to the present" (xvii). Lists 1,624
studies on the *romancero* in Spain, Portugal, Latin America, and in the Judeo-Spanish dialects. It has 7 indexes. This should be an indispensable guide to this field.

396.   Fernández Gómez, Juan F. *Catálogo de entremeses y sainetes del siglo XVIII.*
        Textos y estudios del siglo XVIII 18. Oviedo: Inst. Feijóo de Estudios del
        Siglo XVIII con la colaboración del Excmo. Ayuntamiento de Oviedo,
        1993. 758 pp.
    Provides data on 2,074 *entremeses* and *sainetes*. Items are arranged by title.

Drama

397. Herrera, Jerónimo. *Catálogo de autores teatrales del siglo XVIII.* Publicaciones de la Fundación Universitaria Española. Monografías 58. Madrid: Fundación Universitaria Española, 1993. lvii + 728 pp.
   Biobibliographical catalog of eighteenth-century dramatists. Pages 501–22 are a list of sources.

398. Lafarga, Francisco. *Bibliografía de impresos.* Barcelona: U de Barcelona, 1984. 318 pp. Vol. 1 of *Las traducciones españolas del teatro francés (1700–1835).* 1 vol. to date.
   "Este trabajo consiste, pues, en un catálogo de las traducciones y adaptaciones de piezas dramáticas francesas, impresas o realizadas en España desde 1700 hasta 1835" (11). Includes 674 entries, a section of notes, and indexes of authors, translators, and printers. A projected second volume should be a bibliography of manuscripts of Spanish translations of the French theater for the same period.

Fiction

399. Brown, Reginald F. *La novela española, 1700–1850.* Madrid: Dirección General de Archivos y Bibliotecas, Servicio de Publicaciones del Ministerio de Educación Nacional, 1953. 222 pp.
   ". . . que presento aquí es, pues, un catálogo de cuantos títulos y nombres de autores de novelas se han podido reunir en una extensa búsqueda por la literatura (original, crítica, periodística y bibliográfica) de la época considerada y la posterior, los cuales han sido cotejados con las fichas correspondientes de varias bibliotecas" (12). The chronological arrangement includes translations of Spanish fiction of the period into English, German, French, and other European languages. For fiction of the first half of the nineteenth century the work should be used in conjunction with Ferreras (no. 413).

400. Becerra, Berta. "La novela española, 1700–1850." *Boletín de la Asociación Cubana de Bibliotecarios* 7 (1955): 3–10.
   Additions to Brown's bibliography (no. 399).

Literary Criticism

401. Tucker, Scotti Mae. "Bibliography of Spanish Literary Criticism, 1700–1800." Diss. U of Texas, 1951. xxxix + 301 pp.
   Lists 536 chronologically arranged items and provides brief bibliographical descriptions based on the data on the title page. Tucker either indicates the library, in the United States or Europe, that has the copy she examined or refers to some other bibliography that includes an item she could not examine, giving "in most cases a brief account of its content" (vii). There is an author index.

Press

402.   Aguilar Piñal, Francisco. *La prensa española en el siglo XVIII: Diarios, revistas y pronósticos.* Cuadernos bibliográficos 35. Madrid: CSIC, 1978. xxi + 134 pp.

This volume lists 804 items divided into "Periódicos" and "Pronósticos," with a brief section of additions and an index of personal names. The first section is arranged by city of publication and then by year. Studies on individual publications follow the descriptions of the items discussed. An essential bibliography for those interested in eighteenth-century journalism.

403.   Domergue, Lucienne. "Apéndice 2: Catálogo de obras periódicas que no están comprendidas en el libro de Aguilar Piñal: *La prensa española en el siglo XVIII.*" *Tres calas en la censura dieciochesca.* Collection "Thèses et recherches" 9. Toulouse: Inst. d'Etudes Hispaniques et Hispano-américaines, U de Toulouse-Le-Mirail, 1981. 126–32.

Adds data on 41 periodicals not included in Aguilar Piñal's volume (no. 402). Because of censorship or for other reasons most of these periodicals were not published.

Authors

404.   Zubatsky, David S. *Spanish, Catalan, and Galician Literary Authors of the Eighteenth and Nineteenth Centuries: An Annotated Guide to Bibliographies.* Metuchen: Scarecrow, 1995. vii + 156 pp.

Provides a bibliography of bibliographies of almost 230 authors who lived during these two centuries. Contents or arrangement of the bibliography is stressed. Extremely helpful source for learning of bibliographies on a given author.

405.   Caso González, José Miguel, and Silverio Cerra Suárez. *Bibliografía.* Oviedo: Centro de Estudios del Siglo XVIII, 1981. xxvii + 384 pp. Vol. 1 of *Benito Jerónimo Feijóo. Obras completas.* Colección de autores españoles del siglo XVIII 1-I.

Lists 1,926 works by and about Feijóo published in the eighteenth, nineteenth, and twentieth centuries. Provides an index of "impresores y libreros españoles del siglo XVIII" mentioned in the bibliography and an index of proper names.

406.   Rick, Lillian L. *Bibliografía crítica de Jovellanos (1901–1976).* Textos y estudios del siglo XVIII 7. Oviedo: Cátedra Feijóo, Facultad de Filosofía y Letras, U de Oviedo, 1977. 299 pp.

A bibliography of 506 well-annotated items divided, according to the introduction, into 2 parts. "La primera es un ensayo bibliográfico en el cual he delineado las corrientes críticos sobre Jovellanos desde la muerte de éste, haciendo especial referencia a lo escrito durante el siglo actual. . . . La segunda parte de este libro es una bibliografía crítica de los estudios sobre Jovellanos" (13).

NINETEENTH CENTURY

Current Bibliographies

407.   "The Romantic Movement: A Current Selective and Critical Bibliography for . . ." (title varies). Comp. members of General Topics II and English IX of the MLA. Bibliography for 1936–48: *English Language Notes* 4–16 (1937–49); for 1949–63: *Philological Quarterly* 29–43 (1950–64); for 1965–78: supps. to *English Language Notes* 1–16.3 (1965–78).

408.   *The Romantic Movement: A Selective and Critical Bibliography for 1979–* . Vol. 1 comp. David V. Erdman, with the assistance of Brian J. Dendle, James S. Patty, and Leonard Schuyler. New York: Garland, 1980– .
This bibliography is an indispensable, selective, and critically annotated annual survey of important works on the Romantic movement. Earlier volumes dealt with the movement in both Spain and Spanish America. More recent ones are limited to the movement in Spanish literature.

409.   Elkins, A. C., Jr., and L. S. Forstner, eds. *The Romantic Movement Bibliography, 1936–1970.* . . . 7 vols. Ann Arbor: Pierian, 1973.
The annual bibliographies for these years have been reprinted in photo-offset. Volume 7 contains an index of authors and main entries, a reviewer index, a subject index, an index of personal names as subjects, and an index of categories.

Drama and Drama Journals

410.   Menarini, Piero, Patrizia Garelli, Félix San Vicente, and Susana Vedovato. *El teatro romántico español (1830–1850): Autores, obras, bibliografía.* Milano: Atesa, 1982. 261 pp.
"El presente trabajo está dividido en tres secciones. La primera comprende los repertorios de autores; la segunda de Obras; A) Originales, B) Traducciones, C) Sainetes, D) Obras no clasificadas. La tercera, las bibliografías; A) Romanticismo español, B) Teatro romántico español, C) Autores" (15). A very useful reference work for the study of the Spanish Romantic drama.

411.   Rodríguez Sánchez, Tomás. *Catálogo de dramaturgos españoles del siglo XIX.* Publicaciones de la Fundación Universitaria Española. Monografías 61. Madrid: Fundacion Universitaria Española, 1994. 685 pp.
Biobibliographical catalog of ninteenth-century Spanish dramatists. Pages 629–46 provide a useful guide to the volume's sources.

412.   Gómez Rea, Javier. "Las revistas teatrales madrileñas (1790–1930)." *Cuadernos bibliográficos* 31 (1974): 65–140.
Data are provided on 255 journals. This bibliography is divided into "Revistas exclusivamente teatrales" and "Revistas de teatro y otras materias." The annotations are extremely valuable.

Fiction

413.   Ferreras, Juan Ignacio. *Catálogo de novelas y novelistas españoles del siglo XIX.* Madrid: Cátedra, 1979. 454 pp.
Includes 2,158 authors, anonymous works, and collections. Provides brief biographical data on each author and then lists the author's works, many of which have not survived. "Fuentes" is a useful list of the compiler's sources (19–25).

414.   Labandeira Fernández, Amancio. "Adiciones a un *Catálogo de novelas y novelistas españoles del siglo XIX.*" *Cuadernos para investigación de la literatura hispánica* 4 (1982): 41–93.

415.   ———. "Adiciones y precisiones a un *Catálogo de novelas y novelistas españoles del siglo XIX.*" *Boletín Millares Carlo* 1 (1980): 287–321.

416.   ———. "Cubanos y puertorriqueños que deben figurar en un *Catálogo de novelas y novelistas españoles del siglo XIX:* Identificaciones y precisiones." *Anales de literatura hispanoamericana* 11 (1982): 51–73.
"El presente artículo ha sido dividido en cuatro grandes apartados: 1. Autores nuevos, y la. Autores nuevos no identificados. 2. Autores identificados. 3. Autores completados. 4. Precisiones" (51).

417.   ———. "Identificaciones en un *Catálogo de novelas y novelistas españoles del siglo XIX.*" *Revista de estudios hispánicos* [Alabama] 16 (1982): 379–90.

418.   ———. "Precisiones biográficas y bibliográficas en un *Catálogo de novelas y novelistas españoles del siglo XIX.*" *Cuadernos para investigación de la literatura hispánica* 6 (1984): 7–13.

The bibliographies by Labandeira Fernández (nos. 414–18) supplement and complement Ferreras's (no. 413).

Poety

419.   Rokiski Lazaro, Gloria. *Bibliografía de la poesía española del siglo XIX (1801–1850).* Vol. 1. Madrid: CSIC, 1988– . xi + 607 pp. 1 vol. to date.
Contains "Obras generales" and "Autores y obras anónimas" (A–Ch).

Press

420.   Cazottes, Gisèle. *La presse périodique madrilène entre 1871 et 1885.* Montpellier: Centre de Recherche sur les Littératures Ibériques et Ibéro-Américaines Modernes, U Paul Valéry, 1982. 339 pp.
Divided into "Présentation" and "Catalogues." The first section discusses the various kinds of newspapers and magazines published during this period. "Les revues madrilènes entre 1871 et 1885" is divided into "Revues littéraires," "Revues religieuses," "Revues politiques et satiriques," "Revues féminines," "Revues pour en-

fants," and "Revues éducatives et pédagogiques." An alphabetical list of this material (143–240) is followed by "Catalogue chronologique" and "Catalogue par orientation." Unfortunately, does not give location of files in Spanish and French libraries.

421.   Simón Palmer, María del Carmen. "Revistas españolas femeninas del siglo XIX." *Homenaje a Don Agustín Millares Carlo.* Vol. 1. [Las Palmas de Gran Canaria]: Caja Insular de Ahorros de Gran Canaria, 1975. 401–55. 2 vols.

After an interesting, useful introduction, provides data on 98 women's journals to which numerous important authors contributed.

Romanticism

422.   Jacobson, Margaret D. *The Origins of Spanish Romanticism: A Selective Annotated Bibliography.* Lincoln: Soc. of Spanish and Spanish-American Studies, 1985. 96 pp.

Following an introduction, the bibliography is divided into "Antecedents and Theoretical Foundations" and "The First Romantics." There are author and subject indexes, and the 209 items are carefully annotated.

Spanish Publications in France

423.   Vauchelle-Haquet, Aline. *Les ouvrages en langue espagnole publiés en France entre 1814 et 1833.* Pref. Gérard Dufour. Etudes hispaniques 9. Aix-en-Provence: U de Provence, 1985. 272 pp.

Often for political reasons certain works that could not be published in Spain were published in France. "Présentation" (17–91) discusses the reasons Spanish works were published in France and gives such data as subject matter, distribution, and censorship. "Catalogue" (95–231) is a list of 882 items arranged by year.

Authors

424.   Zubatsky, David S. See no. 404.

425.   Benítez, Rubén. *Ensayo de bibliografía razonada de Gustavo Adolfo Bécquer.* Buenos Aires: Facultad de Filosofía y Letras, U de Buenos Aires, 1961. 158 pp.
Classified, annotated bibliography of 299 items.

426.   Billick, David J., and Walter Dobrian. "Bibliografía selectiva y comentada de estudios becquerianos, 1960–1980." *Hispania* 69 (1986): 278–302.

An excellent classified, annotated bibliography of 198 items. Supplements no. 425.

427.   Ruiz-Fornells, Enrique, comp. and introd. *A Concordance to the Poetry of Gustavo Adolfo Bécquer.* University: U of Alabama P, 1970. xxi + 204 pp.

Based on José Pedro Díaz's edition of *Rimas* (Clásicos castellanos 158, Madrid: Espasa, 1963). Its appendixes are "Concordance to the Attributed Poems," "Concordance to the Variants of *Rimas*," "Word Frequencies—Alphabetical Order," and "Word Frequencies—Numerical Order."

428.   López, Aurora, and Andrés Pociña. *Rosalía de Castro: Documentación biográfica y bibliografía crítica (1837–1990)*. 3 vols. La Coruña: Fundación "Pedro Barrie de la Naza Conde de Fenosa," 1991–93.

An extraordinary critically annotated bibliography of Rosalía de Castro, who wrote in Spanish and Galician. Some of the annotations run to several pages; the table of contents is usually reproduced, and sometimes an article that is hard to annotate is reprinted. The material is arranged chronologically, and within each year there are up to 12 divisions. Volume 1 (xxv + 757 pp.) covers the years 1837–1940, volume 2 (xxii + 835 pp.) covers 1941–84, and volume 3 (xxxi + 829 pp.) covers 1985–90.

429.   Torres, David. *Studies on Clarín: An Annotated Bibliography*. Metuchen: Scarecrow, 1987. 204 pp.

Classified, annotated bibliography of 1,128 entries of material about Clarín.

430.   Valis, Noël. *Leopoldo Alas (Clarín): An Annotated Bibliography*. Research Bibliographies and Checklists 46. London: Grant, 1986. 279 pp.

Excellent classified, annotated bibliography that lists Clarín's works—including films, dramatic adaptations, and dance adaptations—as well as 1,380 entries of secondary material followed by 4 indexes.

431.   Cheyne, George J. G. *A Bibliographical Study of the Writings of Joaquín Costa*. Colección Támesis, Serie A-Monografías 24. London: Támesis, 1972. 189 pp.

Classified bibliography of 834 annotated entries.

432.   Billick, David J. *José de Espronceda: An Annotated Bibliography 1834–1980*. Garland Reference Library of the Humanities 224. New York: Garland, 1981. xiv + 184 pp.

One of the best author bibliographies for a nineteenth-century author. For each item there is a very detailed critical comment. Includes an index of reviewers and one of subjects.

433.   Sánchez, J. Denis. "Mariano José de Larra: A Tentative Critical Bibliography." Diss. U of North Carolina, 1974. 133 pp.

Annotates 441 studies of Larra's life and works. The bibliography covers the period 1837 to 1973.

434.   Scari, Robert M. *Bibliografía descriptiva de estudios críticos sobre la obra de Emilia Pardo Bazán*. Valencia: Albatros; Chapel Hill: Hispanofila, 1982. 142 pp.

Most of the 376 items are well annotated, and the subject index is very useful. The addenda of 41 items are unnumbered and do not appear in the subject index.

435. Clarke, Anthony H. *Manual de bibliografía perediana.* Santander: Inst. de Literatura José María de Pereda, Inst. Cultural de Cantabria, 1974. 148 pp.

"Está dividido en dos partes, y subdividido en varios apartados. Las dos partes generales abarcan: a) Descripciones bibliográficas de la obra de Pereda en su totalidad, obras publicadas y autógrafas, b) catálogo de estudios críticos y biográficos, con lista de las reseñas periodísticas publicadas en la sucesiva aparición de las novelas y otros escritos" (10). Includes an index of titles and concepts as well as an index of proper names.

436. Akers, John. "José María de Pereda: An Annotated Bibliography of Critical Works." *Mester* 9 (1980): 3–20.

This bibliography of 120 books, articles, and dissertations can be considered "an update of and adjunct to the bibliographic work on Pereda found in Anthony Clarke's *Manual . . .* " (3). (See no. 435).

437. Hernández Suárez, Manuel. *Bibliografía de Galdós.* Las Palmas: Excmo. Cabildo Insular de Gran Canaria, 1972 [colophon gives date as 1974]. xiv + 553 pp.

Classified bibliography of Pérez Galdós's works. "De todas las obras de Galdós hemos procurado dar las descripciones bibliográficas completas, en especial de las primeras ediciones y de las traducciones que hemos manejado, de las restantes señalamos sólo las referencias correspondientes" (xii). Omits some translations and material published in newspapers and periodicals.

438. Percival, Anthony. *Galdós and His Critics.* U of Toronto Romance Series 53. Toronto: U of Toronto P, 1985. ix + 537 pp.

"The twofold purpose of this study is to give a reasoned account of the vast body of Galdosian criticism and to provide a general bibliographical guide for use with other bibliographies devoted to specific aspects of the Spanish author and his writings" (vii). This bibliographic essay is divided into "The Biographical Approach"; "Literary History"; "Galdós: The Novels"; "Literature and Ideas"; "Galdós: Drama, Journalism, and Other Writings"; "Conclusions"; "Appendix: Contribution to a Study of Galdós Criticism circa 1975 to circa 1982"; "Notes"; "Selected Bibliography"; "Index of Galdosian Works and Characters Cited"; and "General Index." An extremely valuable bibliography on Galdós.

439. Sackett, Theodore Alan. *Galdós y las máscaras: Historial teatral y bibliografía anotada.* Verona: Faccoltà di Economia e Commercio, Inst. di Lingue e Letterature Straniere di Verona, U degli Studi di Padova, 1982. xi + 212 pp.

Divided into "Metodología," "Escrutinio de la crítica periodística," "Historia de la crítica teatral galdosiana," "Bibliografías generales de contenido teatral galdosiano," "Bibliografía anotada de libros, capítulos y artículos teatrales," "Bibliografía anotada de reseñas periodísticas." There are 3 appendixes and a general index. The 642 items are well annotated. Sackett writes, "La forma empleada para las anotaciones es una de paráfrasis; con pocas excepciones, no se cita directamente el material" (ix).

440.   ———. *Pérez Galdós: An Annotated Bibliography*. U of New Mexico Library Series in Bibliography 3. [Albuquerque]: U of New Mexico P, 1968. 130 pp.
Annotates 625 of its 725 items on the *Novelas españolas contemporáneas*.

441.   Woodbridge, Hensley C. *Benito Pérez Galdós: A Selective Annotated Bibliography*. Metuchen: Scarecrow, 1975. xi + 321 pp.
An annotated, selective, and classified bibliography of biographical and critical studies with author, title, and subject indexes.

442.   ———. *Benito Pérez Galdós: An Annotated Bibliography for 1975–1980*. Watertown: General Microfilm, 1981. iv + 218 pp. Available on microfilm or photocopied.
Supplements no. 441.

443.   de Coester, Cyrus C. *Bibliografía crítica de Juan Valera*. Cuadernos bibliográficos 25. Madrid: CSIC, 1979. 182 pp.
Bibliography of works by and about Valera divided into 20 sections. Annotations are very short, and many items are unannotated.

444.   Lensing, Arvella Hertje. "José Zorrilla: A Critical Annotated Bibliography, 1837–1985." Diss. U of Iowa, 1986. 304 pp.
An annotated bibliography concerning Zorrilla's life and works.

Twentieth Century
General and 1900–31

Dictionaries

445.   *Diccionario de autores iberoamericanos*. Ed. Pedro Shimose. Madrid: Ministerio de Asuntos Exteriores, Dirección General de Relaciones Culturales, Inst. de Cooperación Iberoamericana, 1982. 459 pp.
Provides short biographies, each signed by 1 of the 7 collaborators, and lists each author's principal works with their dates. Covers authors born between 1880 and 1930: "autores españoles de expresión castellana, gallega, vascuence (euskera) y catalana; hispanoamericanos de diecinueve naciones, portugueses, brasileños y chicanos (escritores norteamericanos de origen mexicano)" (7).

446.   Schneider, Marshall J., and Irwin Stern. *Modern Spanish and Portuguese Literatures*. Library of Literary Criticism. New York: Continuum, 1988. lxxxii + 615 pp.
This volume "presents a selection of critical opinions about some eighty twentieth century authors of the Iberian Peninsula, writing in Spanish, Catalan, Galician and Portuguese" (vii).

Bibliographies

447.   Beeson, Margaret E., María Castellanos Collins, Luis T. González del Valle, and Bradley A. Shaw. *Hispanic Writers in French Journals: An Annotated Bibliography.* Manhattan: Soc. of Spanish and Spanish-American Studies, 1978. 155 pp.

Provides data on approximately 2,500 items that deal with Hispanic culture in 18 journals published "between the 1890s and the late 1930s" (7).

448.   Carpenter, Charles A. "Modern Drama Studies: An Annual Bibliography." *Modern Drama* 17–34 (1974–91). Cont. by others, 35– (1992–).

Records, on an annual basis, "current scholarship, criticism, and commentary that may prove valuable to students of modern dramatic literature" (*Modern Drama* 18 [1975]: 61). The "Spanish" section, later changed to "Hispanic," covers drama of Spain, Portugal, Brazil, and Spanish America, regardless of language. Arranged by country and subdivided by dramatist.

449.   ———. "E: Hispanic Drama." *Modern Drama Scholarship and Criticism, 1966–1980: An International Bibliography.* Toronto: U of Toronto P, 1986. 160–210; continued by his *Modern Drama Scholarship and Criticism 1981–1990: An International Bibliography.* Toronto: U of Toronto P, 1996. 175–249.

Drama of Spain, items 1–1558; drama of Spanish America, items 1758A–2585. Continued by no. 448.

450.   Pownall, David E. *Articles on Twentieth Century Literature: An Annotated Bibliography, 1954 to 1970. An Expanded Cumulation of "Current Bibliography" in the Journal* Twentieth Century Literature *Volume One to Volume Sixteen; 1955 to 1970.* 7 vols. New York: Kraus, 1973–80.

Though the coverage of Hispanic literature is not thorough, the annotations are quite useful. The "Current Bibliography" in each issue of *Twentieth Century Literature* lists alphabetically by author the periodical literature on the authors covered. Items are briefly annotated. This bibliography should be consulted for material published since 1971.

451.   Sanz García, María de Pilar Cecilia. *Autores toledanos del siglo XX.* Toledo: Ahorras, 1983. 239 pp.

452.   Vilches de Frutos, María Francisca. "La generación del nuevo romanticismo: Estudio bibliográfico y crítico (1924–1936)." Diss. U Complutense, 1984. 514 pp.

Periodicals and Indexes

453.   Albert, Lorraine, and Nigel Dennis. "Literary and Cultural Periodicals in Spain: 1920–1936." *Ottawa Hispánica* 4 (1982): 126–70.

The introduction to this bibliography should be read carefully. Part 1 lists 200 studies that provide history and criticism of these periodicals; part 2 is "a catalogue of the publications themselves" (129).

454.   Celma Valero, María Pilar. *Literatura y periodismo en las revistas del fin de siglo: Estudio e índices (1888–1907)*. Madrid: Júcar, 1991. 898 pp.
Study of and indexes to 20 journals published between these years.

455.   Osuna, Rafael. "Revistas literarias y culturales españolas: 1920–1936. Bibliografía comentada." *Ottawa Hispánica* 7 (1985): 50–86.
Helpful annotations on about 150 items that deal with studies on the literary and cultural journals of this period.

Second Republic (1931–39)

456.   López-Guerra, Rebecca Jowers. "Apéndice E—Catálogo de las revistas literarias de la época republicana." "Neruda en España: *Caballo verde para la poesía*." Diss. Michigan State U, 1980. 408–60.
Provides data on 94 journals of the period. "El catálogo incluye datos sobre los directores y colaboradores de la revista y los géneros literarios publicados, el lugar, duración y frecuencia de publicación y algo sobre su orientación y su formato. . . . También incluimos información sobre la existencia de reimpresiones de algunas de estas revistas y una nota sobre los estudios críticos que se han dedicado a varias revistas aisladas" (409).

457.   McGaha, Michael D. *The Theatre in Madrid during the Second Republic*. Research Bibliographies and Check Lists 29. London: Grant, 1979. 105 pp.
Chronological arrangement for 14 April 1931–18 July 1934. Includes an index of titles and one of authors, translators, and adapters.

Franco and Post-Franco Period

Current Bibliographies and Annual Surveys

458.   *El año literario español*. 7 vols. (for 1974–80). Madrid: Castalia, 1975–81. Cont. by *Letras españolas* (1976–86, 1987, 1988, 1989). Madrid: Castalia, 1987–90.
This extremely valuable critical survey of literature is produced annually in Spain, with each section by an outstanding authority. The contents vary; the sections in the 1980 (1981) volume (184 pp.) are "La literatura española de los ochenta," "La novela," "La poesía en 1980," "Las preguntas al teatro," "La 'no ficción,' " "La literatura catalana," "Un año del teatro catalán," "La literatura en Andalucía," "La literatura en Canarias," "El año literario en Euskadi," and "El año cultural en el País Valenciano." The bibliographical data provided are incomplete,

with pagination never given. The *Letras españolas* volumes have the same format and coverage as the earlier volumes.

459. *Bibliography. Critical and Biographical References for the Study of French Literature since 1885.* Ed. Douglas W. Alden et al. Vol. 1– . Publisher varies. 1949– .

A current comprehensive annual bibliography useful for material on Arrabal, Buñuel, and other Spanish émigré authors who have lived in France or written in French or in both French and Spanish. Includes references, usually in French, not found in most other current bibliographies.

460. Modern Language Association of America. Spanish Section V. Bibliography Committee. *Bibliography of Contemporary Spanish Literature* 1–4 (1954–58).

Covers 1953–56. Divided into "Literary Genres," "Miscellaneous," "General Criticism," and "Catalan." Apparently planned to do for contemporary Spanish literature what the *French XX Bibliography* (no. 459) does for modern French literature.

Civil War

461. Montes, María José. *La guerra española en la creación literaria (ensayo bibliográfico).* Anejo de Cuadernos bibliográficos de la Guerra de España (1936–39) 3. Madrid: U de Madrid, 1970. 191 pp.

The "Repertorio bibliográfico" is divided into literary genres. The volume also provides indexes to *Hora de España* and *Jeraquía.*

462. Bertrand de Múñoz, Maryse. *La guerra civil española en la novela: Bibliografía comentada.* 3 vols. Madrid: Porrúa Turanzas, 1982.

The first volume has a prologue in both Spanish and English by Gabriel Jackson, an introduction (1–37), and an annotated bibliography divided into "Guerra presentida" and "Guerra vivida." The second volume is divided into "Guerra recordada" and "Guerra referida"; this volume also has 9 useful indexes, 2 appendixes, a critical bibliography of books and articles, a list of libraries with outstanding collections on the Spanish Civil War, as well as an index of names and an index of titles. Volume 3 is subtitled *Los años de la democracia.*

The annotation on each novel has 3 parts: the nationality and dates of the author, a summary of the novel, and a brief critical note. This outstanding bibliography covers not only Spanish authors (those who wrote in Spain as well as those who wrote in exile) but also authors from more than 20 other countries who wrote novels dealing with this civil war.

Dissertations

463.   Blanco Arnejo, María Dolores. "Repertorio bibliográfico de tesis españolas sobre literatura española contemporánea." *Anales de la literatura española contemporánea* 9 (1984): 245–83. Rpt. Lincoln: Soc. of Spanish and Spanish-American Studies, 1985. [39 pp.].
Classified bibliography of 339 "tesis doctorales y de licenciatura" accepted between 1954 and 1984 at 17 Spanish universities. Includes publication data for those later published as books.

Drama

464.   Zeller, Loren L., and Martha T. Halsey. "El drama español del siglo XX: Bibliografía selecta del año 1978." *Estreno* 6.1 (1980): 7–10. Cont. in *Estreno* for 1979 and 1980 in 6.2 (1980): 13–17 and 7.2 (1981): 5–9, 21–24; for 1981 in 9.1 (1983): 19–24; and for 1982 in 11.1 (1985): 30–36 and 11.2 (1985): 29–32.
Partially annotated bibliography divided into "Textos dramáticos," "Libros de crítica," "Artículos críticos," and "General." The compilers' names are sometimes reversed. Extremely useful for its reviews of recently published plays, book reviews, and dissertations. Considerably fuller than the lists in other current bibliographies (nos. 2, 4, 8–10, 220, 223, 227–28, and 458).

465.   Podol, Peter L., and Federico Pérez-Pineda. "El drama español del siglo XX: Bibliografía selecta del año 1983." *Estreno* 11.2 (1985): 29–32.

466.   ———. "El drama español . . . año 1984." *Estreno* 12.2 (1986): 75–78.

467.   ———. "El drama español . . . año 1985." *Estreno* 13.2 (1987): 32–36.

468.   ———. "El drama español del siglo XX: Bibliografía selecta [1986]." *Estreno* 14.1 (1988): 59–63.

469.   Podol, Peter L., and Arie Vicente. "El drama español del siglo XX: Bibliografía selecta del año 1987." *Estreno* 15.2 (1989): 29–36.

470.   ———. "El drama español . . . año 1988." *Estreno* 16.1 (1990): 34–39.

471.   ———. "El drama español . . . año 1989." *Estreno* 17.1 (1991): 31–36.

472.   ———. "El drama español . . . año 1990." *Estreno* 18.1 (1992): 46–51.

473.   ———. "El drama español . . . año 1991." *Estreno* 19.1 (1993): 38–45.

474.   ———. "El drama español . . . año 1992." *Estreno* 20.2 (1994): 38–44.

475. Valdivieso, L. Teresa. *España: Bibliografía de un teatro silenciado*. Lincoln: Soc. of Spanish and Spanish-American Studies, 1979. 120 pp.

For each of the 14 dramatists covered, Valdivieso provides a brief biography; a list of unpublished works, along with any data on their performance or difficulties with the censor; and a bibliography of published works, translations, "Escritos y declaraciones" (often interviews or statements of one kind or another), and critical studies.

476. Vilches de Frutos, María Francisca. *La temporada teatral española 1982–1983*. Supp. to *Segismundo* 8. Madrid: CSIC, 1983. 158 pp.

See comment on no. 477.

477. García Lorenzo, Luciano, and María Francisca Vilches de Frutos. *La temporada teatral española 1983–1984*. Supp. to *Segismundo* 11. Madrid: CSIC, 1984. 341 pp.

This survey and the preceding one are indispensable for the seasons covered. The 1983–84 volume contains 2 parts: "El teatro español de la temporada 1983–84" divided into "Algunas consideraciones generales" and "Tendencias y principales espectáculos," subdivided by city or region; and "Cartelera teatral de la temporada 1983–84" (97–311), also subdivided by city or region. There are indexes of authors, directors, and theatrical companies.

478. ———. "La temporada teatral español 1983–84." *Anales de la literatura española contemporánea* 9 (1984): 201–43.

Briefer version of no. 477.

479. Vilches de Frutos, María Francisca. "La temporada teatral española 1984–85." *Anales de la literatura española contemporánea* 10 (1985): 181–236.

Fiction

480. "Bibliography of Post–Civil War Spanish Fiction, 1978– ." *Anales de la narrativa española contemporánea* 4–5 (1979–80); *Anales de la literatura española contemporánea* 6–8 (1981–83).

". . . a basic research tool for those interested in contemporary Spanish narrative. Creative works, critical books and essays, reviews and other generalized items such as documents and interviews are indexed. All major periodicals and many of the more inaccessible publications are examined" (4: 139).

481. Compitello, Malcolm Alan. "The Novel, the Critics, and the Civil War: A Bibliographic Essay." *Anales de la narrativa española contemporánea* 4 (1979): 117–38.

". . . I have opted for a chronological approach, beginning with the books and dissertations and then analyzing articles on the subject. In the section devoted to the latter, I have made a secondary division: treating first articles written in Spain, and then foreign ones. I will also discuss studies of individual authors in which an evaluation of their work leads to significant critical opinions which I judge to be most relevant to the topic under discussion here" (118). An excellent critical survey.

482.   Martínez Cachero, José María. "Bibliografía crítica 'sobre' la novela española entre 1936 y 1980." *La novela española entre 1936 y 1980: Historia de una aventura*. Literatura y sociedad 37. Madrid: Castalia, 1985. 481–588.

An extremely valuable critically annotated bibliography of 333 items dealing with the Spanish novel for this period in general. There are no studies of individual authors and works. The 10-part index to types of material included is divided into "Bibliografía y cronología," "General," "Grupos y tendencias," "Influjos y relaciones," "Libros colectivos, libros misceláneos, antologías," "Lugares geográficos," "Motivos temáticos," "Panoramas y situación," "Premios y sociología literaria," and "Técnicas." Divided into articles, pamphlets, and books.

483.   Palomo, María del Pilar. *La novela española en 1961 y 1962*. Cuadernos bibliográficos 13. Madrid: CSIC, 1964. 69 pp.

Has a section on monographs and one on authors. Novels, arranged by author, are listed with their reviews, translations, and critical studies.

484.   Soldevila Durante, Ignacio. "Bibliografía fundamental." *La novela desde 1936*. Historia de la literatura española actual 2. Madrid: Alhambra, 1980. 456–70.

A critically annotated bibliography of important works on the novel since 1936. It is divided into "Panoramas generales," "Estudios publicados dentro de libros y en revistas," "Estudios sobre la novela española fuera de España," "Estudios sobre la novela de la guerra civil," "Estudios sobre autores reunidos en volúmenes," and "Estudios sobre aspectos técnicos y formales de la novela."

485.   Villanueva, Darío. "La novela española en 1979." *Anales de la narrativa española contemporánea* 5 (1980): 107–39.

486.   ———. "La novela española en 1980." *Anales de la literatura española contemporánea* 6 (1981): 219–40.

487.   Conde, Rafael. "La novela española en 1981." *Anales de la literatura española contemporánea* 8 (1983): 127–42.

488.   Martín-Maestro, Abraham. "La novela española en 1984." *Anales de la literatura española contemporánea* 10 (1985): 123–41.

These critical essays (nos. 485–88) discuss important novels published during the years covered.

Poetry and Poetry Journals

489.   Bonet, Juan Manuel. *Diccionario de las vanguardias en España 1907–1936.*
Madrid: Alianza, 1995. 654 pp.
Extremely important dictionary of the Vanguard literary movement in Spain.
It supplies data not only on major and minor Spanish authors but also on many
Spanish American ones. It provides hard-to-find information concerning the liter-
ary journals of the movement. The bibliographical data could be more complete.

490.   Agulló y Cobo, Mercedes. *La poesía española en 1961.* Cuadernos bibliográficos 8. Madrid: CSIC, 1965. 88 pp.

491.   ————. *La poesía española en 1962.* Cuadernos bibliográficos 17. Madrid:
CSIC, 1965. 88 pp.

The first section of each of these volumes (nos. 490 and 491) deals with
poetry in the Spanish language. The main divisions are "Revistas de poesía,"
"Revistas literarias, de informaciones, culturales, religiosas, etc. que habitual-
mente publican poesías," "Concursos, juegos florales, premios," "Antologías,"
"Estudios," "Temas," and "Autores."

492.   González Herrán, J. M., Y. Novo Villaverde, M. Santos Zas, and M. A.
Gómez Segade. "La poesía española en 1984." *Anales de la literatura española contemporánea* 10 (1985): 143–80.
After an introduction, briefly reviews 35 volumes of poetry. Includes a bibliography of 150 books of poems published during the year (175–80).

493.   Perna, Michael L., ed. *Twentieth Century Spanish Poets: First Series.* Dictionary of Literary Biography 108. Detroit: Gale, 1991. 400 pp.
Provides biographical, critical, and bibliographical data on 29 twentieth-century Spanish poets. Each author is discussed by an expert; the sketches vary in
length from 7 pages to almost 30. Only 3 of the poets are women.

494.   Rubio, Fanny. *Revistas poéticas españolas, 1939–1975.* Madrid: Turner, 1976.
550 pp.
Bibliographical data on Spanish magazines that publish poetry are scattered
throughout the text. It is a pity that there is no general bibliography of studies on
the individual journals; such information must be gleaned from the footnotes. Of
special interest is "Indice regional de las revistas literarias de posguerra (1939–75)"
(495–513).

495.   Rubio, Fanny, and José Luis Falcó. "Apéndice biobibliográfico." *Poesía española contemporánea (1938–1980).* Clásicos Alhambra 20. Madrid: Alhambra, 1981. 385–423.

Brief bibliographies are provided for 94 poets. More useful for lesser-known poets than for those better known.

496. Siebenmann, Gustav. "Bibliografía cronológica de los libros de poesía aparecidos entre 1883 y 1971." *Los estilos poéticos en España desde 1900*. Biblioteca Románica Hispánica, Estudios y Ensayos 183. Madrid: Gredos, 1973. 491–530.
Provides barest bibliographical data for 77 poets. See also "Apéndice II: Bibliografía de obras consultadas, (B) Estudios" (538–64).

497. Winfield, Jerry Phillips, ed. *Twentieth-Century Spanish Poets: Second Series*. Dictionary of Literary Biography 134. Detroit: Gale, 1994. 410 pp.
Same format as Perna (no. 493). Discusses 23 Spanish and Catalan poets.

Authors

498. Zubatsky, David S. *Spanish, Catalan, and Galician Literary Authors of the Twentieth Century. An Annotated Guide to Bibliographies*. Metuchen: Scarecrow, 1992. 192 pp. Rev. of "An Annotated Bibliography of Twentieth-Century Catalan and Spanish Author Bibliographies." *Hispania* 61 (1978): 654–79.
Comprehensive listing of bibliographies of slightly more than 100 authors. Annotations usually provide an outline of the bibliography's arrangement.

499. Cabey Riley, Julia Elizabeth. *Bibliografía de algunos poetas andaluces de posguerra*. Madrid: Dept. de Bibliografía, U Complutense, 1984. vi + 789 pp.
Bibliographies of José Luis Cano, Juan Ruiz Peña, Ricardo Molina, Leopoldo de Luis, Rafael Montesinos, Alfonso Canales, José María Caballero Bonald, Fernando Quiñones, Manuel Mantero, Aquilino Duque, Mariano Roldán, Julia Uceda, and Joaquín Caro Romero.

500. Albalá Hernández, Paloma. *Bibliografía de Alfonso Albalá*. Trabajos del Dept. de Bibliografía, serie A: Escritores contemporáneos 5. Madrid: U Complutense, 1982. 22 pp.
Items 1–235 are divided into "Obra inédita," "Ediciones," "Poemas sueltos," "Obra crítica" (in chronological order), and "Secciones fijas en la prensa diaria" (in chronological order); items 236–39 are interviews; and items 240–49 are sketches about Albalá.

501. García Gallarín, Consuelo. *Vocabulario temático y característico de Pío Baroja*. Madrid: Verbum, 1991. 174 pp.
The "Vocabulario característico" (17–74) is an alphabetical listing of the vocabulary, along with etymology, meaning, and examples from a Baroja text. The "Vocabulario temático" (75–166) divides the vocabulary by topic, with at least one citation of the word's use. Pages 167–74 are a bibliography.

502.   Smith, Paul. *Vicente Blasco Ibáñez: An Annotated Bibliography*. Research Bibliographies and Check Lists 14. London: Grant, 1976. 127 pp.
The first section is a classified but unannotated bibliography of the works of Blasco Ibáñez. It includes 110 English translations of his post-1894 fiction, films and dramas based on his novels, and his own translations from the French. The second section annotates almost 750 items about Blasco Ibáñez.

503.   Peña Múñoz, Manuel. *Bibliografía de Carmen Bravo-Villasante*. Madrid: [Artes General], 1985. 67 pp.
A classified bibliography of material by and about Spain's outstanding authority on children's literature. Divided into biographies, essays, translations with prologues, editions with prologues, notes, articles, poetry, short stories, literature for children, interviews with her, articles about her, and reviews of her books.

504.   Forys, M. *Antonio Buero Vallejo and Alfonso Sastre: An Annotated Bibliography*. Metuchen: Scarecrow, 1988. 227 pp.
Classified, partially annotated bibliography of studies on Buero Vallejo (1–47), 1512 items, and Sastre (149–95), items 1513–1965.

505.   Calvo-Sotelo Ibáñez-Martín, Pedro. *Bibliografía de Joaquín Calvo Sotelo*. Trabajos del Dept. de Bibliografía, serie A: Escritores contemporáneos 3. Madrid: U Complutense, 1981. 12 pp.
A bibliography of 112 items divided into manuscripts, dramatic works, miscellaneous, translations, and studies on Calvo Sotelo's works.

506.   Suárez Solís, Sara. *El léxico de José Camilo Cela*. Estudios de literatura contemporánea 4. Madrid: Alfaguara, 1969. 565 pp.

507.   Sáez Sánchez, Carmen. *Bibliografía de Jorge Cela Trulock*. Trabajos del Dept. de Bibliografía, serie A: Escritores contemporáneos 4. Madrid: U Complutense, 1981. 12 pp.
A bibliography of 125 items divided into novels, short stories, articles and reviews, and studies on Cela's works.

508.   Fuentes Molla, Rafael, and Carmen Rodríguez Santos. *Bibliografía de "Corpus Barga"* [Andrés García de la Barga y Gómez de la Serna]. Trabajos del Dept. de Bibliografía, serie A: Escritores contemporáneos 8. Madrid: U Complutense, 1982. 55 pp.
A bibliography of 1,358 items divided into novels, poems, articles, translations, and material about "Corpus Barga." Unfortunately the publications he wrote in exile, mostly in Peru, are not included.

509.   Anderson, Andrew A. "Bibliografía lorquiana reciente. . . ." *Boletín de la Fundación Federico García Lorca* 1– (1986–).
Extensive current García Lorca bibliography with the following sections: "I. Obras y ediciones de García Lorca," "II. Libros sobre la vida y obra de García Lorca," "III. Tesis doctorales, tesinas y trabajos inéditos," "IV. Artículos biográficos y críticos en revistas y libros," "V. Reseñas."

510.   *Catálogo general de los fondos documentales de la Fundación Federico García Lorca.* 2 vols. Madrid: Ministerio de Cultura, Dirección de Archivos Estatales, Fundación Federico García Lorca, 1992–93.
Vol. 1: *Manuscritos de obra poética de madurez bajo la dirección de Christian de Paepe*, 1992, 201 pp. Contains 264 numbered entries, though some are merely cross-references.
Vol. 2: *Manuscritos de la obra poética juvenil (1917–1919)*, 1993, 158 pp. Contains 160 entries.

511.   Colecchia, Francesca. *García Lorca: An Annotated Primary Bibliography.* New York: Garland, 1982. xxiv + 281 pp.
Almost 40 compilers produced this classified bibliography of Lorca's works, which includes translations.

512.   ———, ed. *García Lorca: A Selectively Annotated Bibliography of Criticism.* New York: Garland, 1979. xxii + 313 pp.
Almost 40 compilers produced this classified bibliography of 1,882 items, many of which are annotated.

These volumes (nos. 511 and 512) are the best bibliographies now available on Lorca.

513.   Pollin, Alice N. *A Concordance to the Plays and Poems of Federico García Lorca.* Programmed by Daniel C. Weinberger (plays) and Philip H. Smith, Jr. (poems). Ithaca: Cornell UP, 1975. xix + 1,180 pp.

514.   *García Lorca Review* 1–11 (1973–83).
Over the years this journal published a series of bibliographies on Lorca, with an emphasis on translations and critical studies published outside Spain.

515.   López-Vidriero, María Luisa. *Bibliografía de E. Giménez Caballero.* Trabajos del Dept. de Bibliografía, serie A: Escritores contemporáneos 6. Madrid: U Complutense, 1982. 50 pp.
Lists 1,422 items divided into books, prologues, translations, articles, interviews, and material about Giménez Caballero.

516.   López Hernández, Marcela. *Vocabulario de la obra poética de Miguel Hernández.* Extremadura: U de Extremadura, 1992. 711 pp.
This *Vocabulario* is based on Leopoldo de Luis, *Miguel Hernández: Obra poética completa* (Madrid: Zero, 1979, 5th printing), and A. Sánchez Vidal, *Miguel Hernández, Poesías completas* (Madrid: Aguilar, 1979). Defines words and cites their use in Hernández's works. Of special interest is "Inventario de palabras no incluidas en el DRAE ni en el DUE."

517.   Corona Marzol, Gonzalo. *Bibliografía de José Hierro Real.* Zaragoza: Pedro Garcés de Carinena, 1988. 62 pp.

Lists 601 items by and about Hierro arranged chronologically.

518. Campoamor González, Antonio. *Bibliografía general de Juan Ramón Jiménez*. Madrid: Taurus, 1983. 724 pp.
Classified bibliography of 9,070 items by and about Jiménez. Besides the usual material one finds in an author bibliography, there are "Colecciones de poesías y poemas sueltos," "Poemas de J.R.J., en música," and "Grabaciones," as well as "Actos en homenaje a J.R.J.," "Iconografía," "Emisiones por radio y televisión," "Varios," "Filatelia y numismática," "Miscelánea," and "Adaptaciones teatrales y cinematográficas." It includes material published in 1982. There is no index.

519. [Carrión Gútiez, Manuel, ed.]. *Bibliografía machadiana (Bibliografía para su centenario)*. Panoramas bibliográficos de España 2. Madrid: Biblioteca Nacional, 1976. 292 pp.
A highly classified bibliography of works by and about the brothers Antonio and Manuel Machado. The 4,649 items include not only books, articles, and dissertations but also book reviews, interviews, translations, and poems dedicated to the Machados.

520. Sippy, Carol. "A Bibliographical Guide to Critical Works on Antonio Machado y Ruiz." Diss. U of New Mexico, 1978. xxii + 458 pp.
The first part is a chronologically arranged bibliography divided into "Early Criticism: 1930–1949" and "Recent Criticism: 1950–1977." The next 5 parts can be considered an annotated, classified bibliography of Machado criticism; part 2, "A Survey of Preliminary Research," is divided into "Early Criticism," "Introductory and Overview Studies," and "Machado in Literary History"; part 3, "The Major Works," has sections on *Soledades, galerías y otros poemas, Campos de Castilla*, and *Nuevas canciones*; part 4, "Ideology," is divided into "Poetics," "Philosophy," and "Popularism"; part 5 deals with Machado's biography and theater; and part 6 gives the dissertation's conclusions. The 41 appendixes make the bibliography easier to use.

521. Finzi, Alessandro, Ferdinando Rosselli, and Antonio Zampolli. *Concordancias y frecuencias de uso en el léxico poético de Antonio Machado*. Roma: CNR, 1978. 904 pp.

522. Landeira, Ricardo. *An Annotated Bibliography of Gabriel Miró (1900–1978)*. Lincoln: Soc. of Spanish and Spanish-American Studies, 1978. xx + 200 pp.
Partially annotated and classified bibliography of approximately 2,600 items by and about Miró.

523. Fernández Valladares, Mercedes. *Bibliografía de Rafael Morales*. Trabajos del Dept. de Bibliografía, serie A: Escritores contemporáneos 1. Madrid: U Complutense, 1981. 24 pp.
A list of 214 items divided into bibliographies, complete works, works, separately published poems, criticism, translations, interviews, and critical studies.

524.   Donoso, Antón, and Harold C. Raley. *José Ortega y Gasset: A Bibliography of Secondary Sources*. Bowling Green: Philosophy Documentation Center, Bowling Green State U, 1986. xxviii + 449 pp.
Many of the 4,125 entries are incomplete; subject index (407–49) seems quite useful.

525.   Rukser, Ugo. *Bibliografía de Ortega*. Estudios orteguianos 3. Madrid: Revista de Occidente, 1971. 437 pp.
Material by and about Ortega arranged by country.

526.   Ruiz-Fornells, Enrique. *A Concordance to the Poetry of Leopoldo Panero*. University: U of Alabama P, 1978. viii + 725 pp.
Based on Panero's *Obras completas* (Madrid: Nacional, 1973).

527.   Best, Marigold. *Ramón Pérez de Ayala: An Annotated Bibliography of Criticism*. Research Bibliographies and Check Lists 33. London: Grant, 1980. 81 pp.
Comments on 546 items divided into books and studies in books, studies in periodicals, studies in newspapers and dissertations, and unpublished theses.

528.   Doméncha Mira, Francisco J. *Bibliografía de Dionisio Ridruejo*. Trabajos del Dept. de Bibliografía, serie A: Escritores contemporáneos 7. Madrid: U Complutense, 1982. 36 pp.
Classifies 705 items into bibliographies; complete works; separately published works, including prologues in the works of others; contributions to periodicals; materials about the author; and an appendix.

529.   King, Charles I. *Ramón J. Sender: An Annotated Bibliography*. Metuchen: Scarecrow, 1976. xiv + 287 pp.
Classified and annotated bibliography of Sender's works in Spanish and in English translation as well as critical studies and reviews in these two languages.

530.   ———. "Partial Addendum (1975–1982) to *Ramón Sender: An Annotated Bibliography* (1928–1975)." *Hispania* 66 (1983): 209–16.
Supplements no. 529. Divided into "Reprints or Ediciones nuevas" and "New Books, 1975–1982." Includes reviews of books published between 1975 and 1982 as well as reviews omitted from the book.

531.   Vilches de Frutos, María Francisca. "Bibliografía crítica sobre el primer Sender." *Censo de escritores al servicio de los Austrias y otros estudios bibliográficos*. Madrid: CSIC, 1983. 121–42.
Classified and annotated bibliography of 157 items. Includes reviews omitted by King (see nos. 529 and 530), as well as biographical and critical studies published through 1982.

532.	Rodríguez, Rafael, and Ponga Salamanca. *Bibliografía de Mahmud Sobh.* Trabajos del Dept. de Bibliografía, serie A: Escritores contemporáneos 3. Madrid: U Complutense, 1981. 13 pp.
Classifies 124 items into unpublished works, separately published works, interviews, and material about Sobh.

533.	Fernández, Pelayo H. *Bibliografía crítica de Miguel de Unamuno (1888–1975).* Madrid: Porrúa Turanzas, 1976. xxxix + 336 pp.
Lists 4,794 books, articles, dissertations, reviews, interviews, poems dedicated to Unamuno, and so on. "He adoptado el método cronológico-alfabético con índice onomástico" (xi). Despite the title, most of the items are not annotated and many are incomplete.

534.	García Blanco, Manuel. "Crónica unamuniana, 1937–1947." *Cuadernos de la Cátedra Miguel de Unamuno* 1 (1948): 103–26.

535.	———. "Crónica unamuniana. . . ." *Cuadernos de la Cátedra Miguel de Unamuno* 2–14/15 (1951–64/65).
Classified bibliographies of material by and about Unamuno. Many items have very useful annotations, sometimes of review length.

536.	Ibáñez de García Blanco, Leo. "Bibliografía unamuniana." *Cuadernos de la Cátedra Miguel de Unamuno* 19–23 (1969–73).
An unannotated, classified bibliography of material by and about Unamuno for the years covered.

537.	Serrano Alonso, Javier, and Amparo de Juan Bolufer. *Bibliografía general de Ramón del Valle-Inclán.* Santiago de Compostela: U de Santiago de Compostela, 1995, 543 pp.
This volume is a highly classified bibliography of works both by and about Valle-Inclán. Pages 29–278 are the "Bibliografía primaria," while the "Bibliografía secundaria," pages 285–513, consists of more than 3,500 entries. It is more complete than Joaquín del Valle-Inclán and Javier del Valle-Inclán, *Bibliografía de Don Ramón María del Valle-Inclán* (Pretextos 237. Valencia: Pretextos, 1995. 235 pp.), which lists only Valle-Inclán's works. It provides data on 974 items. The majority of the entries are arranged in chronological order; translations are arranged by language.

WOMEN AUTHORS

538.	Alarcón, Norma, and Sylvia Kossnar. *Bibliography of Hispanic Women Writers* (from the *MLA International Bibliography* [1922–78]). Chicano-Riqueño Studies Bibliography Series 1. Bloomington: Chicano-Riqueño Studies, 1980. iv + 86 pp.

This bibliography, marred by inconsistencies, was developed when "several individuals first thought of evolving a course about Women in Hispanic Literature . . ." (Preface, n. pag.). It is extremely useful for its time-saving qualities; it provides data on almost 150 women writers covered in the MLA bibliographies.

539.   Galerstein, Carolyn L. *Women Writers of Spain: An Annotated Biobibliographical Guide*. Non-Castilian materials ed. Kathleen McNerney. Bibliographies and Indexes in Women's Studies 2. New York: Greenwood, 1986. xxi + 389 pp.

About 80 critics provide biographical data (usually extremely brief) on women writers of Spain, regardless of the language in which they wrote or write. After each biography, there is an annotated listing of the author's belles lettres published as books. Writers are not included unless information can be added that is not found in Serrano y Sanz (no. 542). Indispensable for lesser-known women writers. Better editing would have caught the three spellings of Milan and would have insisted on greater consistency in the data provided on the authors' works.

540.   Levine, Linda Gould, Ellen Engleson Marson, and Gloria Feiman Waldman, eds. *Spanish Women Writers: A Bio-bibliographical Source Book*. Westport: Greenwood, 1993. xxxiv + 596 pp.

There are articles on 50 women authors ranging from the sixteenth century to the present. Each sketch is divided into "Biography," "Major Themes," and "Survey of Criticism." The bibliography is divided into the author's works, translations into English, and biographical and critical works about the author. Includes title and subject indexes as well as a list of authors by date of birth and a list of works available in English translation.

541.   McNerney, Kathleen, and Cristina Enríquez de Salamanca, eds. *Double Minorities of Spain: A Bio-bibliographic Guide to Women Writers of the Catalan, Galician, and Basque Countries*. New York: MLA, 1994. 421 pp.

This volume provides data on 421 Catalans, 31 Galicians, and 20 Basques and gives brief biographies and general descriptions of their works. The bibliographical sections list the authors' books, publications in periodicals and newspapers, chapters in books, translations into Castilian or English, and critical studies on them.

542.   Serrano y Sanz, Manuel. *Apuntes para una biblioteca de escritoras españolas desde el año 1401 al 1833*. 4 vols. Madrid: Sucesores de Rivadeneyra, 1903–05. Rpt. as *Biblioteca de autores españoles*. Vols. 268–71. Madrid: Atlas, 1975.

This bibliographical dictionary provides data on 1,065 writers. Includes extensive biographies for some authors and sometimes lists material by them. Excludes critical studies.

543.   Simón Palmer, María del Carmen. "Escritoras españolas del siglo XIX (I)." *Censo de escritores al servicio de los Austrias y otros estudios bibliográficos*. Madrid: CSIC, 1983. 99–119.

Provides, whenever possible, brief biographies and lists of works and studies.

544. ———. *Escritoras españolas del siglo XIX: Manual bio-bibliográfico.* Nueva
biblioteca de erudición y crítica 3. Madrid: Castalia, 1991. xviii + 636 pp.
Outstanding biobibliographical study of Spanish nineteenth-century women
writers. A brief biography is followed by a listing of the author's works and of
studies about her. Has the following indexes: "Indice onomástico," "Indice de materias," "Indice de publicaciones periódicas citadas," and "Indice de obras colectivas." Concludes with "Bibliotecas consultadas" and "Bibliografía."

LITERARY THEORY

545. Alburquerque, Luis. "Producción bibliográfica de la teoría literaria española." *Revista de literatura* 55 (1993): 229–58; 56 (1994): 471–94.

546. Romera Castillo, José. *Semiótica literaria y teatral en España.* Problemata
semiótica 14. Kassel: Reichenberger, 1988. 196 pp.
Part 1 was first published as "Semiótica literaria y teatral en España: Addenda
bibliográfica I" (in *Homenaje al profesor, Ignacio Elizalde. Estudios literarios.* Ed.
Roberto Perez. Bilbao: U de Deusto, 1989. 269–86. Also in *Letras de Deusto* 44
[1989]: 269–86). The volume has the following chapters, each with its own "Referencias bibliográficas" (on the page numbers given): "La semiótica en en España
(30–31), "Semiótica literaria" (42–59), "Narrative" (71–96), "Poesía" (103–17),
"Semiótica del hecho teatral" (137–56), "Addenda bibliográfica" 157–65.

547. ———. "Semiótica literaria y teatral en España: Addenda bibliográfica (I y
II)." *Investigaciones semióticas. III (Retórica y lenguajes).* Madrid: U Nacional
de Educación a Distancia, 1990. 537–61.
Part 1, "Semiótica literaria," is divided into "Teoría," "Narrativa," and
"Poesía." Part 2 is "Semiótica teatral."

548. ———. "Semiótica teatral en español: Ampliación bibliográfica." *Investigaciones semióticas. III (Retórica y lenguajes).* Madrid: U Nacional de Educación a Distancia, 1990. 563–71.
This bibliography supplements the earlier ones on semiotics of the theater.

549. ———. "Semiótica literaria y teatral en España: Addenda bibliográfica
IV." *Investigaciones semióticas IV.* Madrid: Visor, 1992. 1043–55.
Supplements earlier bibliography in regard to the theater as well as to narra-
tive and poetry.

550. ———. "Semiótica literaria y teatral en España: Addenda bibliográfica V."
Signa 2 (1993): 167–84.

STYLISTICS

551.   Hatzfeld, Helmut. "Spain and Portugal." *A Critical Bibliography of the New Stylistics Applied to the Romance Literatures 1900–1952.* U of North Carolina Studies in Comparative Literature 5. Chapel Hill: [U of North Carolina P], 1953. 107–23.
Items 621–95. There is a 1955 Spanish translation.

552.   ———. "Spanish and Ibero-American Literature." *A Critical Bibliography of the New Stylistics Applied to the Romance Literatures 1953–1965.* U of North Carolina Studies in Comparative Literature 27. Chapel Hill: [U of North Carolina P], 1966. 102–18.
Items 1,147–360.

553.   ———. "Títulos españoles 1960–1964 para una nueva edición de la *Bibliografía crítica de la estilística romance.*" *Lengua, literatura, folklore. Estudios dedicados a Rodolfo Oroz.* Santiago: U de Chile, 1967. 205–55.

554.   Hatzfeld, Helmut, and Yves Le Hir. "Littérature espagnole." *Essai de bibliographie critique de stylistique française et romane (1955–1960).* Paris: PU de France, 1961. 149–79.
Items 911–1106.

Each of these volumes (nos. 551–54) annotates all items and provides an index of critics as well as of the authors studied.

555.   Martín, José Luis. *Crítica estilística.* Madrid: Gredos, 1973. 379–402.
Lists 549 unannotated items.

DICTIONARIES OF LITERARY TERMINOLOGY

556.   Ayuso de Vicente, María Victoria, Consuelo García Gallarín, and Sagrario Solano Santos. *Diccionario de términos literarios.* Madrid: Akal, 1990. 420 pp.
Provides useful definitions of literary terms, themes, and movements. Examples cited are generally from Spain, though some references are to Latin American authors and their works.

557.   Marchese, Angelo, and Joaquín Forradellas. *Diccionario de retórica, crítica y terminología.* Barcelona: Ariel, 1991. 446 pp.

Spanish version of Marchese's *Dizionario di retorica e di estilistica* provides useful definitions of Spanish terms that deal with rhetoric, criticism, and literary terminology.

METRICS

558. Domínguez Caparrós, José. *Diccionario de métrica española*. Madrid: Paraninfo, 1985. 200 pp.
"La explicación de cada término responde al siguiente esquema: definición, ejemplo y pequeño comentario" (5).

559. Carballo Picazo, Alfredo. *Métrica española*. Monografías bibliográficas 5. Madrid: Inst. de Estudios Madrileños, 1956. 162 pp.
Some of the 1,203 items are briefly annotated, and book reviews are provided. "Tratados generales" (17–53) includes "los particulares con interés histórico hoy o los que tratan temas amplios" (7). "Tratados especiales" (55–138) lists studies on Spanish metrics. There is also a supplement (139–42).

TRANSLATIONS

General (Worldwide)

560. *Index translationum*. 1–31 (quarterly). Paris: Inst. of International Cooperation, 1932–40; ns 1– (annual, 1948–). Paris: UNESCO, 1949– .
Includes separately published translations from almost 90 countries. Excellent source for those interested in learning which Spanish authors have been translated during the past decades. Provides author, title, translator, place, publisher, date, pagination, often price as well, and usually the title in the original language. The 1986 volume was published in 1992.

Danish

561. Riis, Cleo Roth. *Spansk Skønlitteratur i dansk oversættelse og Danske bidrag til den spanske litteraturhistorie, 1939–1978*. [København]: Danmarks Biblioteksskole, Specialeopgave, Sektion II, 1981. viii + ix + 154 pp.
Pages 1–122 list Danish translations of Spanish and Latin American authors. Includes books, chapters of books, and contributions to periodicals. Often gives the title in Spanish. Pages 123–54 provide Danish critical studies on Spanish and Spanish American authors as well as indexes of critics and titles.

Dutch

562.   Steenmeijer, Maarten. *Literatura española en traducción holandesa: Bibliografía 1946–1979* (title also in Dutch). Cuadernos de Leiden 4. Leiden: U de Leiden, 1980. 94 pp.

"Esta bibliografía trata de ofrecer una sinopsis lo más completa posible de la literatura española traducida al holandés del español desde la Segunda Guerra Mundial, y no solamente la publicada en forma de libro, sino también la aparecida en revistas. Se mencionan además las publicaciones en revistas culturales holandesas y flamencas que tratan de la literatura española" (7).

English

563.   Espadas, Elisabeth, et al. "Spain." *Women Writers in Translation: An Annotated Bibliography, 1945–1982*. Garland Reference Library of the Humanities 228. New York: Garland, 1984. 216–25.

The bibliography, preceded by a short introduction, includes only translations published as books. Entries provide evaluations of the translations and a few lines of biographical information about the author.

564.   O'Brien, Robert A. *Spanish Plays in English Translation: An Annotated Bibliography*. New York: Américas, for American Educational Theatre Assn., 1963. xi + 70 pp.

According to the introduction, "1) Each dramatist and play has been briefly described in a sentence or two. . . . 2) Information useful to potential producers is also included. . . . 3) Plays are arranged, roughly, in order of interest under each dramatist. . . . 4) Similarly, translations have also been listed in order of interest . . ." (vii–viii).

565.   Rudder, Robert S. *The Literature of Spain in English Translation: A Bibliography*. New York: Ungar, 1975. ix + 637 pp.

The fullest bibliography of its kind. The entries are divided by period and followed by addenda, a list of frequently cited anthologies, and indexes of authors and anonymous works. Omits pagination for many items but includes titles of the Spanish originals.

566.   Sader, Marion. *Comprehensive Index to English Language Little Magazines 1890–1970*. 8 vols. Millwood: Kraus, 1976.

Indexes material found in 100 literary journals. Though this index includes biographical and critical studies, it should be particularly useful to those interested in translations.

567.   *Yearbook of Comparative and General Literature* 10– (1961 [for 1960]–).

Since 1961 this annual bibliography has rotated a list of English translations published as books in the United States with a list of translations in periodicals and magazines. The latter list is based on an extremely small sample of some 36 journals. Both bibliographies are arranged by language rather than by countries.

French

568. Horn-Monval, Madeleine. *Répertoire bibliographique des traductions et adaptations françaises du théâtre étranger de XVème siècle à nos jours*. Vol. 4. Paris: CNRS, 1963. 8 vols.
    Divided into "Théâtre espagnol," "Théâtre de l'Amérique latine," and "Théâtre portugais."

German

569. Siebenmann, Gustav, and Casetti Donatella. *Bibliographie der aus dem Spanischen, Portugiesischen, und Catalanischen ins Deutsche übersetzten Literatur (1945–1983)* (title also in Spanish, Portuguese, and Catalan). Beihefte zur Iberoromania 3. Tübingen: Niemeyer, 1985. xx + 190 pp.
    Items 1–2,548 (1–138) are a bibliography of works originally written in Spanish (regardless of subject) that have been published in Switzerland and Germany. Wherever possible, the original Spanish title is given. Unfortunately the contents of anthologies in translation are not included.

Hungarian

570. Tóth, Eva. *Obras traducidas del español al húngaro editadas en Hungría entre 1945 y 1979*. Pref. J. Benybe. Budapest: Magyar Könyvkiadök és Könyvterjestök Egyesülése, 1980. 154 pp.
    Also includes data on translations of Latin American authors.

Norwegian

571. Lorentzen, Eva M. *Spansk poesi i Norge: En bibliografi (Skrifter 17)*. Oslo: Universitetsbiblioteket, 1988. 110 pp.

Polish

572. *El libro polaco en España y el libro español en Polonia: Catálogo de la exposición: Círculo de Bellas Artes*. Madrid: El Centro, 1990. 94 pp.
    Provides data on Spanish literature published in Poland and Polish literature published in Spain.

Romanian

573.   *El libro español en Rumania.* Madrid: Biblioteca Nacional, 1989. 80 pp.
Provides data on books of Spanish literature translated and published in Romania.

Russian (and Other Languages of the Former Soviet Union)

574.   Turkevich, Ludmilla Buketoff. *Spanish Literature in Russia and in the Soviet Union, 1735–1964.* Metuchen: Scarecrow, 1967. xi + 273 pp.
Lists 1,792 items, mostly translations of Spanish literary works into Russian and other languages of the former Soviet Union. Also included are critical and biographical studies on these authors and works.

Serbo-Croatian (and Other Languages of the Former Yugoslavia)

575.   Telecán, Milivoj. "Contribución a la bibliografía de traducciones de literatura hispánica en Yugoslavia (I)." *Studia Románica et Anglica Zagrabiensia* 33–36 (1972–73): 807–39; "Contribución . . . (II)." *Studia Románica y Anglica Zagrabiensia* 23 (1978): 531–48.
A chronological list of 358 books originally in Spanish, published between 1864 and 1977 in Slovenian, Croatian, Serbian, Macedonian, Albanian, and Hungarian.

Swedish

576.   Gyberg, E. *Spanien i svensk litteratur. En bibliografi.* Acta Bibliotecae Universitatis Gothoburgensis 14. Goteborg: ABUG, 1973. xv + 355 pp.
Has sections on Spanish linguistics studies published in Sweden (21–50), on Spanish literature published in Sweden (71–72), on Spanish philosophy (15–17), on Spanish literature translated into Swedish (73–116), and on Swedish literature with a Spanish theme (116–46). It is a pity that the original Spanish titles are not given for the translations.

COMPARATIVE LITERATURE

Bibliographies (General)

577.   Baldensperger, Fernand, and Werner P. Friederich. *Bibliography of Comparative Literature.* U of North Carolina Studies in Comparative Literature 1. Chapel Hill: [U of North Carolina P], 1950. xxiv + 701 pp.

A standard classified bibliography, despite often incomplete bibliographical citations and the absence of an index.

578. *Yearbook of Comparative and General Literature* 1–19 (1952–70).
Annual supplement to no. 577 with the same classified arrangement.

Current Bibliographies

579. "Relaciones con otras literaturas." *Bibliografía de la literatura hispánica*. Vol. 1. Madrid: CSIC, 1983. 604–79.
See no. 239. "Relaciones . . . literaturas" is also a section of the current bibliography found in the *Revista de literatura*.

580. "Relations internationales et littérature comparée." Pt. 8 of "Bibliographie." *Revue d'histoire du théâtre* 1– (1948–).
Notes critical studies and translations of Spanish dramas into foreign languages.

English

581. Stubbins, Hilda U. *Renaissance Spain in Its Literary Relations with England and France: A Critical Bibliography*. Nashville: Vanderbilt UP, 1969. xv + 138 pp.
Annotates 364 items divided into books and monographs and journal articles. Lists materials written in English, French, and Spanish and includes unpublished MA theses and PhD dissertations. "Each item deals with some phase of Renaissance Spanish influence, in literature or culture, on the literature and culture of England and/or culture of England and France during the sixteenth, seventeenth and eighteenth centuries" (viii).

French

582. Cioranescu, Alejandro. *Bibliografía franco-española (1600–1715)*. *Boletín de la Real Academia Española*, Anejo 36. Madrid: Real Acad. Española, 1977. 705 pp.
An outstanding contribution to the study of the cultural relations between Spain and France during the period covered. The 4,769 entries are arranged by year and alphabetized by author within each year. A library location is given for at least one copy of each title. Includes an author index and an index of cryptograms and pseudonyms.

German

583. Blaney, Benjamin. "Spanish and German Literary Relations in United States and Canadian Dissertations." *Revista de Estudios Hispánicos* [Alabama] 15 (1981): 459–71.
"This article is an attempt to bring together all dissertations written in the United States and Canada which deal substantially with German and Spanish

literary relations and to note briefly the main points of contact between the two literatures developed in the dissertations" (459).

Italian

584.   Avila, Pablo Luis. *Contributo a un repertorio bibliografico degli scritti pubblicati in Italia sulla cultura spagnuola (1940–1969)*. Ist. di Letteratura Spagnuola e Ispano-Americana: Serie bibliografica 2. Pisa: Facoltà di Lingue e Letterature Stranieri, U de Pisa, 1971. 109 pp.
Updates Bertini (no. 585).

585.   Bertini, Giovanni Maria. "Contributo a un repertorio bibliografico italiano di letteratura spagnuola (1890–1940)." Ist. Nazionale per le Relazioni Culturali con l'Estero. *Italia e Spagna: Saggi sui rapporti storici, filosofici ed artistici tra le due civiltà*. Firenze: Le Monnier, 1941. 425–518.
Contains 1,236 unannotated items, including some omitted from no. 584, and three indexes: "Indice delle persone citate nelle singole voci," "Indice del nomi di luogo," and "Indice del soggetti." It "comprende libri dedicati per intero a temi di letteratura spagnuola, o soltanto parzialmente (in questo caso l'indicazione dell' opera è preceduta dalla preposizione 'in') e articoli presentati in riviste o giornali" (428). This bibliography often tantalizes the user by including only the initial page number of an article, thus giving no indication of the item's length. For some items, no. 584 offers more bibliographical data than Bertini does.

586.   Laurenti, Joseph L., and Joseph Siracusa. "Literary Relations between Spain and Italy: A Bibliographic Survey of Comparative Literature. First Supplement (1882–1974)." *Annali* [Ist. Universitario Orientale Sezione Romanza] 19 (1970): 127–99.
Divides 291 items into general studies, literature by Spanish authors, and literature by Italian authors.

587.   ———. *Relaciones literarias entre España e Italia: Ensayo de una bibliografía de literatura comparada*. Boston: Hall, 1972. ix + 252 pp.
Arranges 2,188 items by critic and provides an index of Spanish and Italian writers mentioned in these references. Almost all the items in both the book and the supplements are unannotated.

588.   ———. "A Bibliography of Literary Relations between Spain and Italy (1972–1974)." *Hispano-Italic Studies* 1 (1976): 83–96.
Classified bibliography of 133 items.

589.   ———. "Literary Relations between Spain and Italy: A Bibliographic Survey of Comparative Literature (1901–1980)." *Bulletin of Bibliography* 40.1 (1983): 12–39.
Includes 532 items.

Russian

590. Schanzer, George O. *Russian Literature in the Hispanic World: A Bibliography*. [Toronto]: U of Toronto P, 1972. xlvi + 312 pp.
"This work lists Spanish collections and anthologies of Russian literature, individual translations, criticisms both general and specific, and sections of semi-literary writings and pseudo-Russian works . . ." (xxxiii). It contains over 3,700 items and 12 indexes. It is the finest and most comprehensive bibliographical study of Russian influence in the Hispanic world.

DISSERTATIONS

Belgian

591. Jiménez, Pedro. "Información de Bélgica: Tesis sobre temas hispánicos presentadas en las universidades de Bélgica (1964–1971)." *Boletín de filología española* 14–15 (1974–75): 35–37.

British

592. Jones, C. A. "Theses in Hispanic Studies Approved for Higher Degrees by British Universities to 1971." *Bulletin of Hispanic Studies* 49 (1972): 325–54.

593. Hodcroft, F. W. "Theses in Hispanic Studies Approved for Higher Degrees by British and Irish Universities (1972–1974) (with Some Additional Earlier Titles)." *Bulletin of Hispanic Studies* 52 (1975): 325–44.

594. Mackenzie, D. "Theses in Hispanic Studies Approved for Higher Degrees by British and Irish Universities (1975–1978) (with Some Additional Earlier Titles)." *Bulletin of Hispanic Studies* 56 (1979): 283–304.

595. Johnson, M. "Theses in Hispanic Studies Approved for Higher Degrees by British and Irish Universities (1979–1982) (with Some Additional Earlier Titles)." *Bulletin of Hispanic Studies* 61 (1984): 235–61.
Includes a list of theses on Spanish, Catalan, Galician, Hispanic American, Portuguese, and Brazilian languages and literatures (235–39).

596. ———. "Theses in Hispanic Studies Approved for Higher Degrees by British and Irish Universities (1983–1987) (with Some Additional Earlier Titles)." *Bulletin of Hispanic Studies* 66 (1989): 417–52.

These bibliographies of theses and dissertations (nos. 592–96) are arranged alphabetically by author.

European (Western)

597.   Chatham, James R., and Sara M. Scales. *Western European Dissertations on the Hispanic and Luso-Brazilian Languages and Literatures: A Retrospective Index.* Mississippi State: [Dept. of Foreign Languages, Mississippi State U, 1984]. xiii + 145 pp. Rpt. Washington: Eric Clearinghouse on Languages and Linguistics, 1994 [1995]. ED 378 841.

Arranged by author with a detailed subject index. Provides data on 6,050 dissertations written up to the end of 1981 and notes their publication. Extremely important source for this type of information.

French

598.   Fichier Central des Thèses. 200, ave. de la République, U de Paris X, 92001 Nanterre, France.

This organization "enregistre les sujets de thèses de doctorat en préparation et soutenues devant les Universités françaises et les Etablissements d'enseignement supérieur en Lettres. . . . dispose d'un fonds de 120,000 références." Theses in the field of linguistics and literature have been listed since 1970. Since 1981, the Ministère de l'Enseignement Supérieur et de la Recherche (Direction de l'information scientifique et technique et des bibliothèques) has published *Inventaire des thèses de doctorat soutenues devant les Universités françaises: . . . Lettres. . . .* The volume for 1992 was published in 1995.

German (Including Germany, Austria, Switzerland)

599.   Flasche, Hans. "Spanische Literatur" and "Hispano-Amerikanische Literatur." *Romance Languages and Literature as Presented in German Doctoral Dissertations, 1885–1950.* Charlottesville: Bibliographical Soc. of the U of Virginia, 1958. 241–48.

Lists dissertations on Spanish (items 4542–660) and Spanish American literature (4661–68) written for German universities, "including Strassburg up to 1918, and from 1938 to 1945 the Austrian universities" (xviii).

600.   Rodríguez Richart, José. " 'Habilitationsschriften' y tesis de doctorado realizadas en las universidades de Austria, de la República Democrática Alemana y de la República Federal de Alemania, sobre temas de lengua y literatura española y portuguesa (1945–1974)." *Iberoromania* ns 3 (1975): 205–34.

601.   "Die romanistischen Dissertationen" (title varies). *Romanistisches Jahrbuch* 4– (1951–).

A current annual listing of dissertations produced in German and Austrian universities. Arranged by university.

Spanish

602.   *Tesis doctorales aprobadas en las universidades españolas durante el curso 1976–1977.* Madrid: Ministerio de Educación y Ciencias, 1978.
There are also volumes for 1977–78, 1978–79, 1979–80, and 1980–81.

603.   "Tesis doctorales." *Revista de la Universidad de Madrid* 1–20 (1952–71); and *Revista de la Universidad Complutense de Madrid* 21–25 (1972–76).
Arranged by faculties and then by sections. Of interest in the 1978–79 volume are "Sección de filología románica," "Sección de literatura hispánica," and "Sección de filología italiana." Abstracts average about a page.

Both these bibliographies of theses (nos. 602–03) contain abstracts.

604.   Chatham, James R. *Dissertations on Ibero-Romance Languages and Linguistics Accepted at Iberian Universities since 1980.* Washington: ERIC Clearinghouse on Languages and Linguistics, 1995. ED 379 913. 58 pp.

United States

605.   Chatham, James R., and Enrique Ruiz-Fornells, with the collaboration of Sara Matthews Scales. *Dissertations in Hispanic Languages and Literature: An Index of Dissertations Completed in the United States and Canada, 1876–1966.* Lexington: UP of Kentucky, 1970. xiv + 120 pp.
Arranges dissertations by author or topic within chronological periods and provides an index to the authors of the dissertations.

606.   Chatham, James R., and Carmen C. McClendon. *Dissertations in Hispanic Languages and Literature: An Index of Dissertations Completed in the United States and Canada 1967–77.* Lexington: UP of Kentucky, 1981. xi + 162 pp.
Arranges dissertations by author and provides a subject index.

The two preceding volumes (nos. 605 and 606) list 5,310 dissertations. They include dissertations on Brazilian, Catalan, Galician, Portuguese, Spanish, and Spanish American writers as well as those on Catalan, Galician, Portuguese, and Spanish languages. The 1981 volume has "added a retrospective listing of dissertations on the teaching and learning of Catalan, Portuguese, and Spanish as well as those written on bilingualism involving these languages with other tongues" (vii).

Annual dissertation lists appear in both *Hispania* and *Modern Language Journal.* The former list, the more comprehensive of the two, is divided into dissertations completed and those in progress. The latter arranges items by the universities that granted the degrees.

NATIONAL BIBLIOGRAPHY

607.   Maclès, L. N. "Espagne et Amérique latine." *Les sources du travail bibliographique*. Vol. 1. Genève: Droz; Lille: Librairie Girard, 1950. 158–64.

The section on national bibliography devoted to Spain is divided into "Bibliographie nationale retrospective," "Bibliographie courante," "Selection des livres espagnols: 1939–1945," "Complément des bibliographies nationales," "Catalogue de bibliothèques publiques," "Catalogues de collections privées dispersées," "Editions remarquables," "Ouvrages prohibés," "Anonymes et pseudonmyes," and "Revues professionelles." The fullest treatment, though not the most current, of Spanish national bibliography to be found among guides to reference works. See also no. 656.

608.   Palau y Dulcet, Antonio, et al. *Manual del librero hispano-americano: Bibliografía general española e hispano-americana desde la invención de la imprenta hasta nuestros tiempos.* . . . 2nd ed., rev. and enl. 28 vols. Barcelona: Palau y Dulcet, 1948–77.

Agustín Palau Claveras has compiled *Addenda & Corregenda* to volume 1 of the *Manual* (Barcelona: Palau y Dulcet, 1990. 648 pp.), which covers the letter *A*.

609.   Palau Claveras, Agustín. *Indice alfabético de títulos-materias, correcciones, conexiones y ediciones del* Manual del librero hispano-americano *de Antonio Palau y Dulcet*. 7 vols. Empuries: Palacete Palau Dulcet, 1981–87.

This set provides bibliographical data on 381,897 works published in Spain and Spanish America, along with some works that deal with these areas. The imprint varies.

TWENTIETH CENTURY

610.   *Catálogo general de la librería española e hispanoamericana, años 1901–1930: Autores*. 5 vols. Madrid: Inst. Nacional del Libro Español, 1923–51.

Bibliographical data, including price, are given for 92,670 items (separately published books and pamphlets) published during the years covered. Includes Spanish American publications.

611.   *Catálogo general de la librería española, 1931–1950*. 4 vols. Madrid: Inst. Nacional del Libro Español, 1957–65.

Bibliographical data, including price, are given for 69,575 items (separately published books and pamphlets) published during the years covered. This set does not include publications issued outside of Spain.

612. Instituto Bibliográfico Hispánico. *Bibliografía española*. 1958– . Madrid: Ministerio de Cultura, Dirección General del Libro y Bibliotecas, Secretaría General Técnica, 1959– .

Annual cumulations of monthly publications. The volumes for 1964–66 have not yet been published. From 1969 to 1976 only the monthly issues were published. The publication of the annual bibliography began again with the 1977 volume.

". . . registra los materiales producidos en España e ingresados por Depósito Legal. Incluye informes anuales; bibliografías; actas de conferencias; catálogos de exposiciones; publicaciones oficiales; monografías; tanto si se trata de nuevas ediciones como de reimpresiones; separatas de revistas; catálogos de ventas en el caso de sellos; objetos de arte o libros; tesis doctorales; obras en Braille; guiones de películas; radio o televisión; así como otras publicaciones que tengan carácter selectivo.

"Han quedado excluidas las revistas por haber sido objeto de publicación independiente desde 1971 hasta 1978 y como suplemento de *Bibliografía española*, el correspondiente a 1979. A partir de 1980, *Bibliografía española* incluirá en su núcleo, y no por separado, las publicaciones seriadas. Tampoco se incluyen otras obras por ser materiales especiales, objeto de tratamiento distinto, o por considerarse efímeras" (1978 vol., pt. 1, ix).

613. *Libro español* (1958–).

This monthly, issued by the Instituto Nacional del Libro Español, can be considered the Spanish equivalent of *Publishers Weekly*. The most important of the current journals dealing with the Spanish book trade, it includes articles on the business, bibliographies, and lists of books published in Spain.

614. *Libros españoles, en venta, ISBN 1995*. 3 vols. Madrid: Ministerio de Cultura, Inst. Nacional del Libro Español, 1995. Also on CD-ROM.

Includes data on 3,000 publishers and over 400,000 titles from Spain. Lists works published in Bolivia, the Dominican Republic, Guatemala, Panama, Paraguay, Peru, El Salvador, and Uruguay. Arranged by author, title, and subject.

LIBRARY RESOURCES, CATALOGS, AND UNION LISTS

British

615. British Museum. *General Catalogue of Printed Books*. Photolithographic ed. to 1955. 263 vols. London: Trustees of the British Museum, 1961–66.

Catalog of Great Britain's largest library, which has extensive Hispanic holdings.

616. ———. *General Catalogue of Printed Books. 10 Year Supplement 1956–1965*. 50 vols. London: Trustees of the British Museum, 1968.

617.   *British Union-Catalog of Periodicals.* . . . Ed. James D. Stewart, Muriel E.
Hammond, and Erwin Saenger. 4 vols. New York: Academic, 1955–58.
Cont.: *Supplement to 1960.* New York: Academic, 1962. 991 pp. *New Periodical Titles, 1960–68, 1969–73.* 2 vols. London: Butterworths, 1970–76. *New Periodical Titles, 1974 –* . London: Butterworths.
British equivalent to *Union List of Serials* (no. 631).

French

618.   Bibliothèque Nationale. *Catalogue général des livres imprimés de la Bibliothèque Nationale: Auteurs.* 231 vols. Paris, 1897–1981.
Imprint varies.

619.   ———. *Catalogue général des livres imprimés: Auteurs—collectivités–auteurs —anonymes. 1960–64.* 12 vols. Paris, 1965–67.
Catalogs of France's national library.

620.   ———. Département des Périodiques. *Catalogue collectif des périodiques du début du XVIII siècle à 1939.* 5 vols. Paris, 1967–82.
Union list of about 75,000 French and foreign serials in the Bibliothèque Nationale and 70 other large French libraries.

Spanish

621.   Biblioteca Nacional, Madrid. *Catálogo general de libros impresos.* Alexandria: Chadwyck-Healey, 1989.
Includes part 1, "Catálogo general de libros impresos hasta 1981" (approximately 4,000 microfiche); part 2, "Catálogo general de libros impresos, 1982–1987" (579 microfiche); and "Guía para la utilización del Catálogo general de la Biblioteca Nacional, Madrid." "The catalogue contains records for all printed books in the library. It is a single index of authors, corporate authors (since 1964, with place name first), and anonymous works" (advertisement).

622.   Inst. Bibliográfico Hispánico. *Catálogo colectivo de publicaciones periódicas en bibliotecas españolas 5. Humanidades, II. Lingüística y literatura.* Madrid: Ministerio de Cultura, Dirección General del Libro y Biblioteca, 1979. lvii + 693 pp.
". . . se recogen las revistas de Filología, Lingüística y Literatura que se conservan en 525 bibliotecas existentes en el país" (vii). The journals in the Hemeroteca Municipal (Madrid) are not included. "Bibliotecas con máquina de reproducción" are indicated. Data recorded through either 1976 or 1977. Besides the "Lista alfabética de revistas" there is an "Indice alfabético de instituciones y sus publicaciones." Should be useful to Hispanists throughout the world, especially for rarer journals published in Spain.

United States

623. Downs, Robert B. "Spanish, Portuguese, and Latin American Literature." *American Library Resources.* Chicago: American Library Assn., 1950. 247–48.
Items 3687–721.

624. ———. "Spanish, Portuguese, and Latin American Literature." *American Library Resources. Supplement 1950–61.* Chicago: American Library Assn., 1962. 126–27.
Items 1949–62.

625. ———. "Spanish, Portuguese, and Latin American Literature." *American Library Resources. Supplement 1961–70.* Chicago: American Library Assn., 1972. 127–28.
Items 2275–293.

626. ———. "Spanish." *American Library Resources. Supplement 1971–80.* Chicago: American Library Assn., 1981. 94–95.
Items 2209–222.

These lists (nos. 623–26) provide data on descriptions of Spanish literature collections in the United States as well as bibliographies of the holdings of some of these special collections.

627. Hispanic Society of America. *Catalog of the Library.* 10 vols. Boston: Hall, 1962. First supp. 4 vols. Boston: Hall, 1970.
"The Main Catalog, here reproduced, has at least an author card for every book in the Library printed since 1700. . . . Not included are manuscripts, most periodicals, and most books printed before 1701" (Introduction n. pag.).

628. *Library of Congress Catalog . . . Books: Subjects 1950–1954.* 20 vols. 1955; *1955–59.* 22 vols. 1960; *1960–64.* 25 vols. 1965; *1965–69.* 42 vols. 1970; *1970–74.* 100 vols. 1976.
Appears quarterly with annual and 5-year cumulations. Imprint varies. This subject guide to Library of Congress acquisitions since 1950 is an extremely valuable index to material in the largest library in the United States.

629. *The National Union Catalog, Pre-1956 Imprints: A Cumulative Author List Representing Library of Congress Printed Cards and Titles Reported by Other American Libraries. . . .* 685 vols. [London]: Mansell, 1968–80. Supp. 1980– . Vol. 686– . *1958–62.* 50 vols. 1963; *1963–67.* 59 vols. 1969; *1968–72.* 104 vols. 1973; *1973–77.* 135 vols. 1978.
Monthly with quarterly, annual, and 5-year accumulations. Imprint varies. The *NUC* provides bibliographical data on the holdings of numerous academic,

public, and special libraries of the United States and Canada. It is an important source for checking such data as well as for locating copies. The published catalogs of the British Library (formerly British Museum) and of the Bibliothèque Nationale can often be used to supplement the data found in the *NUC*.
Superseded by online databases RLIN and OCLC.

630. *New Serial Titles: A Union List of Serials Commencing Publication after December 31, 1949, 1950–1970 Cumulation.* 4 vols. Washington: Library of Congress; New York: Bowker, 1973. Cont. *1971–1975 Cumulation.* 2 vols. Washington: Library of Congress, 1976; *1976–1979 Cumulation.* 2 vols. Washington: Library of Congress, 1980.
For many years this publication appeared "in eight monthly issues, four quarterly issues and in annual cumulations which have been in turn cumulated over five- or ten-year periods" (*New Serial Titles* Oct.-Dec. 1980: iii).

631. *Union List of Serials in Libraries of the United States and Canada.* 3rd ed. Ed. Edna Brown Titus. 4 vols. New York: Wilson, 1965.

The union lists (nos. 629–31) are essential reference sources for those interested in the location of all types of serial publication, regardless of place of publication. Data have been provided by the major academic, public, and special libraries of the United States and Canada.

Periodical Guides
and Indexes

632. Valis, Noël. "Directory of Publication Sources in the Fields of Hispanic Language and Literature." *Hispania* 64 (1981): 226–57.
Provides data on 265 periodicals. Of special interest to those who wish to submit material for publication to the periodicals covered.

633. *MLA Directory of Periodicals: A Guide to Journals and Series in Languages and Literature.* New York: MLA, 1979–80– .
The 1993–95 edition of this biennial provides data on more than 3,200 currently published journals and series in the fields of modern languages and literatures indexed in the *MLA International Bibliography*. Subscription and advertising information is given as well as editorial descriptions and submission requirements. "Entries in the Directory are arranged alphabetically by title. . . . These entries are supplemented by a series of extensive indexes for subject matter, sponsoring organizations, editorial personnel, and the languages in which articles and monographs are published" (*PMLA* 97 [1982]: 296). The volume for 1993–95, published in 1993, was compiled by Kathleen L. Kent. In addition to the clothbound edition, there is a paperbound version that provides data only on journals and series published in the United States and Canada.

634.   *Periódicos y revistas españolas e hispanoamericanas.* 2 vols. Barcelona: Centro de Investigaciones Literarias Españolas e Hispanoamericanas, 1989.

Despite the title, these volumes offer little information on newspapers of the Spanish-speaking world; instead the emphasis is on journals and magazines. Data provided should be of value to librarians and individuals who might wish to subscribe to a journal. Volume 2 has a subject index as well as separate sections for journals and magazines in Catalan, Basque, and Galician. The introduction speaks of an updated edition that was to appear in 1991. Gives telephone area codes of important cities in Spain, Spanish America, and the United States.

635.   Zubatsky, David S. "An International Bibliography of Cumulative Indices to Journals Publishing Articles on Hispanic Languages and Literature." *Hispania* 58 (1975): 75–101.

This bibliography and the one that follows list journals of general cultural interest; bulletins and memoirs of major learned institutions and societies that include language or literature sections; and literary, critical, and philological journals. "Arrangement is by country and then alphabetical by journal title. Items included in each annotation, when available and applicable, are found in the following order: (1) original place of publication; (2) date the review began, and, if defunct, the date it ceased publication; (3) publishing organization; (4) index(es) of its contents, and, finally, (5) the type of index(es)" (75).

636.   ———. "An International Bibliography of Cumulative Indexes to Journals Publishing Articles on Hispanic Languages and Literature: First Supplement." *Hispania* 67 (1984): 383–93.

Supplements no. 635.

Encyclopedias

There are several contemporary Spanish encyclopedias but no detailed study of them. Such a study would be valuable for students of reference works.

637.   *Enciclopedia universal ilustrada europeo-americana.* 70 vols. in 71. Madrid: Espasa, [190?]–30.

The Espasa, the world's largest encyclopedia, includes numerous maps, diagrams, statistical tables, and so on. Many of the biographical sketches it provides for minor authors cannot readily be found elsewhere.

A 10 volume appendix was published in 1930–33. The following supplements, each with its own index, have been issued (publication dates and pagination in parentheses): 1934 (1935, 1,149 pp.); 1935 (1936, 1,323 pp.); 1936–39 (1944, 2 pts.); 1940–41 (1948, 1,473 pp.); 1942–44 (1950, 1,248 pp.); 1945–48 (1953, 1,548 pp.); 1949–52 (1955, 1,564 pp.); 1953–54 (1957, 1,480 pp.); 1955–56 (1960, 1,381 pp.); 1957–58 (1961, 1,523 pp.); 1958–59 (1964, 1,913 pp.); 1961–62 (1966, 1,449 pp.); 1963–64 (1968, 1,532 pp.); 1965–66 (1970, 1,508 pp.); 1967–68 (1973, 1,419 pp.); 1969–70 (1975, 1,478 pp.); 1971–72 (1978, 1,398 pp.); 1973–74 (1980, 1,363 pp.); 1975–76 (1981, 1,581 pp.); 1977–78 (1982, 1,088 pp.); 1979–80 (l983, 1,283 pp.); 1981–82 (1985, 1,274 pp.); 1983–84 (1987, 1,307 pp.); 1985–86 (1989, 1,126 pp.); 1987–88 (1991, 1,198 pp.); 1989–90 (1992, 1,279 pp.); 1991–92 (1993, 1,406 pp.); 1993–94 (1995, 1,425 pp.).

In 1983 Espasa published an index to its supplements (1,073 pp.).

The supplements have a classified arrangement. None of the articles in either the main body of the encyclopedia or its supplements is signed.

Regional Encyclopedias and Bibliographies

638.   *Gran enciclopedia de Andalucía.* 10 vols. Granada: Anel, 1979.

Published in fascicles of 32 pages. It contains many photographs and colored maps. The quality of the articles seems to vary greatly. The 17-page article on Juan Ramón Jiménez lists his works in Spanish and book-length critical studies about him.

639.   *Gran enciclopedia aragonesa.* 12 vols. Zaragoza: Unión Aragonesa del Libro, 1980–83. Appendix. 1983. 399 pp. Appendix II. Zaragoza: Comercial Aragonesa del Libro, 1987. 397 pp.

640.   *Gran enciclopedia asturiana.* 14 vols. Gijón: Silverio Cañada, 1971–74.

The longer articles are written by leading authorities and signed with initials. They are well illustrated. The article on Clarín is divided into a biography, "El crítico Clarín," and "El narrador Leopoldo Alas." Brief bibliographies conclude the sketch.

641.   *Diccionario enciclopédico ilustrado de la Provincia de Cádiz.* 6 vols. Jérez: Ahorros, 1985.

642.   *Gran enciclopedia de Cantabria.* 8 vols. Santander: Ahorros, 1985.

643.   *Gran enciclopedia gallega.* Dir. Ramón Otero Pedrayo. 30 vols. Gijón: Silverio Cañada, 1974–87. 2 vols. of appendixes.

Longer articles are signed and well illustrated. Brief bibliographies.

644.   *Gran enciclopedia de Madrid, Castilla–La Mancha.* 12 vols. to date. Zaragoza: Unión Aragonesa del Libro, 1982– .

The first 8 volumes, covering A–Neolítico, were published in 1982–85. Well illustrated. Longer articles are signed.

645.   *Gran enciclopedia de la región valenciana.* Dir. Manuel Mas. 12 vols. Valencia: Gran Enciclopedia de la Región Valenciana, 1973–78.

Longer articles are signed. Volumes are well illustrated. If the article on Vicente Blasco Ibáñez is typical, articles provide no bibliography of biographical and critical studies.

646.   *Enciclopedia general ilustrada del país vasco. Cuerpo A: Diccionario enciclopédico vasco.* 38 vols. to date. San Sebastián: Auñamendi, 1969 – .

The volumes published up to 1985 cover A–Inturiza. Even the shortest articles are signed with initials. Well illustrated. Includes articles on writers from the Basque region who have written in Basque or Spanish or in both languages. Articles often include brief bibliographies of biographical and critical material.

647.   Bilbao, J. *Eusko bibliografía.* 10 vols. San Sebastián: Auñamendi, 1970–80.
Publisher describes it as ". . . dando cuenta de todo lo ocurrido en el mundo sobre los vascos. Se trata de una relación impresionante por orden alfabético de todos las libros, folletos, hojas y artículos de revista, tanto de nacionales como extranjeros . . ." (1981–82 publisher's catalog). The bibliographies usually include biographical and critical studies on the authors as well as the authors' separately published works. The material on writers published in journals that specialize in Basque culture often have not been previously included in bibliographies. Proofreading could have been greatly improved, at least in the English entries. This would seem to be the fullest bibliography of the culture of a Spanish region.

648.   ———. *Eusko bibliografía. Diccionario de bibliografía vasca . . . (1976–1980).* 3 vols. Bilbao: U del País Vasco, 1985–87.
Vol. 1: A–E, 1985; Vol. 2: F–M, 1986; Vol. 3: N–Z, 1987.

649.   *Gran enciclopedia vasca.* 14 vols. to date. Bilbao: Gran, 1980– .

650.   *Diccionario enciclopédico del país vasco.* 7 vols. to date. San Sebastián: Haramburu, 1985– .
The volumes published through 1985 cover A–Pheskiza.

Related Bibliographies

651.   Díaz Díaz, Gonzalo, and Ceferino Santos Escudero. *Bibliografía filosófica hispánica (1901–1970).* Madrid: CSIC, 1982. xxxi + 1,371 pp.
Classified bibliography of 35,732 items. Has sections on psychology, philosophy, and the philosophies of religion, education, history, language, and so on. Provides an "Indice alfabético de materias" and an "Indice de autores." An elaborate table of contents shows the work's arrangement. It should be an indispensable starting point for those interested in any phase of Spanish or Spanish American philosophy or in Spanish material on Spanish or non-Spanish-language philosophers.

652.   Foulché-Delbosc, Raymond, and L. Barrau-Dihigo. *Manuel de l'hispanisant.* 2 vols. 1920. New York: Kraus, 1959.
For many decades the outstanding bibliography of bibliographies in the field and still quite useful. Volume 1 is divided into "Généralités," "Type-bibliographies," "Biographie et biobibliographies," "Bibliographies monographiques," "Archives, bibliothèques et musées," and "Collections dispersées." Volume 2 is an

index to collections published between 1579 and 1923, especially in the fields of history and literature.

653.   Gómez-Martínez, José Luis, ed. *Anuario bibliográfico de historia del pensamiento ibero e iberoamericano, 1986–90.* 5 vols. Georgia Series on Hispanic Thought. Athens: Dept. of Romance Languages, U of Georgia, 1989–93.
Numerous contributors provide bibliographies of materials that were published in their countries. Material about Iberian and Iberoamerican thought and philosophy published outside these areas—in places such as Poland, France, and the United States—is also included.

654.   González Ollé, F. *Manual bibliográfico de estudios españoles.* Pamplona: U de Navarra, 1976. xiv + 1,375 pp.
An attempt to provide a bibliographical guide to the study of all phases of Spanish culture. Students of literature should be interested in sections on folklore, literature, language, history, government, and so on. Many of the sections are too short to be as useful as they might have been.

655.   *Índice histórico español.* Barcelona: U de Barcelona, 1953– .
Divided by historical periods with numerous subdivisions within each period. The literary history seems slighted. The work appears 2 times a year. The abstracts should be useful to those chiefly interested in Spain's political history.

656.   Sáinz Rodríguez, Pedro. *Biblioteca bibliográfica hispánica.* 5 vols. Madrid: Fundación Universitaria Española Seminario "M. Pelayo," 1975–80.
The title pages of volumes 1, 3, 4, and 5 state, "Volumen preparado por Amancio Labandeira Fernández." The title page of volume 2 attributes the preparation to Miguel M. Rodríguez San Vicente; volume 6 was prepared by Manuel de Castro. This set is extremely useful, though the sections devoted to Spanish America are considerably less extensive than those devoted to Spain. Most entries are well annotated, and all 6 volumes contain multiple indexes.
Vol. 1: *Repertorios por lugar de nacimiento*, 1975, 151 pp. Provides an annotated bibliography by city and province of biographical and biobibliographical dictionaries.
Vol. 2: *Repertorios por profesiones y otras características personales*, 1976, 300 pp. Divided into 38 sections. Of special interest are "Anónimos y seudónimos," "Archiveros y bibliotecarios," "Bibliófilos y libreros," "Filósofos y pedagogos," "Mujeres," "Periodistas," and "Traductores." General dictionaries are followed by dictionaries for specific provinces and countries of the New World.
Vol. 3: *Tipobibliografías*, 1976, 132 pp. The preface notes, "En el apartado correspondiente a España se han hecho dos grandes divisiones: *Retrospectivas y periódicas*, y dentro de la primera, en donde aparecen los repertorios que reúnen lo publicado en cualquier fecha, aparecen divisiones relativas a repertorios de carácter nacional, regional, provincial y local, según los límites del territorio abarcado. La segunda de estas divisiones—en donde se incluyen todas aquellas obras que dan noticias durante cierto tiempo—se ha dividido a su vez en *Revistas y anuarios*" (5). Contains the fullest bibliography of Spanish national bibliographies arranged

by province (11–57). Some data seem to be almost 5 years old at the time of publication. The rest of the volume is devoted to Spanish America.

Vol. 4: *Indice de publicaciones periódicas*, 1976, 125 pp. Provides data on indexes to journals published in Spain (11–62). The 166 items are divided into "Indices colectivos" and "Indices individuales." The rest of the volume is devoted to Spanish America.

Vol. 5: *Bibliografía sobre historia de la imprenta*, 1980, 130 pp. Lists 235 items on the history of printing in Spain (9–62). This section is divided into "Historia de la imprenta," "España," "Regionales," and "Provinciales y locales." It is the fullest overall bibliography yet produced on this subject for Spain. The rest of the volume deals with lists on printing in Spanish America, arranged by country.

657. Sánchez Alonso, Benito. *Fuentes de la historia española e hispano-americana: Ensayo de bibliografía sistemática de impresos y manuscritos que ilustran la historia política de España y sus antiguas provincias de Ultramar.* 3rd ed., rev. and updated. 3 vols. Publicaciones de la *Revista de filología española* 8. Madrid: CSIC, 1952.

The fullest bibliography in the field of Spanish history. Many items are briefly annotated.

658. Simón Palmer, María del Carmen. "La bibliografía española en 1980–1982." *Censo de escritores al servicio de los Austrias y otros estudios bibliográficos.* Madrid: CSIC, 1983. 161–86.

A bibliography of bibliographies on Spanish culture regardless of place of publication. Items 201–26 are classified as literature (general), and items 227–74 are author bibliographies (published as books, in books, or as articles).

659. ———. "La bibliografía española en 1983–85." *Cuadernos bibliográficos* 47 (1987): 9–46.

Classified bibliography of bibliographies published during these years.

Spanish Literature of the
Western Hemisphere

CURRENT AND
RETROSPECTIVE PERIODICAL
INDEXES AND BOOK
REVIEW INDEX

660.   *Bibliografía de publicaciones japonesas sobre América latina en 1974–* (title also in Japanese). Tokyo: Inst. Iberoamericano de la U de Sofía, 1975– .
Classified bibliography through 1993 of 11,481 items in Japanese that deal with Latin America. It is a source for Japanese translations of Latin American authors. The volume for 1993 was published in 1996.

661.   "Bibliografía hispanoamericana." *Revista hispánica moderna* 1–35 (1934–69).
For almost 35 years this bibliography was the fullest of its kind. It contains more than 80,000 numbered citations and indexes, books, articles, dissertations, and book reviews. From 1967 to 1969 the name was changed to "Bibliografía hispánica."

662.   *Bibliographie latine-américaine d'articles.* Vol. 10– . Paris: Inst. des Hautes Etudes de l'Amérique Latine, 1981– .
Semiannual periodical index to approximately 150 journals and annuals, many of which are published in Latin America. Arranged by country and subdivided by broad subject. Covers United States, German, and British journals on Latin American subjects.

663.   *Bulletin bibliographique Amérique latine: Analyse des publications françaises et recherche bibliographique automatisée sur le fichier FRANCIS.* 1– (1981–).
The prologue notes "— a partir de la base de datos sobre América latina acopiados desde 1980 por el GRECO 26, se han presentado las referencias bibliográficas proporcionadas por los distintos grupos que constituyen la Red de Documentación del GRECO. Esta base de datos incluye a todos los géneros de documentos: artículos de periódicos, libros, tesis, memorias, informes inéditos. . . .
"— a partir de las distintas bases de datos de 'FRANCIS' del Centro de Documentación en Ciencias Humanas del Centro Nacional de Investigaciones Científicas, se realizó una selección automática que vierte sobre los distintos países de América latina (se trata de publicaciones francesas)."
"Analyse des publications françaises" has a section "Langues et littératures" and the following indexes: "Index des revues dépouillées," "Index des concepts," "Index géographique," and "Index des auteurs." "Recherche bibliographique automatisée sur le fichier FRANCIS" has two sections of interest: "Histoire et

sciences de la littérature" and "Sciences du langage." A current source of studies on Latin America published in France by the French. Currently appears twice a year.

664.   *Handbook of Latin American Studies.* See no. 104.

665.   *Hispanic American Periodicals Index, 1970–74.* 3 vols. Los Angeles: U of California Latin American Center, 1984.

An annual since 1975, this index lists articles in over 250 journals on Latin America. Contains subject, book review, and author sections. This important index for research on Latin American literature includes articles on literary themes, literature appearing in journals, reviews, and criticism of Latin American authors.

666.   Leavitt, Sturgis E., Madaline W. Nichols, and Jefferson Rea Spell. *Revistas hispanoamericanas: Indice bibliográfico 1843–1935.* Santiago de Chile: Fondo Histórico y Bibliográfico José Toribio Medina, 1960. xiv + 589 pp.

Classified index to 30,107 items found in slightly more than 50 periodicals published in Spanish America.

667.   Columbus Memorial Library. *Index to Latin American Periodicals: Humanities and Social Sciences.* Vols. 1–2. Boston: Hall, 1961–62; Vols. 3–9. Metuchen: Scarecrow, 1963–69.

Indexes several hundred periodicals received by the library.

668.   ———. *Index to Latin American Periodical Literature 1929–1960.* 8 vols. Boston: Hall, 1962.

Author, title, and subject indexes to over 1,500 periodicals relating to Latin America. Supplements cover the years 1961–70.

See also the *MLA International Bibliography* (no. 8), *Romanische Bibliographie* (no. 9), and *The Year's Work in Modern Language Studies* (no. 10), which include sections on Spanish American literature.

669.   Matos, Antonio. *Guía a las reseñas de libros de y sobre Hispanoamérica, 1972–82.* Detroit: Ethridge, 1976–85.

"The purpose of the Guide is to offer those interested in Hispanic American books an index by author of reviews of books which appear in over 633 of the principal periodicals which include reviews" (1979 ed., vii). Excellent source for reviews, many of which are digested or quoted from.

GENERAL

Dictionaries

670.   Becco, Horacio Jorge. *Diccionario de literatura hispano-americana: Autores.* Buenos Aires: Huemul, 1984. 313 pp.

Brief biographical sketches, each followed by listings of the author's works with pertinent bibliographical details.

671.   Bhalla, Alok. *Latin American Writers: A Bibliography with Critical and Biographical Introductions.* New York: Envoy, 1987. 174 pp.

Each of the 18 biographical sketches of twentieth-century Spanish American writers provides a bibliography of the author's works, including translations as well as criticism.

672.   *Diccionario enciclopédico de las letras de América latina.* 1 vol. to date. Caracas: Biblioteca Ayacucho y Monte Avila, 1995– .

Vol. 1, A–E, 1995, lxiv + 1,706 pp. The 500 contributors from more than 30 countries provide signed articles on authors, works, literary movements, and journals. Each article has a sketch of the author and a selective bibliography of the author's works and of critical studies. This 3-volume set, when completed, will be an outstanding work both for its scholarship and for its inclusiveness, under the term *Latin America*, of those who write in English, French, Dutch, Spanish, and Portuguese.

673.   Flores, Angel. *Spanish American Authors: The Twentieth Century.* New York: Wilson, 1992. 915 pp.

Flores, with an advisory board of 17 scholars and 69 contributors, has produced biographical, critical, and bibliographical sketches of 330 twentieth-century Spanish American authors. Many of the authors provided data about themselves. The bibliography is divided into material by and about the author.

674.   Foster, David William, ed. *Handbook of Latin American Literature.* 2nd ed. New York: Garland, 1992. xxii + 789 pp.

Experts on the literature of different countries have contributed essays on that literature. Foster states that "all of the original essays have been updated, with the exception of the Dominican Republic, Haiti and Paraguay; in the case of Peru, an entirely new chapter has been included" (xiii). Articles on Latino writing, paraliterature, and film have been added to this second edition.

675.   González Echevarría, Roberto, and Enrique Pupo-Walker. *Cambridge History of Latin American Literature.* 3 vols. Cambridge: Cambridge UP, 1996, 3:383–742.

Vols. 1 and 2 deal with Spanish American literature. A general bibliography is followed by briefly annotated bibliographies to individual chapters. Vol. 3 deals with Brazilian literature. The set as a whole is the fullest history of Latin American literature in any language. Numerous scholars have contributed to it. Some might prefer the bibliographies to have appeared at the end of each chapter.

676.   Krstović, Jelena, ed. *Hispanic Literature Criticism*. 2 vols. Detroit: Gale, 1994.
Volume 1 includes 37 authors, Allende to Jiménez. Volume 2 includes 34 authors. One might question the inclusion of Fidel Castro and "Che" Guevara, who are hardly literary figures. Gabriel García Márquez is alphabetized under García, but Federico García Lorca is alphabetized under Lorca. Victor Hernández Cruz is alphabetized under Cruz. One may, from time to time, disagree with provided data. Gives the erroneous idea that very little of César Vallejo exists in English translation.
The set "presents a broad selection of the best criticism of works by major Hispanic writers of the past hundred years" (ix). It is "designed for high school and college students, as well as for the general reader who wants to learn more about Hispanic literature" (ix). Each author is provided with a biographical and critical introduction that is then followed by a chronological anthology of critical comments. The author's principal works are given along with their English translations. There are author, nationality, and title indexes. "The Nationality Index lists all authors featured in *HLC* by nationality or by their professed affiliation" (x). Thus, there are categories for American and Chicano authors, and one author is listed as Mexican even though he was born in the United States, lives in the United States, and writes in English.

677.   Magill, Frank N., ed. *Masterpieces of Latino Literature*. New York: Harper, 1994. xii + 655 pp.
This volume "presents 173 standardized articles — 140 on classical and newly popular works of fiction and nonfiction and 33 general essays about the poetry, plays, short stories, and essays of notable Latino writers and thinkers . . ." (v). Articles are arranged by their English titles. The term *Latino* here includes Spanish American, Brazilian, and Chicano writers. Articles include plot summaries and critical analyses.

678.   Reichardt, Dieter. *Lateinamerikanische Autores: Literaturlexikon und Bibliographie der deutschen Ubersetzungen*. Tübingen: Erdman, 1972. 719 pp.
This German biographical dictionary of Latin American authors is arranged by country; it is a valuable source for German translations.

679.   Ryan, Bryan, ed. *Hispanic Writers: A Selection of Sketches from "Contemporary Authors."* Detroit: Gale, 1991. 514 pp.
Features 400 entries on twentieth-century Hispanic writers. Includes biographical sketches of the authors, a bibliography of their writings, and excerpts of criticism.

680.   Solé, Carlos Alberto, and María Isabel Abreu, eds. *Latin American Writers*. 3 vols. New York: Scribner's, 1989.
Essays by outstanding critics on over 175 authors are followed by bibliographies of the author's first editions, other editions, English translations, and bio-

graphical and critical studies. Includes an overview of the history of Latin American literature and a chronology.

Bibliographies (General)

681. *Apuntes para una bibliografía crítica de la literatura hispano-americana.* Centro di Ricerche per l'America Latina, Ricerche Letterarie 3. Firenze: Valmartina, 1973. viii + 133 pp.
    Critical evaluations of 144 histories of Latin American literature as well as the literature of the individual countries. Ten scholars contributed to this work.

682. Bellini, Giuseppe. *Bibliografia dell'ispanoamericanismo italiano: Letterature e culture dell'America latina.* Vol. 3. Milano: Cisalpino, [1982]. 144 pp.
    Lists 1,191 Italian contributions—both books and articles — to the study of Latin American literature published between 1940 and 1980. Unfortunately, no pagination is given for the items included.

683. *Bibliografía general de la literatura hispanoamericana.* Paris: UNESCO, 1972. 187 pp.
    Sections on 3 chronological periods (colonial, nineteenth-century, and contemporary), compiled by 4 outstanding scholars, are each divided into "Bibliografías generales," "Bibliografías regionales," and "Historias generales."

684. Bryant, Shasta M. *Selective Bibliography of Bibliographies of Hispanic American Literature.* 2nd ed. Austin: Inst. of Latin American Studies, U of Texas, 1976. x + 100 pp.
    Two-thirds of these 662 entries are author bibliographies. Almost all items are annotated.

685. Johnson, Harvey L. "Spanish-American Literary Bibliography—1962." *Hispania* 46 (1963): 557–601.

686. ———. "Spanish-American Literary Bibliography—1963." *Hispania* 47 (1964): 766–71.

687. ———. "Spanish-American Literary Bibliography—1964." *Hispania* 48 (1965): 856–64.

688. ———. "Spanish-American Literary Bibliography—1965." *Hispania* 49 (1966): 793–99.

689. ———. "Spanish-American Literary Bibliography, 1966." *Modern Language Journal* 51 (1967): 402–08.

690. Forster, Merlin. "Spanish-American Literary Bibliography, 1967." *Modern Language Journal* 53 (1969): 85–89.

691.   Foster, David W. "Spanish-American Literary Bibliography, 1968." *Modern Language Journal* 53 (1969): 550–54.

692.   Johnson, Harvey L. "Spanish-American Literary Bibliography, 1969." *Modern Language Journal* 55 (1971): 306–11.

693.   ———. "Spanish-American Literary Bibliography, 1970 and 1971." *Modern Language Journal* 56 (1972): 365–72.

694.   ———. "Spanish-American Literary Bibliography—1972." *Hispanófila* 54 (1975): 61–68.

695.   ———. "Spanish-American Literary Bibliography—1973." *Hispanófila* 54 (1975): 69–78.

696.   ———. "Spanish-American Literary Bibliography—1974." *Hispanófila* 64 (1978): 93–99.

697.   Johnson, Harvey L., and David W. Foster. "Bibliografía literaria hispanoamericana 1976." *Revista iberoamericana* 44 (1978): 221–29.

698.   Foster, David W. "Bibliografía literaria hispanoamericana 1977–78–79." *Revista iberoamericana* 46 (1980): 591–604.

699.   ———. "Bibliografía literaria hispanoamericana 1982–83–84." *Revista iberoamericana* 51 (1985): 347–53.

For more than 2 decades an MLA committee has compiled annotated bibliographies (nos. 685–99) of important reference works in the field of Spanish American literature. These include author bibliographies, genre bibliographies, national bibliographies, bibliographies of the literature of individual countries, dictionaries of authors, and so on that appeared during the years covered. Each was published under the name of a committee member.

700.   Lozano, Stella. *Selected Bibliography of Contemporary Spanish-American Writers*. Latin America Bibliography Series 8. Los Angeles: Latin American Studies Center, California State U, 1979. v + 149 pp.
  ". . . contains critical books, critical essays, dissertations, interviews and book reviews covering literary production of 47 Spanish American writers of the XX Century . . ." (iii). Features material published during the brief period 1974 to 1978, "except for the women writers, in which case material is listed regardless of date" (iii).

701.   Okinschevich, Leo. *Latin America in Soviet Writings*. 2 vols. Hispanic Foundation Publications. Baltimore: Johns Hopkins UP; published for the Library of Congress, [1966].

Pages 159–91 of volume 1 and pages 186–223 of volume 2 list literary criticism, histories of literature, and translations of Latin American authors either in Russian or in the other languages of the former Soviet Union.

702.   Rela, Walter, comp. *A Bibliographical Guide to Spanish American Literature: Twentieth-Century Sources.* Bibliographies and Indexes in World Literature 13. New York: Greenwood, 1988. 381 pp.

Contents include bibliographies, histories, and criticism (general sources arranged by country and genre, anthologies). Indexes contents of anthologies. Supersedes Rela's *Guía* (1971) (no. 703) and supplement (1982) (no. 704).

703.   ———. *Guía bibliográfica de la literatura hispano-americana desde el siglo XIX hasta 1970.* Buenos Aires: Pardo, 1971. 613 pp.

Classified, unannotated bibliography of 6,023 items.

704.   ———. *Spanish American Literature: A Selected Bibliography, 1970–1980. Literatura hispanoamericana: Bibliografía selectiva, 1970–1980.* [East Lansing]: Dept. of Romance and Classical Languages, Michigan State U, 1982. 231 pp.

The 1,502 items could serve as a supplement to the preceding item.

705.   Schnepl, Ryszard, and Krzysztof Smolana. "Cultura." *Bibliografía de publicaciones sobre América latina en Polonia 1945–1977.* Varsovia: Biblioteca Nacional, Inst. de Historia, Acad. de Ciencias en Polonia, Soc. Polaca de Historiadores [y] Soc. Polaca de Estudios Latinoamericanos, 1978. 100–13.

Many items (628–732) are Latin American literary works translated into Polish and their Polish reviews. Spanish titles are given for works in Polish.

Black Authors

706.   Bansart, Andrés. *El negro en la literatura hispanoamericana: Bibliografía y hemerografía.* Colección de bolsillo 2. Caracas: Equinoccio, [1986]. 113 pp.

The 661 items of "Presencia del descendiente de negro-africanos en la literatura hispanoamericana" are divided into "Hemerografía" (11–56) and "Bibliografía" (57–76).

707.   Jackson, Richard L. *The Afro-Spanish American Author: An Annotated Bibliography of Criticism.* New York: Garland, 1980. xix + 129 pp.

Jackson, an outstanding expert on Afro-Spanish American authors, has divided this well-annotated bibliography of 562 items into general bibliographies, general studies, anthologies, and authors.

708.   ———. *The Afro-Spanish American Author II, the 1980s: An Annotated Bibliography of Recent Criticism.* West Cornwall: Locust Hill, 1989. xxviii + 154 pp.

Contains 466 well-annotated items divided into (1) creative works and translations published since 1979; (2) general bibliographies; (3) general studies and anthologies; (4) studies on individual authors. Excellent supplement to no. 707. Includes works in progress.

709.   ———. "Afro-Hispanic Literature (Caribbean and South America)." Part of "Studies in Caribbean and South American Literature: An Annual Annotated Bibliography, [1985–1988]." Ed. Brenda F. Berrian et al. *Callaloo* 9.4 (1986); 653–60; 10.4 (1987); 732–39; 11.4 (1988): 825–34; 12.4 (1989): 152–60. Cont. by others.

Excellent annotated serial bibliography for the study of Afro-Hispanic literature. Includes translated works, interviews, general studies on individual genres, and studies on individual authors.

710.   Williams, Lorna V. "Recent Works on Afro-Hispanic Literature." *Latin American Research Review* 22 (1987): 245–54.

Drama

711.   Acuña, René. *El teatro popular en Hispanoamérica: Una bibliografía anotada.* México: Inst. de Investigaciones Filológicos, Centro de Estudios Literarios, UNAM, 1979. 114 pp.

Despite the title, not all items are annotated; some obviously are known secondhand. Contains 380 items on Hispanic American popular theater. Also has a section of 141 items on Spain's popular theater.

712.   Allen, Richard E. *Teatro hispanoamericano: Una bibliografía anotada. Spanish American Theatre: An Annotated Bibliography.* Boston: Hall, 1987. 633 pp.

Arranged by country. Provides brief plot summaries and critical comment. Locates at least one copy in the United States.

713.   Becco, Horacio Jorge. *Bibliografía general de las artes del espectáculo en América latina.* Paris: UNESCO, 1977. 118 pp.

Valuable bibliography of 1,797 items, many of them on the theater and its history. Arranged by country.

714.   Carpenter, Charles A. "Latin American Theater Criticism, 1966–1974: Some Addenda to Lyday and Woodyard." *Revista interamericana de bibliografía* 30.2 (1980): 246–53.

Praises Lyday and Woodyard (no. 719) and adds 97 items.

715.   ———. "Spanish-American Drama." *Modern Drama Scholarship and Criticism, 1966–1980: An International Bibliography.* Toronto: U of Toronto P, 1986. 193–210.

Supplemented by the annual bibliography in *Modern Drama* (no. 448).

716. Finch, Mark Steven. "An Annotated Bibliography of Recent Sources on Latin American Theater: General Section, Argentina, Chile, Mexico and Peru." Diss. U of Cincinnati, 1979. ii + 372 pp.

Lists 884 well-annotated items concerning the Latin American theater and in particular the four countries mentioned in the title. Each section is divided into books and book reviews, articles, anthologies, bibliographies, and miscellaneous. The general section also has a section called "Other: Chicano, Puerto Rico."

717. Hebblethwaite, Frank P. *A Bibliographical Guide to the Spanish American Theater*. Basic Bibliographies 6. Washington: Pan American Union, 1969. viii + 84 pp.

Classified bibliography "on the history and criticism of the Spanish American theater in its entirety. It is not a compilation of dramatic works, nor of studies concerning individual authors, plays, or playhouses" (vi). Many items are annotated.

718. Hoffman, Herbert H. *Latin American Play Index*. 2 vols. Metuchen: Scarecrow, 1983–84.

Volume 1 covers 1920–62; volume 2, 1962–80. These volumes provide data on 3,300 plays by more than 1,000 dramatists who have written or write in Spanish, French, or Portuguese.

719. Lyday, Leon F., and George W. Woodyard. *A Bibliography of Latin American Theater Criticism 1940–1974*. Guides and Bibliographic Series 10. Austin: Inst. of Latin American Studies, U of Texas, 1976. xvii + 243 pp.

Many of the 2,360 items are annotated.

720. Neglia, Erminio Guiseppe, and Luis Ordaz. *Repertorio selecto del teatro hispanoamericano contemporáneo*. 2nd ed. Tempe: Center for Latin American Studies, Arizona State U, 1980. xix + 110 pp.

Lists contemporary dramatists alphabetically by country. Includes many anthologies.

721. Obregón, Osvaldo. "Apuntes sobre el teatro latinoamericano en Francia." *Caravelle* 40 (1983): 17–43.

The article's appendix, with its references to Latin American theater in French periodicals, should interest students of this theater in France.

722. "Recent Publications, Materials Received and Current Bibliographies." *Latin American Theater Review* 3– (1969–).

Published in each issue of the *Review* since volume 3, this bibliography is the best current source for data on recently published plays as well as for critical studies on the Latin American theater.

723. Rhoades, Duane. *The Independent Monologue in Latin American Theater: A Primary Bibliography with Selective Secondary Sources*. Bibliographies and Indexes in World Literature 5. Westport: Greenwood, 1985. xxvi + 242 pp.

"This bibliography aspires to incorporate all independent monologue pieces written in Spanish and Portuguese" (ix).

724.   Rojo, Grinor. "Estado actual de las investigaciones sobre teatro hispanoamericano contemporáneo." *Revista chilena de literatura* 2–3 (1970): 133–61.

Useful, though now dated, critical essay on Spanish American theater.

725.   Toro, Fernando de, and Peter Roster. *Bibliografía del teatro hispanoamericano contemporáneo (1900–1980).* 2 vols. Editionen der Iberoamericana Reihe 2. Bibliographische Reihe 3. Frankfurt: Vervuert, 1985.

Most complete bibliography yet published of the contemporary Spanish American theater. Volume 1, "Obras originales," is a classified bibliography of 6,952 items, while volume 2, "Crítica," is a classified bibliography of 3,132 items. No index.

726.   Trenti Rocamora, José Luis. *El repertorio de la dramática colonial hispanoamericana.* Buenos Aires: ALEA, 1950. 110 pp.

Deals with the published drama of the colonial period; a supplement makes reference to unpublished texts preserved in repositories.

Fiction

727.   Balderston, Daniel, comp. *The Latin American Short Story: An Annotated Guide to Anthologies and Criticism.* Bibliographies and Indexes in World Literature 24. New York: Greenwood, 1992. xx + 529 pp.

"Primary Materials: Anthologies" is a bibliography of anthologies divided into general anthologies, general anthologies in English translation, regional anthologies, and anthologies by country. "Secondary Materials: Criticism" is divided into short story theory; general criticism, literary history, and bibliography; regions of Latin America; and critical studies on the short story in each country. There are indexes of authors, critics, titles, and themes.

728.   Becco, Horacio Jorge. "Antologías del cuento hispano-americano: Notas para una bibliografía." *Narradores latinoamericanos 1929–1979.* Vol. 2. Memoria del XIX Congreso del Inst. Internacional de Literatura Iberoamericana 2. Caracas: Centro de Estudios Latinoamericanos Rómulo Gallegos, 1980. 287–327.

Valuable for its listing of 350 anthologies of the Spanish American short story (293–327).

729.   Becco, Horacio Jorge, and David William Foster. *La nueva narrativa hispanoamericana: Bibliografía.* Buenos Aires: Pardo, 1976. 226 pp.

Unannotated list of 2,257 items on the "new" novel and short story. Lists the works, translations, and criticism of 15 authors in its first part. The second part is "Referencias generales," and the third is "Referencias nacionales."

730.   Brower, Keith H. *Contemporary Latin American Fiction: An Annotated Bibliography*. Pasadena: Salem, 1989. 218 pp.

Basic annotated list of selected English-language criticism on contemporary Latin American novelists and their works. Important beginning point for locating criticism and general commentaries. Includes 600 citations to 23 contemporary Latin American narrativists and over 100 of their works. Cites books, articles, and essays.

731.   Calimano, Iván E. *Index to Spanish Language Short Stories in Anthologies*. Albuquerque: SALALM Secretariat, 1994. 332 pp.

This index "analyzes the contents of more than 200 anthologies of Spanish language short stories published in Spanish America, Spain, and the United States from 1979 to the present . . ." (1). The arrangement is by author. There are indexes of titles and of authors by country, as well as a full key to the anthologies. A very useful bibliography for this literary genre.

732.   Foster, David William. *The Twentieth-Century Spanish American Novel: A Bibliographical Guide*. Metuchen: Scarecrow, 1975. vii + 227 pp.

Provides "a working bibliography on the criticism pertaining to the 56 Spanish American novelists most commonly studied in the U.S." (vi). This unannotated bibliography includes "Basic Monographic Studies on the Spanish-American Novel" and divides the material on authors in much the same way as no. 731.

733.   Foster, Jerald. "Towards a Bibliography of Latin American Short Story Anthologies." *Latin American Research Review* 12.2 (1977): 103–08.

Critically annotated bibliography of over 50 items. Includes anthologies of Latin American short stories in English translation.

734.   Luis, William, ed. *Modern Latin-American Fiction Writers*. First Series. Dictionary of Literary Biography 113. Detroit: Gale, 1992. xvii + 317 pp.

Treatment of 30 authors; similar to material in no. 735.

735.   Luis, William, and Ann González, eds. *Modern Latin-American Fiction Writers*. Second Series. Dictionary of Literary Biography 145. Detroit: Gale, 1994. 413 pp.

Sketches of 39 authors, both Spanish American and Brazilian, written by experts on the authors. Each sketch provides a listing of the author's works, often with any English translations, a biographical critical discussion, and a classified bibliography of material about the author.

736.   Matlowsky, Bernice. *Antologías del cuento hispanoamericano: Guía bibliográfica*. Monografías bibliográficas 3. Washington: Pan American Union, 1950. 48 pp.

Alphabetizes 75 annotated items by author or editor and provides an author index.

737.   Ocampo de Gómez, Aurora M. *Novelistas iberoamericanos contemporáneos: Obras y bibliografía crítica*. Cuadernos del Centro de Estudios Literarios 2, 4, 6, 10, 11. México: UNAM, 1971–81.
Provides dates and nationality of important contemporary novelists. Lists their books and critical studies of them.

738.   Roinat, Christophe. *Romans et nouvelles hispano-américains. Guide des œuvres et des auteurs*. Paris: L'Harmattan, 1992. 209 pp.
Lists novels and short story collections by twentieth-century Spanish American authors along with French translations of these works. Of special interest is "101 œuvres caractéristiques" (145–83), which provides French summaries of 101 works.

739.   Zeitz, Eileen M., and Richard A. Seybolt. "Hacia una bibliografía sobre el realismo mágico." *Hispanic Journal* 3.1 (1981): 159–67.
Provides a bibliography of general critical studies on magical realism and studies on 7 specific authors.

Essays

740.   Horl, Sabine. *Der Essay als literarische Gattung in Lateinamerika*. Frankfurt: Lang, 1980. xiii + 100 pp.
Classified bibliography of 722 items.

741.   *Los ensayistas*. Vols. 1–31. Athens: U of Georgia, 1976–91.
Bibliographies of studies on Spanish and Spanish American essayists. Published at irregular intervals.

Gay Authors and Literature

742.   Foster, David William, ed. *Latin American Writers on Gay and Lesbian Themes: A Bio-critical Sourcebook*. Westport: Greenwood, 1994. 544 pp.
"Each entry assesses and analyzes homoerotic elements in the work of a particular author and closes with a bibliography of primary and secondary material" (Greenwood catalog). Provides entries for more than 100 authors.

743.   Howes, Robert. "The Literature of Outsiders: The Literature of the Gay Community in Latin America." *Latin American Masses and Minorities: Their Images and Realities*. Ed. Dan C. Hazen. Vol. 1. [Madison]: SALALM, 1987. 288–304.
Includes data on literature with homosexuality as a theme and literature by homosexuals, as well as comments on homosexual periodicals.

744.   ———. "Select Bibliography of Latin American Publications Dealing with Homosexuality." *Latin American Masses and Minorities: Their Images and Realities*. Ed. Dan C. Hazen. Vol. 2. [Madison]: SALALM, 1987. 580–91.

Has sections on Spanish American and Brazilian imaginative literature; items marked with an asterisk have homosexuality as their central theme. Contains a valuable listing of gay movement serials published in both Brazil and Spanish America.

Indigenist Authors

745. Echeverría, Evelio. "La novela indigenista hispano-americana: Definición y bibliografía." *Revista interamericana de bibliografía* 35 (1985): 287–96.

746. Foster, David William. "Bibliografía del indigenismo hispano-americano." *Revista iberoamericana* 50.127 (1984): 587–620.
   After listing general studies, the bibliography covers 11 authors. Sections on each author are divided into works, bibliographies, monographs and dissertations, and critical articles. The critical material is limited to studies that deal with "cuestiones del indigenismo o cuestiones paralelas a las obras señeras del mismo" (587).

Modernismo

747. Anderson, Robert Roland. *Spanish American Modernism: A Selected Bibliography*. Tucson: U of Arizona P, 1970. xxii + 167 pp.
   Provides data on critical studies for 17 authors of this period. Individual index for each author. Extremely useful for period covered.

748. Fretes, Hilda Gladys, and Esther Barbará, comps. *Bibliografía anotada del modernismo*. Cuadernos de la biblioteca 5. Mendoza: Biblioteca Central, U ، Central de Cuyo, 1970. 138 pp.
   Annotates 245 items. Emphasis is on the movement rather than individual authors.

Poetry

749. Forster, Merlin H. "Bibliografía." *Historia de la poesía hispanoamericana*. Clear Creek: American Hispanist, 1981. 209–34.
   This classified bibliography, though extremely selective, is quite useful.

750. Hoffman, Herbert H. *Hoffman's Index to Poetry: European and Latin American Poetry in Anthologies*. Metuchen: Scarecrow, 1985. xiii + 672 pp.
   Indexes poems from these areas found in almost 100 anthologies. There are indexes both by title and by first line.

Vanguard Literature

751.   Forster, Merlin H., and K. David Jackson. *Vanguardism in Latin American Literature: An Annotated Bibliographical Guide*. Westport: Greenwood, 1990. xii + 214 pp.
Includes a general list of sources for the period and a listing by country of reference sources, journals, writings, and critical studies. Name index.

Authors

752.   Mundo Lo, Sara de. *The Andean Countries*. Boston: Hall, 1981. 496 pp. Vol. 1 of *Index to Spanish American Collective Biography*. 4 vols to date. 1981– .
An index to biographical studies published in books. The annotation for each volume almost always lists the biographies included. This volume provides such data for Chile, Bolivia, Ecuador, Colombia, and Venezuela. It should be emphasized that the index is to biographies in collections and that book-length studies do not appear. It is a valuable source for biographical data. See also nos. 782, 836, 975.

753.   Zubatsky, David S. *Latin American Literary Authors: An Annotated Guide to Bibliographies*. Metuchen: Scarecrow, 1986. ix + 332 pp.
This indispensable guide to bibliographies of Latin American authors "includes citations that appear in periodicals, books, dissertations, and *Festschrift* volumes" (v).

Women Authors

754.   Cortina, Lynn Ellen Rice. *Spanish-American Women Writers*. New York: Garland, 1983. xi + 292 pp.
Arranged by countries. Provides the author's dates and lists her publications.

755.   Corvalán, Graciela N. V. *Latin American Women Writers in English Translation: A Bibliography*. Latin American Bibliography Series 9. Los Angeles: Latin American Studies Center, California State U, 1980. iv + 109 pp.
Data provided on 282 women writers whose works have either been translated into English or for whom there are critical or biographical studies in English.

756.   Cypess, Sandra Messinger, David R. Kohut, and Rachelle Moore. *Women Authors of Modern Hispanic South America: A Bibliography of Literary Criticism and Interpretation*. Metuchen: Scarecrow, 1989. xii + 156 pp.
Lists criticism of the writings of 169 modern women authors from Argentina, Bolivia, Chile, Colombia, Ecuador, Paraguay, Peru, Uruguay, and Venezuela. Arranged by country. Critical studies are listed under each author and grouped by genre.

757. Knaster, Meri. "Literature, Mass Media, and Folklore." *Women in Spanish America: An Annotated Bibliography from Pre-Conquest to Contemporary Times*. Boston: Hall, 1977. 39–94.
Items 160–414 of this extremely selective annotated list deal with women writers of this area.

758. Marting, Diane E., ed. *Spanish American Women Writers: A Bio-bibliographical Source Book*. New York: Greenwood, 1990. xxvi + 645 pp.; *Escritoras de Hispano-américa: Una guía bio-bibliográfica*. Prólogo, coordinación y revisión de la edición en español por Montserrat Ordoñez. Bogotá: Siglo XXI, 1990. 638 pp.
Excellent biobibliographical source for information on 50 prominent women writers of Latin America and the Caribbean, from colonial to contemporary times. Each entry provides biographical information, a discussion of major themes, and a survey of criticism. Includes a bibliography of the author's works and literary criticism. An essay on Indian women writers and one on Latinas include extensive bibliographies. The work concludes with an extensive bibliography of sources and criticism (569–76) as well as a listing of authors by genre and country.

759. ———. *Women Writers of Spanish America: An Annotated Bio-bibliographical Guide*. Bibliographies and Indexes in Women's Studies 5. New York: Greenwood, 1987. 448 pp.
Annotated guide to the literary works of women writers in Latin America. Includes Hispanic American women if their works are principally in Spanish. Occasionally includes biographical information. Has the following appendixes: an annotated list of anthologies on women writers; a list of authors born before 1900; a list of authors by country; a list of translations; and bilingual editions.

760. Sonntag Grigera, María Gabriela. "Lesser-Known Latin American Women Authors: A Bibliography." *Revista interamericana de bibliografía* 42 (1992): 463–88.
Provides data on works by and about 17 contemporary women authors.

ARGENTINA

Dictionaries

761. Organbide, Pedro G., and Roberto Yahni. *Enciclopedia de la literatura argentina*. Buenos Aires: Sudamericana, 1970. 639 pp.
Provides biographies and critical comments on Argentine authors. Most entries are signed by 1 of the 19 contributors, and many include very brief biographical data about the author.

762. *Diccionario de la literatura latinoamericana: Argentina*. 2 vols. Washington: Pan American Union, 1960–61.

The material on each author is divided into 2 sections. The first is a biographical and critical sketch; the second is a bibliography of the author's separately published works and critical studies on them.

763.   Prieto, Adolfo. *Diccionario básico de literatura argentina*. Biblioteca Argentina Fundamental. [Buenos Aires: Centro Editor de América Latina, 1968]. 159 pp.
Provides brief biographies of important authors and entries on literary works and movements but no bibliography of critical studies.

Bibliography (General)

764.   Foster, David William. *Argentine Literature: A Research Guide*. 2nd ed. New York: Garland, 1982. xliii + 778 pp.
Fullest bibliography of critical studies on Argentine literature. General references are divided into 30 sections. The sections devoted to 73 authors are divided into bibliographies, critical monographs and dissertations, and critical essays.

Bibliographies (Current)

765.   *Bibliografía argentina: Indice de revistas, registro selectivo de artículos correspondientes a las siguientes materias de interés nacional: . . . cultura*. Nos. 1–2. Buenos Aires: Centro de Estudios Bibliográficos de Argentina, 1977, 1981.
The publisher hoped to have this bibliography appear twice a year but apparently issued only 2 numbers. It is a classified bibliography with a subject index.

766.   *Bibliografía argentina de artes y letras*. 52 vols. Buenos Aires: Fondo Nacional de las Artes, 1959–71.
Bibliographies of current books and articles arranged by subject. *Compilaciones especiales* contain bibliographies on special topics such as Argentine literary periodicals and theater criticism.

Drama

767.   Ferdis, Rubén. *Diccionario sobre el origen del teatro argentino*. Buenos Aires: Kleiner, 1988. 104 pp.

768.   Foppa, Tito Livio. *Diccionario teatral del Río de la Plata*. Buenos Aires: Carro de Tespis, 1961. 1,046 pp.
Includes dramatists from the beginning of the Argentine theater up to the present, as well as data on theaters, theatrical groups, and so on.

769.   Martínez, Martha. "Bibliografía sobre teatro argentino (1955–1976)." *Ottawa Hispánica* 5 (1983): 89–100.

The 122 entries do not include studies on individual dramatists; they deal only with the Argentine theater.

770. Pepe, Luz E., and María Luisa Punte. *La crítical teatral argentina, 1880–1962*. Spec. issue of *Bibliografía argentina de artes y letras* 27–28 (1966): 6–78.
Classified bibliography of the Argentine theater (including the circus, puppets, children's theater, and so on) for the period covered.

771. Zayas de Lima, Perla. *Diccionario de autores teatrales argentinos, 1950–1980*. Buenos Aires: Alonso, [1981]. 188 pp.
Provides brief biographical sketches of the dramatists of the period and a list of their published works, as well as data on the performances of their plays.

Fiction

772. Chertudi, Susana. *El cuento folklórico y literario regional*. Spec. issue of *Bibliografía argentina de artes y letras* 16 (1962): 1–35.
Annotated classified bibliography.

773. Trevia Paz, Susana N. *Contribución a la bibliografía del cuento fantástico argentino en el siglo XX*. Spec. issue of *Bibliografía argentina de artes y letras* 29–30 (1966): 1–49.
Provides classified bibliographies of fantasy short stories by 12 authors.

Jewish Authors

774. Weinstein, Ana E., and Miryam E. Gover de Nasatsky. *Escritores judeo-argentinos: Bibliografía 1900–1987*. 2 vols. Buenos Aires: Milá, 1994.
Classified, unannotated bibliography of material by and about Jewish Argentine writers. 10,066 entries.

Library Catalog

775. Universidad de Buenos Aires. *Bibliografía argentina: Catálogo de materiales argentinos en las bibliotecas de la Universidad de Buenos Aires*. 7 vols. Boston: Hall, 1980.
Dictionary catalog of books and pamphlets held at the university through 1978. Includes Argentine authors published outside the country.

Poetry

776. Frugoni de Fritzche, Teresita. *Indice de poetas argentinos.* 4 vols. in 1. Guías bibliográficas 8. Buenos Aires: Facultad de Filosofía y Letras, Inst. de Literatura Argentina "Ricardo Rojas," U de Buenos Aires, 1963–68.
Alphabetical by author; titles in chronological order.

777. Gobello, José, and Jorge A. Bossio. *Tangos, letras y letristas.* 5 vols. Buenos Aires: Plus Ultra, 1993–95.
Anthologies usually have not been listed; however, the introductions to the poetry selections provide data about the poets not readily available elsewhere.

778. González Castro, Augusto. *Panoramas de las antologías argentinas.* Buenos Aires: Colombo, [1966]. 293 pp.
Extensively annotated bibliography of poetry anthologies published mainly between 1839 and 1937.

779. Prosdocimi, María del Carmen. *Las antologías poéticas argentinas, 1960–1970.* Guías bibliográficas 10. Buenos Aires: Facultad de Filosofía y Letras, Inst. de Literatura Argentina "Ricardo Rojas," U de Buenos Aires, 1971. 32 pp.
Evaluates the almost 20 poetry anthologies listed in her "Bibliografía de las antologías poéticas" (6–7).

Pseudonyms

780. Cutolo, Vicente Osvaldo. *Diccionario de alfónimos y seudónimos de la Argentina, 1900–1930.* Buenos Aires: Elche, 1962. 160 pp.
Provides an introduction, "Para una historia de alfónimos y seudónimos de la Argentina" (7–8), followed by 1,099 entries.

781. Durán, Leopoldo. *Contribución a un diccionario de seudónimos en la Argentina.* Buenos Aires: Huemul, [1961]. 60 pp.
Divided into "Iniciales y seudónimos/nombres" and "Nombres/seudónimos e iniciales."

Authors

782. Mundo Lo, Sara de. *The River Plate Countries.* Boston: Hall, 1985. xxxi + 388 pp. Vol. 4 of *Index to Spanish American Collective Biography.* 4 vols. to date. 1981– .
See no. 752. Indexes individuals from Argentina, Paraguay, and Uruguay whose biographies are found in collective biographies.

783. Becco, Horacio Jorge, and Oscar Mascotta. *Roberto Arlt.* Guías bibliográficas 2. Buenos Aires: Facultad de Filosofía y Letras, Inst. de Literatura Argentina "Ricardo Rojas," U de Buenos Aires, 1959. 10 pp.
Classified bibliography of material by and about Arlt.

784. López, Susanna Beatriz. *Contribucción a la bibliografía de Rafael Alberto Arrieta.* Spec. issue of *Bibliografía argentina de artes y letras* 37–38 (1970): 1–71.
A classified bibliography of 873 items by and about Arrieta.

785. Lacunza, Angélica Beatriz. *Bibliografía de Francisco Luis Bernárdez.* Guías bibliográficas 7. Buenos Aires: Facultad de Filosofía y Letras, Inst. de Literatura Argentina "Ricardo Rojas," U de Buenos Aires, 1962. 26 pp. Rpt. in *La obra poética de Francisco Luis Bernárdez.* . . . By Lacunza. Buenos Aires: Huemul, 1964. 199–208.
A bibliography of works by and about Bernárdez.

786. Balderston, Daniel. *The Literary Universe of Jorge Luis Borges: An Index to References and Allusions, to Persons, Titles and Places in His Writings.* Bibliographies and Indexes in World Literature 9. New York: Greenwood, 1986. xxxi + 305 pp.

787. Becco, Horacio Jorge. *Jorge Luis Borges: Bibliografía total, 1923–1973.* Buenos Aires: Pardo, 1973. 244 pp.
This bibliography of 1,381 items is divided into "Obras del autor," "Obras en colaboración," "Prólogos y ediciones," "Ediciones privadas," "Traducciones de su obra," "Discografía," "Crítica y biografía," "Diálogos y reportajes," and "Bibliografías e iconografía."

788. Foster, David William. *Jorge Luis Borges: An Annotated Primary and Secondary Bibliography.* Introd. Martin S. Stabb. New York: Garland, 1984. xlv + 328 pp.
Fullest bibliography of this author. Includes an index of original titles of Borges's works and an index of critics, translators, illustrators, and coauthors.

789. Istituto Italo-Latino Americano. *Jorge Luis Borges (In occasione del "Colloquio con Jorge Luis Borges," che si terrá il 12 octobre, 1984).* Centro documentazione. Bibliographía 5. Roma: Ist. Italo-Latino Americano, 1984. 50 pp.
This bibliography is especially useful for Italian items on Borges. It was produced on the occasion of Borges's winning the Novecento Prize in 1984. Divided into "Borges autore"; "Borges e *Sur*: 1) Autore. 2) Critico letterario. 3) Critico cinematografico"; "Borges e la stampa italiana"; and "Borges e la stampa estera." Numerous items are incomplete.

790. Isbister, Rob, and Peter Standish, comps. *A Concordance to the Works of Jorge Luis Borges (1899–1986) Argentine Author.* 7 vols. Lewiston: Mellen, 1991.
Concordance based on *El Aleph, Ficciones, El libro de arena,* and *El informe de Brodie.* Title should perhaps have indicated that the work is a concordance to 4 of his prose works.

791.   Loewenstein, C. Jared. *A Descriptive Catalogue of the Jorge Luis Borges Collections at the University of Virginia.* Charlottesville: UP of Virginia, 1993. 254 pp.

This catalog describes one of the finest Borges collections in the United States.

792.   Scarano, Tommaso, and Manuela Sassi. *Concordanze per lèmma dell'opera in versi di J. L. Borges con repertorio metrico e rimario.* Viareggio-Lucca: Baroni, 1992. 957 pp.

A concordance of the poetry based on Borges's *Obras completas* (Buenos Aires: Emecé, 1989).

793.   Mundo Lo, Sara de. *Julio Cortázar: His Work and His Critics. A Bibliography.* Urbana: Albatross, 1985. 274 pp.

Highly classified bibliography of 2,619 items of material by and about Cortázar, with an index of Cortázar's works in book form, an author index, a list of journals cited, and a chronology.

794.   Rossi, Iris. *Contribución a la bibliografía de Juan Carlos Dávalos.* Spec. issue of *Bibliographía argentina de artes y letras* 23 (1966): 1–91.

A bibliography of material by and about Dávalos.

795.   Aldecua, Francisco F. *Bibliohemerografía de María Elena Dubecq.* Buenos Aires: Agon, 1985. 46 pp.

A classified bibliography of material by and about Dubecq.

796.   Kisnerman, Natalio. *Contribución a la bibliografía de Esteban Echeverría (1805–1970).* Buenos Aires: Publicaciones de la Facultad de Filología y Letras, U Nacional, 1971. 123 pp.

Divided into "Bibliografía (de obras y crítica)," which lists 740 partially annotated items; "Iconografía . . ."; "Addenda a la bibliografía de obras"; "Bibliografía general"; and "Indice de autores y temas."

797.   Fernández Moreno, César, and Manrique Fernández Moreno. *Bibliografía de [Baldomero] Fernández Moreno.* Guías bibliográficas 5. Buenos Aires: Facultad de Filosofía y Letras, Inst. de Literatura Argentina "Ricardo Rojas," U de Buenos Aires, 1961. 105 pp.

Lists 1,059 items by and about Fernández Moreno.

798.   Kisnerman, Natalio. *Bibliografía de Manuel Gálvez.* Spec. issue of *Bibliografía argentina de artes y letras* 17 (1964): 1–75.

Classified bibliography of 1,165 items by and about Gálvez.

799.   Gover de Nasatsky, Miryam Esther. *Bibliografía de Alberto Gerchunoff.* Buenos Aires: Fondo Nacional de las Artes, Soc. Hebraica Argentina, 1976. 255 pp.

Classified bibliography of Gerchunoff's publications and of critical studies on them. The 1,845 items have both a proper name index and a title index.

800. Becco, Horacio Jorge. *Ricardo Güiraldes.* Guías bibliográficas 1. Buenos Aires: Facultad de Filosofía y Letras, Inst. de Literatura Argentina "Ricardo Rojas," U de Buenos Aires, 1959. 35 pp.
Divided into "Libros," "Separatas y folletos," and "Obras completas."

801. Benson, Nettie Lee, et al. *Catalog of* Martín Fierro *Materials in the University of Texas Library.* Guides and Bibliographies Series 6. Austin: Inst. of Latin American Studies, U of Texas, 1972. 135 pp.
Classified bibliography of 787 items about *Martín Fierro.*

802. Scroggins, Daniel C. *A Concordance of José Hernández'* Martín Fierro. U of Missouri Studies 53. Columbia: U of Missouri P, 1971. 251 pp.
Based on the critical edition by Eleuterio Tiscornia (Buenos Aires: Coni, 1925).

803. Montero, María Luisa, and Angélica L. Tórtola. *Contribución a la bibliografía de Enrique Larreta.* Spec. issue of *Bibliografía argentina de artes y letras* 19 (1964): 1–59.
Classified bibliography of works by and about Larreta.

804. Becco, Horacio Jorge. *Leopoldo Lugones: Bibliografía de su centenario (1876–1974).* [Buenos Aires]: Culturales Argentinas, 1978. 169 pp.
Contains an introduction as well as several indexes. Divided into "Obras del autor" (a classified bibliography), "Crítica y biografía," "Bibliografías," and "Addenda."

805. Cohen, Howard Randolph. "Critical Approaches to Mallea and Sábato: An Annotated Bibliography." Diss. U of Virginia, 1977. 288 pp.
A bibliography of critical studies on Mallea and Sábato. The items are arranged chronologically and are well annotated. Cohen is also the compiler of "Eduardo Mallea: A Selective Annotated Bibliography of Criticism" (*Hispania* 62 [1979]: 444–67), which is based on the dissertation. This article has 134 well-annotated items published between 1935 and 1978.

806. Giannengeli, Liliana. *Contribución a la bibliografía de José Mármol.* Textos, documentos y bibliografías 5. La Plata: Facultad de Humanidades y Ciencias de la Educación, Dept. de Letras, Inst. de Literatura Argentina e Iberoamericana, U Nacional de La Plata, 1972. 254 pp.
Classified bibliography of 811 items by and about Mármol. Those about him are not well annotated.

807. Adam, Carlos. *Bibliografía y documentos de Ezequiel Martínez Estrada.* . . . Textos, documentos y bibliografías 3. La Plata: Facultad de Humanidades y Ciencias de la Educación, U Nacional de La Plata, 1968. 247 pp.
Classified bibliography of 1,056 items by and about Martínez Estrada. The review by S. R. Wilson (*Hispanic Review* 38 [1970]: 446–51) contains useful additions and corrections.

808.   Tuninetti, Beatriz T. *Contribución a la bibliografía de Victoria Ocampo.* Guías bibliográficas 6. Buenos Aires: Facultad de Filosofía y Letras, Inst. de Literatura Argentina "Ricardo Rojas," U de Buenos Aires, 1962. 26 pp.
Classified bibliography of 304 items by and about Ocampo.

809.   Lena Paz, Marta. *Bibliografía crítica de Carlos Mauricio Pacheco, aporte para su estudio.* Spec. issue of *Bibliografía argentina de artes y letras* 14 (1963) 1–94.
Classified bibliography of works by and about Pacheco.

810.   Kisnerman, Natalio. *Bibliografía de Antonio Pagés Larraya.* Buenos Aires: Argentino, 1963. 25 pp.
Lists 301 items by and about Pagés Larraya.

811.   Fernández de Vidal, Stella Maris. *Bibliografía de Roberto J. Payró.* Supp. to *Bibliografía argentina de artes y letras* 13 (1962): 1–73.
Classified bibliography of 1,065 items by and about Payró.

812.   Baralis, Marta. *Contribución a la bibliografía de Alfonsina Storni.* Spec. issue of *Bibliografía argentina de artes y letras* 18 (1964): 1–64.
Classified bibliography of material by and about Storni.

813.   Buffa Peyrot, Yolanda H. *Contribución a la bibliografía de Eduardo Wilde.* Spec. issue of *Bibliografía argentina de artes y letras* 31 (1967): 1–106.
Classified bibliography of 933 items of material by and about Wilde.

Bolivia

Dictionaries

814.   Guzmán, Augusto. *Biografías de la literatura boliviana: Biografía, evaluación, bibliografía.* Enciclopedia boliviana. Cochabamba: Amigos del Libro, 1982. 307 pp.
Does not include literary criticism.

815.   ———. *Diccionario de literatura latinoamericana: Bolivia.* Washington: Pan American Union, 1957. xi + 121 pp.
The material on each author is divided into 2 sections: the first is a biographical and critical sketch; the second is a bibliography of the author's separately published works and critical studies on them.

816.   Ortega, José, and Adolfo Cáceres Romero. *Diccionario de la literatura boliviana.* La Paz: Amigos del Libro, 1977. 337 pp.
Provides data on authors since 1825, when Bolivia became independent. Includes a brief biography, a list of works, and a bibliography of criticism.

Bibliographies

817. Arze, José Roberto. "Ensayo de una bibliografía biográfica boliviana." *Bio-bibliografía boliviana, 1978.* La Paz: Amigos del Libro, 1980. 203–72. Rpt. as *Ensayo.* . . . La Paz: Amigos del Libro, 1981. 71 pp.
Lists 367 biographies, autobiographies, memoirs, and *repertorios biográficos.*

818. Costa de la Torre, Arturo. *Catálogo de la bibliografía boliviana: Libros y folletos 1900–1963.* Vol. 1. La Paz: U Mayor de San Andrés, 1966. 1,254 pp.
Brief biographies of 3,003 authors, each followed by a chronological listing of the author's separately published works. (Volume 2 deals with other subjects.)

819. Ortega, Julio. "Manual de bibliografía de la literatura boliviana." *Cuadernos hispanoamericanos* 263–64 (1972): 657–71.
Divided into history and literary criticism, anthologies and literary collections, bibliographical works and Bolivian catalogs, Bolivian periodicals and newspapers, and general sources.

820. ———. "Bibliografía selecta de la literatura de Bolivia, 1969–1974." *Revista de crítica literaria latinoamericana* 1.1 (1975): 159–69.
Classified and annotated.

Drama

821. Soria, Mario T. "Bibliografía de teatro boliviano del siglo XX." *Teatro boliviano en el siglo XX.* La Paz: Biblioteca Popular Boliviana de "Ultima Hora," 1980. 211–26.
Plays, often with incomplete bibliographical data, are arranged in chronological order under the name of the dramatist. Pages 227–30 are a valuable list of articles and essays on the Bolivian theater and dramatists.

Fiction

822. Echeverría, Evelio. "Panorama y bibliografía de la novela social boliviana." *Revista interamericana de bibliografía* 27 (1977): 143–52.
The bibliography (149–52) is divided into 1904–52 and 1952–70.

823. Paz Soldán, Alba María. "Indice de la novela boliviana (1931–1978)." *Revista iberoamericana* 52.134 (1986): 311–20.
Within each decade, arranged alphabetically by novelist.

824. Poppe, René. *Indice de los libros de cuentos bolivianos: Primera parte.* Cuadernos de investigación 2. La Paz: Inst. Boliviano de Cultura, Inst. Nacional de Historia y Literatura, 1979. 13 pp.

825.   ———. *Indice del cuento minero boliviano*. La Paz: Inst. Boliviano de Cultura, Inst. Nacional de Historia y Literatura, Dept. de Literatura, 1979. 16 pp.

Useful lists (nos. 824 and 825) of Bolivian short stories.

Author

826.   Siles Guevara, Juan. *Bibliografía preliminar de Ricardo Jaimes Freyre*. Cuadernos de bibliografía 2. La Paz: Ministerio de Informaciones, Cultura y Turismo, 1969. 36 pp.

CARIBBEAN AREA

827.   Coll, Edna. *Las Antillas. Indice informativo de la novela hispanoamericana*. Vol. 1. Río Piedras: U de Puerto Rico, 1974. 418 pp.
Bibliographical dictionary of novelists in Cuba, Puerto Rico, and the Dominican Republic.

828.   Fenwick, M. J. *Writers of the Caribbean and Central America: A Bibliography*. 2 vols. New York: Garland, 1992.
An overambitious work arranged by country (it includes the English-, French-, Dutch-, and Spanish-speaking areas that the Caribbean touches). Compiler gives only the titles and dates of the authors' works. Since he has not personally examined all works listed, bibliographical ghosts sometimes appear, such as the attribution to Juan Rulfo of *La Cordillera* (1966), which was never published.

829.   Herdeck, Donald E., et al. "Spanish Language Literature from the Caribbean." *Caribbean Writers: A Bio-bibliographical Encyclopedia*. Washington: Three Continents, 1979. 599–943.
Includes a biobibliographical dictionary of the writers of Cuba, the Dominican Republic, and Puerto Rico (629–910). Attempts to list the important works of all the authors covered. Many more entries could have been added to the biographical-critical bibliographies. The volume concludes with sections on critical studies, bibliographies, and anthologies for Cuba, the Dominican Republic, and Puerto Rico, including brief essays on the literatures of these areas.

830.   Paravisini-Gebert, Lizabeth, and Olga Torres-Seda. *Caribbean Women Novelists: An Annotated Critical Bibliography*. Westport: Greenwood, 1993. xv + 427 pp.
Includes 23 novelists from Cuba, 10 from the Dominican Republic, and 18 from Puerto Rico. A biographical sketch of 3 or 4 lines is followed by a listing of

and an annotation of the author's novels. Other works by the author are listed by their literary genre; translations, critical studies, and reviews are also given.

831.   Perrier, José Luis. *Bibliografía dramática cubana, incluye a Puerto Rico y Santo Domingo*. New York: Phos, 1926. 115 pp.
The authors of the 3 areas appear in 1 alphabetical list; gives no critical studies of authors and their works.

CENTRAL AMERICA

832.   Arellano, Jorge Eduardo. "Bibliografía general de la literatura centroamericana." *Boletín nicaragüense de bibliografía y documentación* 29 (1979): 1–5.
Contains 55 unannotated items divided into reference works, anthologies, and critical studies.

833.   Coll, Edna. *Centroamérica. Indice informativo de la novela hispanoamericana*. Vol. 2. Río Piedras: U de Puerto Rico, 1977. 343 pp.
Biographical dictionary of novelists of Central America.

834.   Flores, Carlos Gregorio. *Biografías de escritores salvadoreños*. [San Salvador: Editorial Libertad, 1994]. 178 pp.
Biographical sketches of 79 authors and brief selections of their work.

835.   Fenwick, M. J. See no 828.

836.   Mundo Lo, Sara de. *The Central American and Caribbean Countries*. Boston: Hall, 1984. xxxiii + 360 pp. Vol. 3 of *Index to Spanish American Collective Biography*. 4 vols. to date. 1981– .
See no. 752.

CHILE

Dictionaries

837.   *Diccionario de la literatura latinoamericana: Chile*. Washington: Pan American Union, 1958. 234 pp.
The material on each author is divided into 2 sections; the first is a biographical and critical sketch; the second is a bibliography of the author's separately published works and critical studies on them.

838.   Neghme Rodríguez, Amador. *La obra literaria de los médicos chilenos*. Santiago: Bello, [1984]. 257 pp.
Biographical dictionary of Chilean physicians who have also been writers.

839.   Rafide Batarce, Matias. *Diccionario de autores de la región del Maule.* Talca: Rafide, 1984. 572 pp.
Biobibliographical and critical data on the writers of this area.

840.   Rojas, Luis Emilio. *Biografía cultural de Chile.* 2nd ed. Santiago: Gong, 1988. 343 pp.
Includes biographies of authors.

841.   Szmulewicz, Efraín. *Diccionario de la literatura chilena.* 2nd ed., corrected and enlarged. Santiago: Bello, 1984. xviii + 494 pp.
Contains brief biographical information and a list of authors' works. Appendix includes information on literary groups and organizations, literary prizes and recipients, and a general bibliography on Chilean literature. Numerous errors.

Bibliographies

842.   *Bibliografía chilena de obras en el exilio. Lista parcial. 1973–1985.* Santiago: Comité Pro-Retorno de Exiliados Chilenos, SEREC, 1986. 34 leaves. Mimeographed.
Has 637 items that include works by exiled Chilean authors. Because of the difficulties in obtaining works by exiled Chilean authors, the material is not exhaustive, and the bibliographical entries are not complete.

843.   Domínguez D., Marta. *Biobibliografía de nuevos escritores de Chile.* Santiago: SEREC, 1993. 35 leaves. Mimeographed.
". . . reúne una muestra de escritores chilenos nacidos desde el año 1945, aquellos que se cuentan entre los escritores jóvenes" (presentación).

844.   ———. *Bibliografía anotada de escritores de Chile, 1569–1976.* Santiago: SEREC, 1994. 192 leaves. Mimeographed.
The "Presentación" states that "Esta obra, ordenada por generaciones bien definidas, cubre a narradores, poetas ensayistas, críticos, periodistas, dramaturgos, bibliógrafos e historiadores chilenos que produjeron sus obras en el período señalado. Concluye con un índice alfabético de los autores y la bibliografía revisada, que enriquecen la información." Gives the barest bibliographical details: author, dates, titles of works, literary genre, and dates of works.

845.   Foster, David William. *Chilean Literature: A Working Bibliography of Secondary Sources.* Boston: Hall, 1978. xxii + 236 pp.
Divided into 2 main sections: general references and bibliographies of the 46 authors, which are divided into bibliographies, critical books and theses, and critical essays. Index of critics.

846.   Jofré, Manuel Alcides. *Literatura chilena en el exilio.* Santiago: CENECA, 1986. 89 pp.
Except for the interesting prefatory material concerning Chilean exile literature, the data duplicate some of those in the *Bibliografía chilena de obras en el exilio* (no.

842). Material, regardless of genre, is arranged chronologically by author. Many of the items listed are known to the compiler secondhand; consequently, it is incomplete.

847.   Rojas Piña, Benjamín. "Bibliografía de la literatura chilena, 1967–1968." *Revista chilena de literatura* 1 (1970): 97–117.

848.   ———. "Bibliografía de la literatura chilena, 1969–1970." *Revista chilena de literatura* 2–3 (1970): 215–39.

Classified bibliographies (nos. 847 and 848) that often provide the contents of the works cited.

Current Bibliography

849.   Biblioteca Nacional de Chile. *Referencias críticas sobre autores chilenos* 1–9 (1968–74) pub. 1969–77; cont. by *Referencias . . . chilenos. Con apéndice sobre autores españoles e iberoamericanos* 10–18 (1975–83) pub. 1978–91; 22–23 (1987–88) pub. 1992–94.
Chile has been one of the few countries to produce a current bibliography of criticism of its authors and of authors from Spain and the Iberoamerican countries. The volume for 1988 indexes material in 111 journals; it also indexes literary material in newspapers. For many years it was produced under the supervision of Justo Alarcón. Steps should be taken to bring it out more promptly.

Drama

850.   Durán Cerda, Julio. *Repertorio del teatro chileno: Bibliografía, obras inéditas, obras estrenadas*. Publicaciones del Inst. de Literatura Chilena, serie C: Bibliografías y registros 1. Santiago: Inst. de Literatura Chilena, 1962. 247 pp.
Essential bibliography on the Chilean theater that lists 1,710 plays as well as important studies on the theater in Chile since 1910.

Fiction

851.   Castillo, Homero, and Raúl Silva Castro. *Historia bibliográfica de la novela chilena*. Charlottesville: Bibliographical Soc. of the U of Virginia, 1961. 214 pp.
Provides data on Chilean novels and short story collections.

852.   Echeverría, Evelio. "La novela histórica de Chile: Deslinde y bibliografía (1852–1990)." *Revista interamericana de bibliografía* 42 (1992): 643–50.
Lists 65 novels that fit the compiler's 7-point criteria for being historical novels.

853. Goić, Cedomil. "Bibliografía de la novela chilena del siglo XX." *Boletín de filología de la Universidad de Chile* 14 (1962): 51–168.
Excludes short stories and anthologies. Lists 1,232 items written chiefly between 1910 and 1961.

854. Guerra-Cunningham, Lucía. "Fuentes bibliográficas para el estudio de la novela chilena, 1843–1960." *Revista iberoamericana* 42.96–97 (1976): 601–19.
Classified bibliography of general studies on the Chilean novel.

855. Lastra, Pedro. "Registro bibliográfico de antologías del cuento chileno, 1876–1976." *Revista crítica literaria latinoamericana* 5 (1977): 89–111.
Chronological arrangement. Indicates contents of anthologies.

856. Román-Lagunas, Jorge. *The Chilean Novel: A Critical Study of Secondary Sources and a Bibliography.* Lanham: Scarecrow, 1995. xi + 560 pp.
Extremely important bibliography of the Chilean novel based on the author's dissertation ("La novela chilena: Estudio bibliográfico." 2 vols. Diss. U of Arizona, 1985. 752 pp.). The two translators are noted in the acknowledgments. The main sections are "Preface," "Classification of the Material," "Part I. Critical Analysis of the General Studies," "Part II. Secondary Sources on Special Topics," and "Part III. Secondary Sources on Chilean Novelists." The sections on the 48 authors are often divided into "Bibliographies," "Books and Doctoral Dissertations," "Monographic Studies," "Nonmonographic Studies," "Reviews," "Histories of Literature, Panoramas, Dictionaries, etc.," "Notes and References," and "Interviews and Statements." It is not obvious how up-to-date Román-Lagunas has tried to be. He refers to the 1977 edition of Efraín Szmulewicz, *Diccionario de la literatura chilena,* rather than to that of 1984. One wonders at the omission of Skármeta.

857. Villacura Fernández, Maúd. "Bibliografía de narradores chilenos nacidos entre 1935–1949." *Revista chilena de literatura* 4 (1973): 109–28.
Lists books and short stories published in anthologies, periodicals, and newspapers, both Chilean and foreign, as well as translations between 1956 and 1970.

Library Catalog

858. Welch, Thomas L. *Catálogo de la colección de la literatura chilena en la Biblioteca Colón.* Documentation and Information Series 7. Washington: Columbus Memorial Library, 1983. ix + 154 pp.
Lists works by and about Chilean authors and works about Chilean literature in the Columbus library.

Literary Movements

859. Múñoz González, Luis, and Dieter Oelker Link. *Diccionario de movimientos y grupos literarios chilenos*. Concepción: U de Concepción, 1993. 344 pp.

According to the back cover, this volume "está constituido por un conjunto de dieciocho monografías abreviadas sobre los movimientos y grupos literarios que ha venido estableciendo nuestra tradición creadora y crítica en el ámbito de la Literatura Chilena. Comprende el período que va desde la Independencia manifestada en 'El movimiento literario de 1842' hasta la llamada 'Generación de 1950,' en plena vida democrática." Each monograph is signed by its author. The bibliographies at the end of each section are extremely valuable. Unfortunately there is no index of authors or titles mentioned in the text.

Poetry

860. Escudero, Alfonso M. "Fuentes de consulta sobre los poetas románticos chilenos." *Aisthesis* 5 (1970): 295–307.

Provides biographical and critical materials on 9 Chilean romantic poets.

Pseudonyms

861. Torres Marín, Manuel. *Aproximación al seudónimo literario chileno*. Santiago: Universitaria, 1985. 83 pp.

General remarks on the uses of pseudonyms in Chile. Contains 2 lists: "Elenco de seudónimos" (65–73) and "Elenco de autores" (74-81).

Authors

862. Biblioteca Nacional. Sección Referencias Críticas. *Indice general de artículos de Juan Marín Rojas*. Prod. under the direction of Justo Alarcón, 1991. 176 leaves.

Chronological, unannotated bibliography of 2,011 entries with a useful index. Marín was a journalist, doctor, and critic.

863. Escudero, Alfonso M. *La prosa de Gabriela Mistral: Fichas de contribución a su inventario*. 2nd ed. Santiago: Anales de U de Chile, 1957. 62 pp.

Annotates 549 works by Mistral, including books, journals, and newspaper articles.

864. Guillón Barret, Ivonne. "Bibliografía anotada de la prosa." *Antología mayor. Gabriela Mistral vida y obra*. Ed. Luis Alberto Ganderas. Vol. 4. Santiago: Cochrane, 1992. 206–544.

Classified bibliography of 947 entries, of which 927 are annotated.

865.   Rubio, Patricia. *Gabriela Mistral ante la crítica: Bibliografía anotada.* Santiago: Dirección de Bibliotecas, Archivos y Museos, Centro de Investigaciones Diego Barros Arana, 1995. 437 pp.

This work is an outstanding, highly classified, extremely well-annotated bibliography of 3,908 entries followed by "Indice de poemas y prosa," "Indice de revistas y diarios citados," and "Indice onomástico."

866.   Becco, Horacio Jorge. *Pablo Neruda: Bibliografía.* Buenos Aires: Pardo, 1975. 261 pp.

Lists 1,057 items divided into "Obras," "Homenajes," "Crítica," and "Bibliografía" and provides 3 indexes. The emphasis is on material published in Argentina and Chile.

867.   Shur, Leonid Avel'evich, comp. *Pablo Neruda: Bio-bibliograficheskii.* Moscow: Izdatel'stvo Vsesoiuznoi Knizhnoi Palaty, 1960. 74 pp.

Especially valuable for its bibliography of Russian translations of Neruda and Russian critical studies about him.

868.   Woodbridge, Hensley C., and David Zubatsky. *Pablo Neruda: An Annotated Bibliography of Biographical and Critical Studies.* New York: Garland, 1988. xviii + 629 pp.

Highly classified, annotated bibliography of 2,384 items with material in such languages as English, French, Romanian, Italian, Japanese, and Spanish. Includes much Chilean material.

Women Authors

869.   González-Vergara, Ruth. *Nuestras escritoras chilenas. Una historia por descifrar.* 1 vol. to date. Santiago: Hispano-chilena, 1992– .

Volume 1 (274 pp.) discusses Chilean women writers from colonial times through the early twentieth century. Volume 2 should bring this study of women writers through 1993. Pages 211–58 are "Primer diccionario biobibliográfico de las escritoras chilenas. I Parte, A–L." Entries include name, dates, a biography of several lines, and a list of works with genre and dates. Volume 2 should complete the biobibliography.

870.   Medina, José Toribio. *La literatura femenina en Chile: Notas bibliográficas y en parte críticas.* Santiago: Universitaria, 1923. 334 pp.

Annotated, critical bibliography of books and pamphlets by Chilean women authors. Includes chapters on poetry, novels, and the theater.

871.   Rojas Piña, Benjamín, and Patricio Pinto Villaroel. *Escritoras chilenas: Teatro y ensayo.* Vol. 1. Santiago: Cuarto Propio, 1994. 236 pp.

Planned as a 3-volume set. Volume 2 will deal with narrative, while volume 3 will deal with poetry. According to the introduction, "El objetivo principal del trabajo es centrar la atención sobre la literatura y la producción intelectual de las mujeres chilenas desde el siglo XIX hasta el presente. Buscamos así, proponer lecturas de escritoras que han sido injustamente ignoradas, y de revisar y/o complementar con nuevas perspectivas las lecturas que se han hecho de la producción de las escritoras que han recibido mayor atención de la crítica." The 19 sketches are divided into "Referencia biográfica," "Análisis," sometimes "Revisión de la crítica," and "Bibliografía" of material by and about the author.

COLOMBIA

Dictionaries

872.   Sánchez López, Luis María. *Diccionario de escritores colombianos.* 3rd enl. and rev. ed. [Bogotá]: Plaza y Janés, 1985. 903 pp.
This edition is no improvement over the editions of 1978 and 1982. Gives only the barest biographical data and omits dates of authors' works.

873.   García Prada, Carlos. *Diccionario de la literatura latinoamericanana: Colombia.* Washington: Pan American Union, 1959. ix + 179 pp.
The material on each author is divided into 2 sections: the first is a biographical and critical sketch; the second is a bibliography of the author's separately published works and critical studies on them.

874.   Madrid Malo, Néstor. "Ensayo de un diccionario de la literatura colombiana." *Boletín cultural y bibliográfico* 7 (1964): 401–05, 613–18, 823–28, 1004–11, 1183–94, 1377–86, 1615–21; 9 (1966): 1766–74, 1973–82, 2206–16, 2430–37; 10 (1966): 630–37; 10 (1967): 530–38, 817–25; 10.11 (1967): 84–91; 12.5 (1969): 69–81.
Biographies of Colombian authors, A–E.

Bibliography

875.   Orjuela, Héctor H. *Fuentes generales para el estudio de la literatura colombiana.* Publicaciones del Inst. Caro y Cuervo, serie bibliográfica 7. Bogotá: Inst. Caro y Cuervo, 1968. xl + 863 pp.
Classified, often annotated bibliography of Colombian literature. Locates copies in the United States and in Colombian libraries.

Drama

876.   Orjuela, Héctor H. *Bibliografía del teatro colombiano*. Publicacions del Inst. Caro y Cuervo, serie bibliográfica 10. Bogotá: Inst. Caro y Cuervo, 1974. xxvii + 312 pp.
Lists plays written by Colombians as well as critical studies on Colombian dramatists and their works.

877.   González Cajiao, Fernando. "Adiciones a la *Bibliografía del teatro colombiano*." *Materiales para una historia del teatro en Colombia*. Bogotá: Inst. Colombiano de Cultura, 1978. 690–713.
Additions and corrections to Orjuela's bibliography (no. 876).

878.   Vitoria Bermúdez, Xorge. "Indice biobibliográfico de autores colombianos de teatro hasta el siglo XIX." *Logos* [Cali] 10 (1974): 7–22.
Provides few bibliographical details; gives the date of the first performance for the play listed. Covers the period between 1610 and 1900.

Fiction

879.   Coll, Edna. *Colombia. Indice informativo de la novela hispanoamericana*. Vol. 4. Río Piedras: U de Puerto Rico, Universitaria, 1980. 587 pp.
Bibliographical dictionary of Colombian novelists.

880.   Mena, Lucile Inés. "Bibliografía anotada sobre el ciclo de la violencia en la literatura colombiana." *Latin American Research Review* 13.3 (1978): 95–107.
Lists 74 novels of the period and annotates 35 critical studies that deal with the Colombian novels of *violencia*.

881.   Porras Collantes, Ernesto. *Bibliografía de la novela en Colombia: Con notas de contenido y crítica de las obras y guías de comentarios sobre los autores*. Publicaciones del Inst. Caro y Cuervo, serie bibliográfica 11. Bogotá: Inst. Caro y Cuervo, 1976. xix + 888 pp.
Bibliographical data on 2,326 novels published through 1974. Provides a list of pseudonyms, a title index, and a chronological index.

882.   Williams, Raymond L. "La novela colombiana, 1960–1974: Una bibliografía." *Chasqui* 5.3 (1976): 27–39.
Bibliographical data on 149 Colombian novels.

Poetry

883.   Cobo Borda, J. G. "La nueva poesía colombiana: Una década, 1970–1980." *Boletín cultural y bibliográfico* 16.9–10 (1979): 75–122.

884. Orjuela, Héctor H. *Las antologías poéticas de Colombia: Estudio y bibliografía.* Publicaciones del Inst. Caro y Cuervo, serie bibliográfica 6. Bogotá: Inst. Caro y Cuervo, 1966. xii + 514 pp.
Provides data on 389 anthologies. Lists authors for each volume and locates at least one copy in a library either in the United States or in Colombia.

885. ———. *Bibliografía de la poesía colombiana.* Publicaciones del Inst. Caro y Cuervo, serie bibliográfica 9. Bogotá: Inst. Caro y Cuervo, 1971. xxii + 486 pp.
Provides data on the principal books, pamphlets, and translations of each poet as well as on anonymous poetry. Lists translations under the name of the Colombian translator.

886. Romero Rojas, Francisco José, et al. *Bibliografía de la poesía colombiana 1970–1992.* Publicaciones del Inst. Caro y Cuervo, serie bibliográfica 14. Bogotá: Inst. Caro y Cuervo, 1993. 286 pp.
Supplements no. 885.

Pseudonyms

887. Pérez Ortiz, Rubén. *Seudónimos colombianos.* Publicaciones del Inst. Caro y Cuervo, serie bibliográfica 2. Bogotá: [Inst. Caro y Cuervo], 1961. 276 pp.
The first part is a list of pseudonyms and real names; the second part reverses the data.

Authors

888. Valle, Rafael Heliodoro. "Bibliografía de Porfirio Barba Jacob." *Thesaurus* 15 (1960): 70–173. Rpt. Bogotá: Inst. Caro y Cuervo, 1961. 107 pp.
A posthumously published work by the outstanding Honduran bibliographer seen through the press by his wife, Emilia Romero de Valle. This bibliography of Ricardo Arenales, who adopted the pseudonym Porfirio Barba Jacob, is divided into material by and about him. Many items are briefly annotated.

889. Torres Quintero, Rafael. *Bibliografía de Rufino José Cuervo.* Publicaciones del Inst. Caro y Cuervo, serie minor 2. Bogotá: [Lit. Colombia], 1951. 104 pp. Rpt. in *Rufino José Cuervo.* . . . Filólogos colombianos 1. Bogotá: Inst. Caro y Cuervo, 1954. 145–221.
Includes material by and about Cuervo.

890. Fau, Margaret Eustella. *Gabriel García Márquez: An Annotated Bibliography, 1947–1979.* Westport: Greenwood, 1980. viii + 198 pp.
A classified bibliography of material by and about García Márquez. Numerous bibliographical errors mar what could have been an even more useful work.

891.   Fau, Margaret Eustella, and Nelly Sefeir de González. *Bibliographic Guide to Gabriel García Márquez, 1979–1985*. Westport: Greenwood, 1986. xvii + 181 pp.
Supplement to and continuation of no. 890. Title and subject indexes in each volume would have been useful additions to the name index.

892.   Ossorio de Abenoza, Bianca. "Gabriel García Márquez juzgado por la crítica: Una bibliografía analítica y comentada, 1955–1974." Diss. U of Virginia, 1979. 374 pp.
The most important sections are "La bibliografía García Marquina" (4–69), a "sinopis de los patrones y tendencias seguidas por los críticos" (3), and "Síntesis de los trabajos críticos sobre las obras de García Márquez" (70–360), a classified bibliography of 360 items.

893.   Sefeir de González, Nelly. *Bibliographical Guide to Gabriel García Márquez, 1986–1992*. Westport: Greenwood, 1994. xx + 430 pp.
A classified, often annotated bibliography of 2,812 entries by and about García Márquez.

894.   McGrady, Donald. *Bibliografía sobre Jorge Isaacs*. Publicaciones del Inst. Caro y Cuervo, serie bibliográfica 8. Bogota: [Inst. Caro y Cuervo], 1971. 100 pp.
Bibliography of books, articles, and dissertations on Isaacs with an appendix, "Selección de alusiones a Isaacs en estudios de asunto general."

Women Authors

895.   Solari, M. "Ecriture féminine dans la Colombie contemporaine." Diss. U Toulouse, 1982. 335 pp.
Provides biobibliographical data on the most representative women prose writers of this country for the period 1950–80.

Costa Rica

896.   *Diccionario de la literatura latinoamericana: América Central*. 2 vols. Washington: Pan American Union, 1963.
See no. 834.

897.   Dobles Segreda, Luis. "Novela, cuento y artículo literario" and "Teatro." *Indice bibliográfico de Costa Rica*. Vol. 4. San José: Lehmann, 1934. 3–378, 385–429.

898.   Kargleder, Mary, and Warren H. Mory. *Bibliografía selectiva de la literatura costarricense*. San José: Costa Rica, 1978. 109 pp.

Bibliographies of Costan Rican literature from 1869 through 1976. No references to material published in anthologies, journals, or newspapers unless the works have been separately published. Lists translations under the name of the translator if the individual is Costa Rican.

899.   Menton, Seymour. "Indice bibliográfico del cuento costarricense." *El cuento costarricense: Estudio, antología y bibliografía.* Antologías Studium 8. México: Andrea; Lawrence: U of Kansas P, 1964. 163–82.
This outstanding study on the Costa Rican short story has a bibliography of stories published in anthologies, short story collections, and magazines.

900.   Ovares R., Flora. *Literatura de kiosko: Revistas literarias de Costa Rica 1890–1930.* Heredia: EUNA, 1994.
Contains the following 5 appendixes: "Principales revistas literarias, ilustradas, y culturales (1880–1935)"; "Revistas literarias, culturales e ilustradas según fechas de aparición"; "Revistas pedagógicas"; "Revistas teosóficas, humorísticas y otras"; "Canjes de *Athenea Páginas ilustradas y Renovación.*" The "Referencias bibliográficas" covers an area that has not been widely studied, but many studies of individual journals of this period have still been omitted.

901.   Portuguez de Bolaños, Elizabeth. "Bibliografía." *El cuento en Costa Rica: Estudio, bibliografía y antología.* San José: Lehmann, 1964. 309–40.
Classified bibliography of the Costa Rican short story and of Costa Rican novels that have "cuadros costumbristas."

902.   Welch, Thomas L., and René L. Gutiérrez. *Bibliografía de la literatura costarricense.* Washington: OAS, 1993. 213 pp.
Contains 3,285 citations to novels, plays, poetry, speeches, literary history, and criticism; includes name and title indexes.

CUBA

Dictionaries

903.   Instituto de Literatura y Lingüística de la Academia de Ciencias de Cuba. *Diccionario de la literatura cubana.* 2 vols. La Habana: Letras Cubanas, 1980–84.
An indispensable source for the study of Cuban authors, cultural institutions, and literary journals. Each author entry includes a biographical sketch, a chronological listing of the author's works, and a bibliography of critical and biographical studies about the author. Cuban exile authors are omitted, and a certain political bias is noticeable with the omission of a writer of the stature of Guillermo Cabrera Infante. It ranks, along with the dictionaries for Mexican and Venezuelan literature, as one of the best produced in Latin America.

904.   Martínez, Julio A. *Dictionary of Twentieth-Century Cuban Literature*. New York: Greenwood, 1990. 537 pp.
Excellent source for information on contemporary Cuban writers in Cuba or in exile. Also describes literary genres, publications, and movements. Includes bibliographical references.

Bibliographies

905.   "Bibliografía de la crítica literaria cubana." *Revista de literatura cubana* 1 (1983): 101–31.
Books, articles, and book reviews published in 1981 that deal with Cuban literature. The first part is for the seventeenth to the nineteenth centuries; the second deals with twentieth-century Cuban literature.

906.   "Bibliografía de la crítica literaria cubana, 1959–1983: La crítica." *Revista de literatura cubana* 3.5 (1985): 132–40.
Includes Cuban criticism of both Cuban and non-Cuban authors.

907.   Rolo, Lázaro. "Bibliografía de la crítica literaria cubana." *Revista de la literatura cubana* 3.5 (1985): 373–93.
Continuation of no. 906.

908.   Casal, Lourdes. "A Bibliography of Cuban Creative Literature: 1958–1971." *Cuban Studies Newsletter* 2.2 (1972): 2–29.
Divided by literary genres. It includes works both by Cubans living in Cuba and by those living outside Cuba. Also lists translations of Cuban works.

909.   "Classified bibliography." *Cuban Studies: Estudios cubanos* 1– (1970–).
Each issue of this semiannual journal has a classified bibliography with sections on literature and language.

910.   Fernández, José B., and Roberto G. Fernández. *Índice bibliográfico de autores cubanos, diáspora 1959–1979*. Miami: Universal, 1983. 106 pp.
Classified bibliography of the literary and linguistic works of Cuban exiled writers.

911.   Foster, David William. *Cuban Literature: A Research Guide*. Garland Reference Library of the Humanities 511. New York: Garland, 1985. 522 pp.
Critical references on 98 Cuban authors preceded by a classified bibliography of general references on Cuban literature.

912.   Martínez, Julio A. "Fuentes bibliográficas para el estudio de la literatura cubana moderna." *Revista interamericana de bibliografía* 36 (1984): 473–85.
Classified and annotated bibliography in essay form.

Black Authors

913. Trelles y Govín, Carlos Manuel. "Bibliografía de autores de la raza de color, de Cuba." *Cuba contemporánea* 43 (1927): 30–78.
Divided into material on black writers during the period of slavery, material after the slavery period, periodicals published by blacks, and works of all kinds by whites about blacks.

Drama

914. Inerarity Romero, Zayda. "Ensayo de una bibliografía para un estudio del teatro cubano hasta el siglo XIX." *Islas* 36 (1970): 151–71.
Classified, annotated bibliography of 100 items that the author considers to be the principal bibliographical sources for the study of the Cuban theater.

915. Palis, Terry L. "Annotated Bibliographical Guide to the Study of Cuban Theater after 1959." *Modern Drama* 22.4 (1979): 391–408.
"The 121 entries include books and articles which contain bibliographical information on contemporary Cuban theater or critical studies concerning the effect of the Cuban revolution on the nature of the dramatic activity there, and a list of seventy-four plays, written, staged, and published after 1959" (392).

916. Rivero Muñiz, José. *Bibliografía del teatro cubano*. La Habana: Biblioteca Nacional "José Martí," 1957. 120 pp.
Based on the library that once belonged to Francisco de Paula Coronado. Authors range from the early 1800s to the 1950s. It includes unpublished manuscripts as well as published dramatic works.

917. Skinner, Eugene R. "Research Guide to Post-Revolutionary Cuban Drama." *Latin American Theatre Review* 7.2 (1974): 59–68.
Divided into bibliographies, articles and books, and reviews. Attempts to provide "a specialized guide to post-Revolutionary Cuban theatre" (59).

Fiction

918. Abella, Rosa. "Bibliografía de la novela publicada en Cuba, y en el extranjero por cubanos, desde 1959 hasta 1965." *Revista iberoamericana* 32.62 (1966): 307–11.
Lists data on 76 novels written by Cubans, regardless of place of publication.

919. Casal, Lourdes. "The Cuban Novel, 1959–1969: An Annotated Bibliography." *Abraxas* 1.1 (1970): 77–92.
Briefly summarizes 77 novels and sometimes provides critical studies on them.

920. Menton, Seymour. "Bibliography." *Prose Fiction of the Cuban Revolution.* Latin American Monographs 37. Austin: U of Texas P, 1975. 287–317.

Outstanding classified and partially annotated bibliography of Cuban novels, short story anthologies, and short stories by Cubans in exile, as well as foreign prose fiction of the Cuban Revolution.

921. Sánchez, Julio C. "Bibliografía de la novela cubana." *Islas* 3 (1960): 321–56. Lists 800 titles.

Library Catalog

922. Figueras, Myriam, comp. *Catálogo de la colección de la literatura cubana en la Biblioteca Colón.* Documentation and Information Series 9. Washington: Columbus Memorial Library, 1984. x + 114 pp.

Classified bibliography divided into 8 sections with author and title indexes.

Poetry

923. *Bibliografía de la poesía cubana en el siglo XIX.* La Habana: Dept. de Colección Cubana, Biblioteca Nacional "José Martí," 1965. 89 pp.

Lists in chronological order 1,111 separately published works of poetry by Cubans, regardless of place of publication.

924. Le Riverend, Pablo. *Diccionario biográfico de poetas cubanos en el exilio (contemporáneo): Premio cintas, 1987–1988.* Newark: Q-21, 1988. 208 pp.

925. Montes Huidobro, Matías, and Yara González. *Bibliografía crítica de la poesía cubana, exilio 1959–1971.* Madrid: Playor, 1973. 138 pp.

In addition to providing bibliographical data on the poetry of Cubans outside Cuba, many of the comments on these works are several hundred words long.

Authors

926. García-Carranza, Araceli. *Bibliografía de Alejo Carpentier.* La Habana: Letras Cubanas, 1984. 644 pp.

A classified bibliography of 4,932 items by and about Carpentier with several indexes. Includes material not usually found in bibliographies, such as posters concerning him.

927. González Echevarría, Roberto, and Klaus Müller-Bergh. *Alejo Carpentier: Bibliographical Guide/Guía bibliográfica.* Westport: Greenwood, 1983. xxvi + 271 pp.

A classified primary and secondary bibliography. Includes a listing of recordings of Carpentier's works. Another especially valuable index covers individuals dealt with in Carpentier's newspaper columns.

928.   Gutiérrez-Vega, Zenaida. *Estudio bibliográfico de José Ma. Chacón (1913–1969)*. Biblioteca histórica hispanoamericana 5. Madrid: Fundación Universitaria Española, 1982. 163 pp.
A classified bibliography of material by and about Chacón.

929.   Dihigo y López-Trigo, Ernesto. *Bibliografía de Juan Miguel Dihigo y Mestre*. La Habana: Talleres del Archivo Nacional, 1964. 91 pp.
Classified bibliography with 19 sections of 893 items by and about Dihigo y Mestre.

930.   Antuña, María Luisa, and Josefina García Carranza, comps. *Bibliografía de Nicolás Guillén*. La Habana: Inst. Cubano del Libro, 1975. 379 pp.
Includes a bibliography of works by Guillén (items 1–2052) and of material about him (2053–737), as well as "Indice de títulos," "Indice de autores," and "Relación de publicaciones consultadas."

931.   ———. "Bibliografía de Nicolás Guillén. Suplemento 1972–1977." *Revista de la Biblioteca Nacional José Martí* 19.3 (1977): 61–123.
Supplement to no. 930.

932.   Robaina, Tomás F. *Bibliografía sobre José María Heredia*. La Habana: Biblioteca Nacional "José Martí," 1970. 111 pp.
Classified bibliography of Heredia's works (155 items) and of material about him (444 items).

933.   Toussaint, Manuel. *Bibliografía mexicana de Heredia*. Monografías mexicanas 2, serie 5. México: Secretaría de Relaciones Exteriores, Dept. de Información para el Extranjero, 1953. 146 pp.
Classified bibliography of works by and about Heredia.

934.   Rovirosa, Dolores F. *Jorge Mañach: Bibliografía*. Bibliography and Reference Series 13. Madison: SALALM, 1985. xxxi + 257 pp.
Each of the 2 main classifications, works by Mañach and material about him, has subdivisions. Includes 2,516 items and provides subject and author indexes.

935.   Antuña, María Luisa, and Josefina García Carranza. "Bibliografía de Juan Marinello." *Revista de la Biblioteca Nacional* 35 (Sept.-Dec. 1974): 25–474. Rpt. La Habana: Ciencias Sociales del Inst. Cubano del Libro, 1975. 473 pp.
Material by and about Marinello.

936.   *Anuario martiano* [La Habana] 1– (1969–).
Each number publishes a current Martí bibliography.

937.   Blanch y Blanco, Celestino. *Bibliografía martiana, 1954–1963*. La Habana: Dept. de Colección Cubana, Biblioteca Nacional "José Martí," 1965. 111 pp.
Classified bibliography of 1,008 items by and about Martí.

938.   González, Manuel Pedro. *Fuentes para el estudio de José Martí: Ensayo de bibliografía clasificada*. Bibliografía cubana 1. La Habana: Ministerio de Educación, Dirección de Cultura, 1950. 517 pp.
Includes material by and about Martí.

939.   Peraza Sarausa, Fermín. *Bibliografía martiana, 1853–1955*. La Habana: Anuario Bibliográfico Cubano, 1956. 720 pp.
More than 10,000 items by and about Martí.

DOMINICAN REPUBLIC

Dictionaries

940.   Tarazona Hijo, Enrique. *Guía biobibliográfica. 123 escritores dominicanos vivos —1983–* . [Santo Domingo: Alfa y Omega, 1983]. 139 pp.
Provides a brief biographical sketch for each author as well as a list of the author's works. Excludes critical studies.

941.   Vallejo de Paredes, Margarita. *Apuntes biográficos y bibliográficos de algunos escritores dominicanos del siglo XIX*. 2 vols. Santo Domingo: Onap, 1995.
Provides biographies of 109 Dominican nineteenth-century authors as well as bibliographies of their works and of critical and biographical material concerning them.

Bibliographies

942.   Collado, Miguel. *Apuntes bibliográficos sobre la literatura dominicana*. Santo Domingo: Biblioteca Nacional, 1993. 535 pp.
Contains the following sections of interest: "Acotaciones bibliográficas" (67–70), 24 items added to Manuel Mora Serrano's "La novela dominicana en los ochenta" (*Coloquio* [supp. to *El siglo*] 30 Dec. 1989: 11–12); "El cuento dominicano en los 80s" (71–79); "Narrativa dominicana 80: Breve reseña bibliográfica" (80–105), 40 well-annotated titles, as well as a listing of works that have won literary prizes; "Presencia de Trujillo en la narrativa dominicana: Una mini-antología" (106–21); "Más apuntes para la bibliografía poética dominicana" (133–243), 573 entries published between 1969 and 1990 with contents given of anthologies; "Una bibliografía cronológica de la narrativa dominicana (1841–1969)" (244–73), 269 entries; "Bibliografía dominicana: Obras narrativas de los 70s" (274–88), 110 entries; "Una bibliografía de la novela dominicana (1970–1990)" (289–300), 109 entries; "Obras dominicanas publicadas en 1990" (301–10), 74 entries divided into nonfiction and fiction; "Literatura infantil dominicana: Una bibliografía prelimi-

nar" (311–28), 156 entries; the first appendix reprints Vetilio Alfau Durán's "Apuntes para la bibliografía poética dominicana" (367–449), originally published in *Clio* (see no. 947).

943.   Olivera, Otto. *Bibliografía de la literatura dominicana (1960–1982)*. Lincoln: Soc. of Spanish and Spanish-American Studies, 1985. 86 pp.
Classified bibliography of 1,181 entries with a section on periodical publications and an index.

944.   Romero, Guadalupe. "Bibliografía comentada de la literatura dominicana." *Eme Eme* 3.14 (1974): 104–56.
Contains 173 annotated entries divided into anthologies, bibliographies, critical studies, and literary histories.

945.   Waxman, Samuel Montefiore. *A Bibliography of the Belles-Lettres of Santo Domingo*. Cambridge: Harvard UP, 1931. 31 pp. Suppl. by Vetilio Alau Durán. "Minucas [sic] bibliográficas dominicanas. . . ." *Clio* 198 (1956): 154–61. Rpt. as *Apuntes de bibliografía dominicana en torno a las rectificaciones hechas a la obra del prof. Waxman*. Ciudad Trujillo: Dominicana, 1956. 8 pp. Supp. by Pedro Henríquez Ureña and Gilberto Sánchez Lustrino. *Revista de filología española* 21 (1934): 293–309.

Fiction

946.   Alfau Durán, Vetilio. "Apuntes para la bibliografía de la novela en Santo Domingo." *Anales de la Universidad de Santo Domingo* 23 (1958): 203–24; 24 (1958): 405–35; 26 (1960); 87–100.
Covers A–F. Includes brief biographies of authors and, often, summaries of the novels, with occasional critical comments taken from reviews or critical studies.

Poetry

947.   Alfau Durán, Vetilio. "Apuntes para la bibliografía poética dominicana." *Clio* 122 (1965): 34–60; 123 (1968): 107–19; 124 (1969): 53–68; 125 (1970): 50–77.
Provides a bibliography of critical studies and of Dominican poetry; works are arranged by author.

Pseudonyms

948.   Rodríguez Demorizi, Emilio. *Seudónimos dominicanos*. 2nd ed. Santo Domingo: Taller, 1982. 280 pp.

ECUADOR

Dictionaries

949.   Barriga López, Franklin, and Leonardo Barriga López. *Diccionario de la literatura ecuatoriana*. 2nd ed. 5 vols. Colección letras del Ecuador 103, 104, 106–08. Guayaquil: Cultura Ecuatoriana, Núcleo del Guayas, 1980.
    Includes biographies of Ecuadorian authors as well as entries on institutions and corporations interested in culture. It includes titles and dates of an author's works and sometimes cites critics. There are, however, no bibliographies of critical studies on individual authors.

950.   *Diccionario de la literatura latinoamericana: Ecuador*. Washington: Pan American Union, 1962. xi + 172 pp.
    The material on each author is divided into 2 sections: the first is a biographical and critical sketch; the second is a bibliography of the author's separately published works and critical studies on them. Contains a helpful, though now dated, "Bibliografía de las letras ecuatorianas" (167–72).

Bibliographies

951.   *Bibliografía de autores ecuatorianos*. [Quito]: Biblioteca Nacional, 1977. 474 pp.
    Classified bibliography based on the national library's collection.

952.   Rolando, Carlos A. *Las bellas letras en el Ecuador*. Guayaquil: Imprenta i Talleres Municipales, 1944. xii + 157 pp.
    An important bibliography that could have been greatly improved.

Drama

953.   Luzuriaga, Gerardo. *Bibliografía del teatro ecuatoriano 1900–1980*. Quito: Cultura Ecuatoriana, 1984. 131 pp.
    Provides a bibliography of reference works for the study of Ecuadorean literature and drama of the period covered, a bibliography of published or performed plays, and critical references on Ecuadorian drama and dramatists.

954.   Welch, Thomas L., and René L. Gutiérrez. *Bibliografía de la literatura ecuatoriana*. Hipólito Unanue Bibliographic Series 5. Washington: OAS, 1990. 291 pp.
    Bibliography of 4,790 citations to novels, plays, poetry, short stories, essays, speeches, literary criticism, and history. Name and title indexes.

Modernist Journals

955.   Handelsman, Michael H. "Una bibliografía crítica de las revistas literarias del modernismo ecuatoriano (1895–1930)." *El modernismo en las revistas li-*

terarias del Ecuador: 1895–1930. Ensayo preliminar y bibliografía. Cuenca: [Cultura Ecuatoriana, Núcleo del Azuay], 1981. 37–127.

Based on the Colección Rolando in Guayaquil, this bibliography discusses and describes the Ecuadorean journals of the *modernismo* movement.

Women Authors

956. Rodríguez-Arenas, Flor María, and Raúl Neira. *Guía bibliográfica de escritoras ecuatorianas.* Bogotá: Codice, 1993. vii + 211 pp.

Excellent source for material by and about Ecuadorean women authors. Occasional incomplete references.

El Salvador

See no. 834.

Guatemala

Dictionary

957. López, Carlos. *Diccionario bio-bibliográfico de literatos guatemaltecos.* México: Praxis, 1993. 384 pp.

The fullest and most recent biobibliographical dictionary of Guatemalan writers, produced by a Guatemalan exile living in Mexico. Provides data on 336 authors and gives brief biographical sketches, which may vary from a single line to more than a page. A classified listing of the author's works follows, sometimes without imprint data. The "Referencias" section enables users to become familiar with some of the chief studies on the author. One might question why Asturias is given a 14-line biography and a 2-page list of critical material, while Luis Cardoza y Aragón's sketch occupies 62 lines. The bibliography of critical studies of Carlos Illescas Hernández is more than twice that of Asturias. Better proofreading and bibliographical completeness of many of the entries would have greatly added to this volume's usefulness. Pages 377–84 are a general bibliography of some of the compiler's sources.

Fiction

958. Ciruti, Joan. "The Guatemalan Novel: A Critical Bibliography." Diss. Tulane U, 1959. 263 pp.

Includes a critical annotated bibliography of 558 Guatemalan novels (106–253).

959. Menton, Seymour. "Los Señores Presidentes y los Guerrilleros: The New and the Old Guatemalan Novel (1976–1982)." *Latin American Research Review* 19.2 (1984): 93–117.

Divided into critical commentary and criticism on the novels of the period (93–110) and a chronological, briefly annotated list of 84 novels published between 1955 and 1982 (110–17).

Authors

960.   Andrea, Pedro F. de. "Miguel Angel Asturias: Anticipo bibliográfico." *Revista iberoamericana* 23.67 (1969): 133–268. Rpt. México: Andrea, 1969. 135 pp.
Classified bibliography of 1,460 items.

961.   Moore, Richard E. *Asturias: A Checklist of Works and Criticism.* Bibliographical Series 13. New York: American Inst. for Marxist Studies, 1979. 121 pp.
Divided into Asturias's major works and criticism, his minor works and criticism, translations by Asturias, prologues, books of criticism, general items on Asturias, and an author index. Has a good number of incomplete references.

962.   Estévez, Irma I. de, and Arely Mendoza de León. *Bibliografía de César Brañas.* Guatemala: EU de U de San Carlos, 1983. 57 pp.
An unusual bibliographical arrangement with only 2 pages dealing with criticism of Brañas's works (31–32). Includes a bibliography of his works, one of his prologues, one arranged by subject or literary genre, and a chronological bibliography covering 1920 to 1978.

963.   Castillo López, Victor. *Bibliografía de Enrique Gómez Carrillo.* Guatemala: EU de U de San Carlos, 1984. 22 pp.
Lists material by and about Gómez Carrillo based chiefly on Guatemalan libraries and sources. Ignores much published by and about him outside the country.

964.   Valenzuela de Garay, Carmen. *Bibliografía de José Milla y Vidaurre 1822–1882.* Guatemala: EU de U de San Carlos, 1982. 27 pp.
Divided into a bibliography of Milla y Vidaurre's works from 1844 to 1981, a bibliography of the prologues to his works, a listing of critical studies with brief annotations, and a bibliography of studies that celebrate the centennial of his birth or that appeared the year he died.

965.   Andrea, Pedro F. de. *Carlos Solórzano: Bibliografía.* México: Hojas Volantes de la Comunidad Latinoamerica de Escritores, 1970. 37 pp.
A bibliography of 356 items by and about Solórzano.

Honduras

See no. 834.

966.   Argueta, Mario R. *Diccionario crítico de obras literarias hondureñas.* Tegucigalpa: Gaymuras, 1993. 170 pp.

The compiler describes this volume as "una obra de referencia que contiene, en ordenamiento por títulos en secuencia alfabética, libros de contenido literario escritos por hondureños. Se incluyen comentarios, reseñas y opiniones por el mismo autor o por críticos en la materia" (17). An author index would have been helpful, as would have a bibliographical key to the critics cited.

967.   ———. *Diccionario de escritores hondureños*. Tegucigalpa: Universitaria, 1993. 147 pp.
Provides an extremely short biographical sketch along with a listing of the author's works and their dates. Critical evaluations only for selected authors.

968.   González, José. *Diccionario de autores hondureños*. Tegucigalpa: Unidos, 1987. 129 pp.
Includes a glossary of literary terms by S. Turaiev (85–120). Both González and Argueta (no. 967) should probably be consulted for the authors of this country. On the whole, González provides fuller data on the writers than Argueta does, but dates and information occasionally differ. Both must be used with care.

969.   Welch, Thomas L., and René L. Gutiérrez. *Bibliografía de la literatura hondureña*. Washington: OAS, 1992. 161 pp.
Includes 1,287 references to novels, essays, literary history, theater, and bibliographies. Has name and title indexes.

MEXICO

Dictionaries

970.   Agraz García de Alba, Gabriel. *Biobibliografía de los escritores de Jalisco*. Serie bibliografías 9. 2 vols. to date. México: Inst. de Investigaciones Bibliográficas, UNAM, 1980– .
Volumes 1 (cxxvii + 622 pp.) and 2 (cx + 247 pp.) cover A–B.

971.   Aranda Pamplona, Hugo. *Biobibliografía de los escritores del estado de México*. Serie bibliografías 5. México: Inst. de Investigaciones Bibliográficas, UNAM, 1978. 105 pp.

972.   Cortés, Eladio, ed. *Dictionary of Mexican Literature*. Westport: Greenwood, 1993. xliii + 768 pp.
". . . contains approximately 500 entries in English covering the most important writers, literary schools, and cultural movements in Mexican literary history" (xiii). Bibliographical sketches are followed by a listing of the author's works and of critical studies on them. Spanish titles are translated into English.

973. Lara Valdez, Josefina, and Russell M. Cluff. *Diccionario biobibliográfico de escritores de México nacidos entre 1920 y 1970*. 2nd. ed. México: Inst. Nacional de Bellas Artes, Centro Nacional de Información y Promoción de la Literatura, 1994. 458 pp.

This edition is almost twice the size of the 1988 volume, which included writers born between 1930 and 1960. Listings of the authors' works follow brief biographical sketches.

974. Montejano y Aguiñaga, Rafael. *Biobibliografía de los escritores de San Luis Potosí*. Serie bibliografías 6. México: Inst. de Investigaciones Bibliográficas, UNAM, 1979. lxxx + 439 pp.

Biobibliographical dictionary. Provides biographical data on the writers as well as a list of their published works and critical studies. Each entry is preceded by lengthy prefatory material.

975. Mundo Lo, Sara de. *Mexico*. Boston: Hall, 1982. xxx + 378 pp. Vol. 2 of *Index to Spanish American Collective Biography*. 4 vols. to date. 1981– .
See no. 752.

976. Múñoz Fernández, Angel. *Fichero bio-bibliográfico de la literatura mexicana del siglo XIX*. 2 vols. México: Factoria, 1995.

Múñoz, a collector of Mexican nineteenth-century literature, has compiled a useful guide to the writers of the period. For each author, he provides an extremely brief biography, a list of the author's pseudonyms, a list of first editions (title and date only), a list of newspapers and journals to which the author contributed, and occasional notes. For first editions, Múñoz gives references where fuller data can be found in other bibliographies. Pages 792–880 list pseudonyms in one column and the author's name in another column. Includes José Zorrilla, though is it difficult from the biographical sketch to discover how long he spent in Mexico.

977. Ocampo de Gómez, Aurora M., ed. *Diccionario de escritores mexicanos del siglo XX: Desde las generaciones del Ateneo y novelistas de la Revolución hasta nuestros días*. 3 vols. to date. México: UNAM, 1988– .

Vol 1: A–Ch, 1988, xlii + 456 pp. Vol. 2 D–F, 1992, xxlvi + 267 pp. Vol. 3: G, 1993, xlvi + 371 pp. This multivolume dictionary of twentieth-century Mexican writers provides a brief biography and critical study on each author as well as an extensive primary and secondary bibliography of the author's works. When completed, it will be the fullest biobibliographical dictionary of any Latin American country's twentieth-century writers.

978. Ocampo de Gómez, Aurora M., and Ernesto Prado Velázquez. *Diccionario de escritores mexicanos*. México: UNAM, 1967. xxvii + 442 pp.

Extraordinarily useful biobibliographical dictionary of Mexican writers. Provides a biographical sketch and a list of the works for each author, as well as a list of critical studies.

Bibliographies

979. Foster, David William. *Mexican Literature: A Bibliography of Secondary Sources*. 2nd ed. Metuchen: Scarecrow, 1992. x + 686 pp.
More than 15,000 unannotated items. Divided into 28 sections with data on 82 Mexican authors. Each author entry is divided into bibliographies, critical monographs and dissertations, and critical essays.

980. "Historia literaria." *Bibliografía histórica mexicana* [Colegio de México] 1– (1967–).
The annual includes chiefly histories and anthologies of Mexican literature as well as biographies of authors. Excludes literary criticism.

981. *Bibliografía literaria: Boletín destinado a informar de los artículos literarios aparecidos en las publicaciones periódicas recibidas por la Hemeroteca Nacional el mes próximo pasado*. México: Hemeroteca Nacional, Mar. 1973–Jan. 1976. Renamed *Hemerografía literaria* Feb. 1976– .
The first issue contains 119 items found in 23 issues of 16 periodicals and includes a subject index. It seems to be the first attempt at indexing the literary material in current Mexico periodicals.

Autobiographies

982. Woods, Richard D. *Mexican Autobiography: An Annotated Bibliography. La autobiografía mexicana: Una bibliografía razonada*. Trans. Josefina Cruz Mélendez. Bibliography and Indexes in World History 13. New York: Greenwood, 1988. 228 pp.

983. ———. "Mexican Autobiography: An Essay and Annotated Bibliography." *Hispania* 77 (1994): 750–802.
Contains 347 well-annotated autobiographies published chiefly between 1980 and 1993. Woods is one of the few scholars to be interested in this type of literature.

Drama

984. Lamb, Ruth S. *Mexican Theatre of the Twentieth Century: Bibliography and Study*. Claremont: Ocelot, 1975. 143 pp.
Except for the introductory essay, this work appears to be a facsimile reproduction of Lamb's *Bibliografía del teatro mexicano del siglo XX* (México: Andrea, 1962. 143 pp.). Includes a bibliography, arranged by author, on the Mexican twentieth-century theater; a critical bibliography; and a bibliography of Mexican magazines and newspapers that contain criticism, bibliography, or texts of plays.

985. Mendoza-López, Margarita, Daniel Salazar, and Tomás Espinosa. *Teatro mexicano del siglo XX, 1900–1986: Catálogo de obras teatrales*. 2 vols. México: Inst. Mexicano del Seguro Social, 1987.

986.   Monterde García Icazbalceta, Francisco. *Bibliografía del teatro en México.* 1933. Bibliography and Reference Series 369. New York: Franklin, [1970]. 649 pp.

Extensive bibliography of plays by and about Mexicans written by Mexicans and writers of other nationalities.

Essay

987.   Polasky, Sulema Laufer. "Bibliografía selecta anotada sobre la crítica de cinco ensayistas mexicanos." Diss. U of Cincinnati, 1983. 222 pp.

Bibliographies on Antonio Caso, Samuel Ramos, José Vasconcelos, Alfonso Reyes, and Octavio Paz as essayists in the fields of philosophy, sociology, and psychology. Useful, though there are numerous omissions and bibliographical inconsistencies.

Fiction

988.   Carballo, Emmanuel. *Bibliografía de la novela mexicana del siglo XX.* Materiales de extensión universitaria, serie textos 2. México: Coordinación de Difusión Cultural, UNAM, 1988. 233 pp.

This bibliography of the twentieth-century Mexican novel is divided into 2 parts. The first part lists the works in chronological order (1900–87); the second part lists the novels by author.

989.   Hoffman, Herbert H. *Cuento mexicano index.* Newport Beach: Headway, 1978. 600 pp.

This volume indexes 7,230 short stories by 490 Mexican authors born after 1870 or so. All books analyzed have been published since 1945. The compiler refers to these books only by numbers keyed to a "List of Books Analyzed."

990.   Iguiniz, Juan B. *Bibliografía de novelistas mexicanos: Ensayo biográfico, bibliográfico y crítico.* Monografías bibliográficas mexicanas 3. México: Monografías Bibliográficas Mexicanas, 1926. xxxv + 432 pp.

Provides brief biographical data for important authors. Lists authors' books but not critical studies.

991.   Leal, Luis. *Bibliografía del cuento mexicano.* Colección Studium 21. México: Andrea, 1958. 162 pp.

Indexes stories found in books, anthologies, newspapers, and magazines up to 1957.

992.   Rutherford, John. *An Annotated Bibliography of the Novels of the Mexican Revolution of 1910–1917 in English and Spanish.* Troy: Whitston, 1972. 180 pp.

Locates copies in Mexican libraries. Volume is in both English and Spanish.

Periodical Lists and Indexes

993. Forster, Merlin H. *An Index to Mexican Literary Periodicals.* Metuchen: Scarecrow, 1966. 276 pp.
Indicates the literary genre of 4,036 articles found in 16 journals published during the period 1920–60.

994. *Hemerografía literaria de 1976.* México: UNAM, 1979. 269 pp.
A list of 3,293 items.

995. *Hemerografía literaria de 1977.* México: UNAM, 1980. 221 pp.
A list of 3,045 items.

996. *Hemerografía literaria de 1978.* México: UNAM, 1983. 208 pp.
A list of 2,888 items.

Most of the journals and newspaper literary supplements indexed in these 3 guides (nos. 994–96) are Mexican. Unfortunately, no further issues seem to be planned.

997. *Nueva hemerografía potosina, 1828–1978.* Introd. and ed. Rafael Montejano y Aguiñaga. Serie hemerografías, Universidad Autónoma de México, Inst. de Investigaciones Bibliográficas, Biblioteca de Historia Potosina, serie documentos 6. México: UNAM, 1982. 376 pp.
Provides data on 1,372 journals and newspapers published in San Luis Potosí. Includes indexes of places of publication, titles, and names of journalists.

998. Universidad de Guanajuato. Dirección General de Bibliotecas. Departamento de Investigaciones Bibliotecnológicas. *Directorio de publicaciones periódicas mexicanas. 1981.* Guanajuato: U de Guanajuato, 1982 [1983]. iii + 200 pp.
Provides data on 453 periodicals published in Mexico. Most of them are scholarly; omits more or less popular journals like *Tiempo, Hoy,* and *Mañana.* Contains an above-average number of errata. It has the following indexes: "Indice de editores," "Indice de frecuencia," "Indice de fuentes secundarias," "Indice de instituciones," "Indice ISSN," "Indice de temas," and "Indice geográfico."

Poetry

999. González, Aurelio, coord. *Bibliografía descriptiva de la poesía tradicional y popular de México.* México: Colegio de México, 1993. xvi + 577 pp.
Each of the 500 entries has an extensive annotation. This outstanding bibliography provides 10 indexes: "Indice de autores," "Indice geográfico," "Indice de materias," "Indice de lenguas," "Indice por géneros de textos transcritos," "Indice de transcripciones musicales," "Indice de instrumentos," "Indice de dazas," "Indice de fiestas," and "Indice de textos transcritos y primeros versos."

The bibliography is on pages 1–227; the indexes appear on pages 237–575. There is a "Glosario," pages 229–34.

1000. Torres Ríoseco, Arturo, and Ralph Emerson Warner. *Bibliografía de la poesía mexicana*. Cambridge: Harvard UP, 1934. 86 pp.
Arranged alphabetically by poet.

Pseudonyms

1001. Ruiz Castañeda, María del Carmen, and Sergio Márquez Acevedo. *Catálogo de seudónimos, anagramas, iniciales y otros alias usados por escritores mexicanos y extranjeros que han publicado en México*. Instrumenta bibliographica. México: UNAM, 1985. lxxi + 290 pp.
The back cover notes that this volume "comprende los seudónimos literarios en la más amplia acepción del término: no sólo de poetas, novelistas y cuentistas, ensayistas, autores teatrales y periodistas, sino de cronistas, historiadores, autores de memorias y discursos, políticos que se han servido de la pluma, etc., lo mismo que caricaturistas, letristas y compositores de música popular.
"Asienta la correspondencia entre el seudónimo y el nombre verdadero de cerca de 1700 autores embozados bajo más de 5000 falsos nombres."
The prologue (xiii–xxxiii), by Sergio Márquez Acevedo, explains the volume's arrangement and discusses the different kinds of pseudonyms. It is followed by an anthology of articles that have previously been published in Mexico on the subject. The bibliography (279–90) is a useful listing of the compilers' sources.

Authors

1002. Warner, Ralph E. *Bibliografía de Ignacio Manuel Altamirano*. Serie letras 19. México: Universitaria, 1955. 220 pp.
Items 1–360d are a classified bibliography of Altamirano's works. The second part, on his life and works, has 95 items.

1003. Pasquel, Leonardo. *Bibliografía diazmironiana*. Colección suma veracruzano, serie bibliográfica. México: Citlaltépetl, 1966. 63 pp.
Lists 485 items by and about Salvador Díaz Mirón. Bibliographic data are often incomplete, and many studies published outside Mexico are omitted.

1004. Verani, Hugo. *Octavio Paz: Bibliografía crítica*. México: UNAM, 1983. 257 pp.
Includes 2,247 items by and about Paz and an index of critics, translators, and editors. The thoroughness and accuracy of this classified bibliography make it an outstanding example of its type.

1005. Robb, James Willis. *Repertorio bibliográfico de Alfonso Reyes*. Publicaciones 14, serie bibliografías 2. México: Inst. de Investigaciones Bibliográficas, UNAM, 1974. 294 pp.

Lists literary works by Reyes (3–15) and 2,858 items about him.

1006. Fernández-Cuesta, Marino. "Juan Rulfo: Bibliografía anotada." Diss. U of New Mexico, 1983. 320 pp.
Would have been an outstanding bibliography of its kind except for the errata and the many unannotated items. Where annotations do occur, they are excellent, sometimes running to 400 words.

NICARAGUA

Dictionaries

1007. Arellano, Jorge Eduardo. *Diccionario de autores nicaragüenses.* 2 vols. Managua: Convenio Biblioteca Real de Suecia, Biblioteca Nacional "Rubén Darío," 1994.
The sketch of each of the 600 authors in this biobibliographical dictionary usually includes "una reseña biográfica, una valoración crítica, una bibliografía activa (títulos publicados por él) y una pasiva (trabajos sobre el autor); más, también en algunos casos, reconocimientos o textos ajenos que aprecian, en general, la trayectoria del autor incluído" (1: 5).

1008. ———. "Diccionario de las letras nicaragüenses. Primera entrega: Escritores de la época colonial y el siglo XIX." *Cuadernos de bibliografía nicaragüense* 3–4 (1982): 1–144.
Biobibliographical dictionary of 100 Nicaraguan writers of the colonial period and of the nineteenth century. Extremely useful study for the period covered.

Bibliographies

1009. Arellano, Jorge Eduardo. *Panorama de la literatura nicaragüense.* 5th ed. Managua: Nueva Nicaragua, 1986. 197 pp.
Especially valuable for its bibliographical data. Includes "Bibliografía fundamental" and "Fichero de autores nicaragüenses," a bibliography of works and about contemporary Nicaraguan authors.

1010. Cerutti, Franco. "Datos para un futuro diccionario de escritores nicaragüenses (primera parte)." *Revista del pensamiento centro-americano* 168–69 (1980): 1–16; 172–73 (1981): 6–17.
Biobibliographical and critical sketches of 16 authors. Bibliographies include critical studies.

English Translations

1011. Woodbridge, Hensley C. "Una bibliografía de la literatura nicaragüense en inglés." *Boletín nicaragüense de bibliografía y documentación* 8 (1975): 1–5; 18 (1977): 84–97.
 The first part is a bibliography of English translations of Nicaraguan authors, with the exception of Rubén Darío. The second part is a bibliography of English translations of Rubén Darío. Attempts to identify the Spanish title of as many translations as possible.

Pseudonyms

1012. Cuadra Downing, Orlando. *Seudónimos y apodos nicaragüenses.* Managua: [Alemania], 1957. 341 pp.
 Considers pseudonyms as a contribution to the study of literature and political ideas of Nicaragua as well as to the study of philology and psychology of the Nicaraguan people.

Authors

1013. Smith, Janet Lynne. *An Annotated Bibliography of and about Ernesto Cardenal.* Special Studies 21. Tempe: Center for Latin American Studies, Arizona State U, 1979. 61 pp.
 This classified bibliography lists only works in Spanish and in English translation, thus ignoring Cardenal's tremendous popularity outside the Spanish- and English-speaking worlds. Critical studies are also limited to those in Spanish or English.

1014. Del Greco, Arnold Armand. *Repertorio bibliográfico del mundo de Rubén Darío.* New York: Américas, 1969. 666 pp.
 Fundamental classified bibliography for the study of Darío's life and works. Many of the 3,179 items are annotated.

1015. Jirón Terán, José. "Bibliografía general de Rubén Darío (julio 1883–enero 1967)." *Cuadernos universitarios* 2nd ser. 2 (1967): 315–440. Rpt. as *Publicaciones del centenario de Rubén Darío.* Managua: San José, 1967. 128 pp.
 Contains 1,447 items based on the compiler's collection of Darío materials. Divided into works by and about him, it is especially valuable for Central American publications on Darío.

1016. Lozano, Carlos. *Rubén Darío y el modernismo en España 1888–1920: Ensayo de bibliografía comentada.* New York: Américas, 1968. xxii + 158 pp.
 A chronological bibliography not only of critical studies but also of Darío's contributions to Spanish journals. Most of the 947 items have annotations of 4 or 5 lines.

1017. Woodbridge, Hensley C. *Rubén Darío: Bibliografía selectiva clasificada y anotada.* León: UNAN, 1975. vii + 146 pp.
A slightly enlarged translation of the English version (Metuchen: Scarecrow, 1975. xiv + 231 pp.). An annotated, classified bibliography of about 500 items about Darío, most of them published between 1950 and 1974. Two supplements list later works (see nos. 1018 and 1019).

1018. ———. "Rubén Darío: Bibliografía selectiva, clasificada y anotada, suplemento para los años 1974–1976." *Cuadernos universitarios* 2nd ser. 20 (1977): 33–66.
See no. 1017.

1019. ———. "Rubén Darío . . . anotada, suplemento II para los años 1975–1978." *Cuadernos de bibliografía nicaragüense* 2 (1981): 70–92.
See no. 1017.

PANAMA

1020. García Saucedo, Jaime. "Cronología de la novela panameña, 1849–1985." *Lotería* 360 (1986): 109–22.

1021. King, Charles A. "Apuntes para una bibliografía de la literatura de Panamá." *Revista interamericana de bibliografía* 14 (1964): 262–302.
Classified by literary genres.

1022. Miró, Rodrigo. *Bibliografía poética panameña.* Panamá: Imprenta Nacional, 1942. 61 pp.
Provides bibliographical data on Panamanian and foreign authors. There is also a chronological listing of titles.

1023. ———. *El cuento en Panamá: Estudio, selección, bibliografía.* Panamá: n.p., 1950. 203 pp.
The bibliography section (191–201) is divided into "Autores nacionales," "Libros de material vario, que incluyen cuentos," and "Novelas de tema o ambiente panameño."

PARAGUAY

Dictionaries

1024. Mendez-Faith, Teresa. *Breve diccionario de la literatura paraguaya.* Colección literaria 22. Asunción: Lector, 1994. xv + 178 pp.
This volume is the fullest attempt yet at a dictionary of Paraguayan authors as well as of literary movements and journals. Barest bibliographical details of

published books provide only title and date. Gives no data concerning biographical and critical materials about the author.

1025.   Pérez Mavievich, Francisco. *Diccionario de la literatura paraguaya (I parte).* 1 vol. to date. Biblioteca colorados contemporáneos 7. Asunción: América, 1983– . 291 pp.
Volume 1 covers A–Cuento. Provides a biography, an evaluation of the author's works, and a bibliography of material by and about the author. Includes articles on literary genres; the article on the Paraguayan short story covers pages 157–291.

1026. Welch, Thomas L., and René L. Gutiérrez. *Bibliografía de la literatura paraguaya.* Hipólito Unanue Bibliographic Series 6. Washington: OAS, 1990. 180 pp.
Has 1,501 citations to Paraguayan literature and literary criticism. Indexes novels, plays, poetry, short stories, essays, speeches, literary history, and criticism. Author arrangement with name and title indexes.

Bibliographies

1027.   Fernández-Caballero, Carlos F. S. *The Paraguayan Bibliography: A Retrospective and Enumerative Bibliography of Printed Works of Paraguayan Authors.* 3 vols. Washington: Arandú, 1983.
Vol. 1: *Aranduká ha kuatiañeé paraguái rembiapocué;* vol. 2: *Paraguái tai hũme: tove paraguái arandú taisarambi ko yvy apére* (Amherst: SALALM, U of Massachusetts Library, 1975); vol. 3: *Paraguái rembiapokúe ha paraguái rehegúa tembiapo oñembokuatiavaekúe.* Provides bibliographical data on almost 4,000 separately published works written either by Paraguayans or about Paraguay and published between 1724 and 1974.

1028.   Jones, David Lewis. "Literature." *Paraguay: A Bibliography.* New York: Garland, 1979. 372–415.
Certain portions, especially of better-known authors, appear to be very selective. Divided into general studies, individual authors before 1935, and individual writers after 1935.

1029.   Vallejos, Roque. *Antología de la prosa paraguaya. Generación del 900.* Vol. 1. Asunción: Pueblo, 1973. 154 pp.
Brief biographies of 29 Paraguayan authors followed by biographical and critical studies.

PERU

Dictionaries

1030.   Arriola Grande, Maurilio. *Diccionario literario del Perú: Nomenclatura por autores.* 2nd ed. 2 vols. Lima: Universo, 1983.

Includes some non-Peruvians who have written about Peru's history and literature. Provides a brief biography, critical note, and an evaluation of each author. Lists no references about the author.

1031. Romero de Valle, Emilia. *Diccionario manual de literatura peruana y material afines.* Lima: Dept. de Publicaciones, U Nacional Mayor de San Marcos, 1966. 356 pp.
Provides data on literary movements in Peru, journals, and newspapers that are ignored by Arriola Grande (no. 1030).

Bibliographies

1032. Foster, David William. *Peruvian Literature: A Bibliography of Secondary Sources.* Westport: Greenwood, 1981. xxix + 324 pp.
The first section, a classified bibliography of general studies on Peruvian literature, is divided into 24 sections. The second section provides data on critical studies of 38 authors.

1033. Pinto Gamboa, Willy E. *Contribución a la bibliografía de la literatura peruana en la prensa española.* [Lima: U Nacional Mayor de San Marcos], 1965. 170 pp.
Bibliographies of Peruvian literature appearing in Spanish journals and newspapers. Sections include Peruvian authors and non-Peruvian writing about Peruvian themes, each arranged by author. Occasional annotations.

1034. Tauro, Alberto. "Bibliografía peruana de literatura." *Boletín de la Biblioteca Nacional* 13–14, 19–20 (1957–59): 109–298. Rpt. Lima: [Villanueva], 1959. 194 pp.
Classified bibliography of 2,097 items. Principally lists works on Peruvian literature that have appeared since 1931.

1035. Fuente Benavides, Rafael de la. "Autores del primer siglo de la literatura peruana." *Boletín bibliográfico* [Biblioteca de la U de San Marcos] 9.12.3–4 (1939): 268–332; 10.12.1–2 (1940): 81–133.
Biobibliographical dictionary of sixteenth- and seventeenth-century Peruvian authors. Covers A–F only.

Drama

1036. Natella, Arthur A., Jr. "Bibliography of the Peruvian Theatre, 1946–1970." *Hispanic Journal* 2.2 (1981): 141–47.
"The list includes works which have been presented on the Peruvian stage, published, or both" (141).

1037. Reverte Bernal, Concepción. "Guía bibliográfica para el estudio del teatro virreinal peruano." *Historiografía y bibliografía americanistas* 29 (1985): 129–50.

Fiction

1038.   Escajadillo, Tomás G. "Bibliografía selectiva sobre el indigenismo (posterior a 1971)." *La narrativa indigenista peruana.* Lima: Amaru, 1994. 259–333.
Divided into a general section and sections on José Carlos Mariátegui, Clorinda Matto de Turner, Enrique López Albújar, Ventura García Calderón, César Vallejo, Ciro Alegría, José María Arguedas, Eledoro Vargas Vicuña, Carlos Eduardo Zavaleta, and Manuel Scorza.

1039.   Rodríguez Rea, Miguel Angel. "El cuento peruano contemporáneo: Indice bibliográfico. I. 1900–1930." *Lexis* 7 (1983): 287–309.
Provides bibliographical data and the contents of 62 short story anthologies.

1040.   Vidal, Luis Fernando. "Las antologías del cuento en el Perú." *Revista de crítica literaria latinoamericana* 1.2 (1974): 121–38.
Provides contents of anthologies published between 1908 and 1975.

1041.   Villanueva de Puccinelli, Elsa. *Bibliografía de la novela peruana.* Lima: Biblioteca Universitaria, 1969. 88 pp.
Besides listing the works of Peruvian novelists, Villanueva de Puccinelli provides a chronology.

Library Catalog

1042.   Biblioteca Nacional del Perú. *Catálogo de autores de la colección peruana.* 6 vols. Boston: Hall, 1979.
". . . includes catalog cards for Peruvian imprints and for publications about Peru from 1553 through 1977 which are found in the National Library" (1: vii).

Literary Journals

1043.   O'Brien, MacGregor. "Bibliografía de las revistas literarias peruanas." *Hispania* 71 (Mar. 1988): 61–74.

Poetry

1044.   Cabel, Jesús. *Bibliografía de la poesía peruana 65/79.* [Lima]: Amaru, [1980]. 143 pp.
Lists Peruvian poets published either in Peru or abroad. Volume is divided into books, anthologies, *plaquetas*, and a supplement.

1045.   ———. *Bibliografía de la poesía peruana 80/84.* [Lima: Biblioteca Universitaria, 1986]. 45 pp.

1046.   Rodríguez Rea, Miguel Angel. "Poesía peruana del siglo XX." *Hueso húmero* 7 (1980): 133–50; 8 (1981): 132–49; 9 (1981): 148–58.

This 3-part bibliography covers 1900–20, 1921–30, and 1931–35 and includes data on 351 works of poetry by Peruvians, regardless of the place of publication.

Pseudonyms

1047. Angeles Caballero, César Augusto. "Diccionario de seudónimos peruanos." *Boletín bibliográfico* [Biblioteca de la U de San Marcos] 32.1–2 (1962): 37–90. Lists 1,449 pseudonyms along with the authors' real names.

1048. ———. "Diccionario de seudónimos peruanos." *Boletín bibliográfico* [Biblioteca de la U de San Marcos] 33.3–4 (1962): 162–64.

1049. ———. "Diccionario de sobrenombres literarios peruanos." *Boletín bibliográfico* [Biblioteca de la U de San Marcos] 34.1–2 (1963): 134–42.

1050. Castro, Emma. "Seudónimos de autores peruanos." *Fénix* 4 (1946): 86–93.

1051. Pastor Delgado, Amadeo. "Contribución para un catálogo de seudónimos de autores peruanos." *Boletín bibliográfico* [Biblioteca de la U de San Marcos] 18.3–4 (1948): 254–64.

1052. Tauro, Alberto. *Hacia un catálogo de seudónimos peruanos.* Lima: U Nacional Mayor de San Marcos, 1967. 66 pp. Lists 861 pseudonyms along with the authors' real names.

Authors

1053. Weller, Hubert P. *Bibliografía analítica y anotada de y sobre Martín Adán (Rafael de la Fuente Benavides) (1927–1974).* Lima: Inst. Nacional de Cultura, 1975. 139 pp. Lists 169 items by Adán and 534 about him.

1054. Cornejo, Raúl Estuardo. *López Albújar, narrador de América: Bibliografía general.* [Lima: n.p., 1963]. 84 pp.

1055. Rouillón, Guillermo. *Bio-bibliografía de José Carlos Mariátegui.* Biblioteca de Estudios Superiores. Lima: [Dept. de Publicaciones, U Mayor de San Marcos], 1963. 345 pp. The 3,462 items are divided into "Obra," "Estudios críticos y biográficos sobre J. C. Mariátegui," and "Referencias e iconografía."

1056. *Literature and Politics in Latin America: An Annotated Calendar of the Luis Alberto Sánchez Correspondence, 1919–1980.* Trans. and comp. Donald C. Henderson and Grace R. Pérez. University Park: Pennsylvania State U Libraries, 1982. xix + 498 pp. Annotates 1,993 letters to and from the Peruvian author.

1057. Sobrevilla, David. *Introducción bibliográfica a César Vallejo.* Lima: Amaru, 1995. 143 pp.

Sobrevilla, an outstanding Peruvian scholar on Vallejo, has produced an excellent critical bibliographical introduction to this author's life and works as well as indicating, in "Consideraciones finales" (133–41), where further research is needed. Its major parts are "Fuentes y medios auxiliares de investigación," "La investigación sobre Vallejo y su obra," and "Consideraciones finales." Some of his annotations are 3 or 4 pages. Christian Pixis, *Bibliografía de la crítica vallejiana* (München: Pixisverlag, 1990), could have been a work of great value, but its incomplete references and errors make one doubt that Pixis has personally examined all his items.

1058.   Rosselli, Fernando, Alessandro Finzi, and Antonio Zampolli. *Diccionario de concordancia y frecuencias de uso en el léxico poético de César Vallejo*. Firenze: Inst. di Lingue Straniere Facoltà di Economia e Commercio; Pisa: Cattedra di Linguistica dell'U de Pisa, [1978]. 1,070 pp.
  This concordance is divided in "Concordancias" and "Frecuencias." The introduction to this volume previously appeared as "Diccionario de concordancias y frecuencias del léxico poético de César Vallejo," by Rosselli and Finzi, in *Quaderni latinoamericani* 2 (1977): 47–68. This concordance is based on *Heraldos negros, Trilce, Poemas en prosa, Poemas humanos,* and *España, aparta de mí este cáliz.* My data are taken from Sobrevilla's *Introducción* (1057) 16–17.

PUERTO RICO

Dictionary

1059.   Rivera de Alvarez, Josefina. *Diccionario de literatura puertorriqueña*. 2nd ed. 2 vols. in 3. San Juan: Inst. de Cultura Puertorriqueña, 1974.
  After a "Panorama histórica de la literatura puertorriqueña," there is a biobibliographical dictionary of Puerto Rican authors. It also includes entries on Puerto Rican cultural institutions and literary terms.

Bibliographies

1060.   Foster, David William. *Puerto Rican Literature: A Bibliography of Secondary Sources*. Westport: Greenwood, 1982. 324 pp.
  The first section is a classified bibliography of general studies on Puerto Rican literature. The second part provides bibliographies of critical studies on 80 Puerto Rican authors.

1061.   Hill, Marnesba D., and Harold B. Schleifer. *Puerto Rican Authors. A Bibliographic Handbook*. Metuchen: Scarecrow, 1974. 267 pp.
  Bilingual biobibliographical dictionary of Puerto Rican authors that lists their works but extremely few biographical and critical materials.

1062. Bravo, Enrique R. *An Annotated Selected Puerto Rican Bibliography: Bibliografía puertorriqueña selecta y anotada.* New York: Urban Center of Columbia U, 1972. 60–84.
Bilingual bibliography with a classified literature section.

1063. Pedreira, Antonio S. *Bibliografía puertorriqueña (1493–1930).* Bibliography and Reference Series 496. New York: Franklin, 1974. 487–558.
Originally published in 1932. A classified bibliography on literary history that may occasionally prove useful.

1064. Rivera, Guillermo. *A Tentative Bibliography of the Belles-Lettres of Puerto Rico.* Cambridge: Harvard UP, 1931. 61 pp.
Arranged alphabetically by author within 15 subject categories. Also contains a list of periodicals and a bibliography of Eugenio María de Hostos.

1065. Vivó, Paquita. *The Puerto Ricans: An Annotated Bibliography.* New York: Bowker, 1973. 113–46, 215–16.
Useful annotations on Puerto Rican literature, literary history, and criticism in periodicals.

Drama

1066. González, Nilda. *Bibliografía de teatro puertorriqueño, siglos XIX y XX.* [Río Piedras]: U de Puerto Rico, EU, 1979. xx + 223 pp.
Extremely useful bibliography of the Puerto Rican theater and criticism concerning it. Includes data on both published and unpublished plays as well as information on certain performances.

Fiction

1067. Quiles de la Luz, Lillian. "Indice bibliográfico del cuento en la literatura puertorriqueña, 1843–1963." *El cuento en la literatura puertorriqueña.* [San Juan]: U de Puerto Rico, EU, 1968. 141–293.
Extensive bibliography of the Puerto Rican short story as found in books, anthologies, and periodicals.

Literature in Translation

1068. *Puerto Rican Literature: Translations into English. Literatura puertorriqueña, traducciones al inglés.* Río Piedras: Biblioteca José M. Lázaro, 1974. 38 pp.

1069. Mohr, Eugene V. "Fifty Years of Puerto Rican Literature in English: 1923–1973. An Annotated Bibliography." *Revista/Review Interamericana* 3 (Fall 1973): 290–98.

Provides an annotated listing of English translations of Spanish works by Puerto Ricans (295–96), but all the other works in the bibliography were originally written in English.

UNITED STATES

Chicano Literature

1070. Eger, Ernestina N. *A Bibliography of Criticism of Contemporary Chicano Literature*. Chicano Studies Library Publications 5. Berkeley: U of California Chicano Studies Library, 1982. xxi + 295 pp.
An excellent classified bibliography that lists books, articles, reviews, and dissertations published or written on this subject chiefly between 1960 and 1979.

1071. Foster, Virginia Ramos. "Literature." *Sourcebook of Hispanic Culture in the United States*. Chicago: American Library Assn., 1982. 86–111.
A classified bibliography of 76 well-annotated items.

1072. Kanellos, Nicolás. *Biographical Dictionary of Hispanic Literature in the United States: The Literature of Puerto Ricans, Cuban Americans, and Other Hispanic Writers*. New York: Greenwood, 1989. 357 pp.
Biobibliographical dictionary of 50 contemporary writers. Each entry includes biographical information, a discussion of major themes, a survey of criticism, and a brief bibliography of the author's works and of literary criticism.

1073. Lomelí, Francisco A., and Carl R. Shirley, eds. *Chicano Writers*. First Series. Dictionary of Literary Biography 82. Detroit: Gale, 1989. 388 pp.
Features 52 Chicano authors, including Amado Muro. Biographical-critical sketches include bibliographies, some with illustrations.

1074. Martínez, Julio A., and Francisco A. Lomelí, eds. *Chicano Literature: A Reference Guide*. Westport: Greenwood, 1985. xii + 492 pp.
The biographical-critical articles on Chicano authors written by several dozen specialists are followed by a listing of the authors' most important works and of their critical studies. There are also articles on various literary genres.

1075. Trujillo, Roberto G., and Andrés Rodríguez. *Literatura Chicana: Creative and Critical Writings through 1984*. Oakland: Floricano, 1985. xi + 95 pp.
The 783 items are divided by literary genre. Besides the usual types of materials that one would expect to find, the compilers include data on Chicano literary periodicals, videos, and sound recordings.

1076. Zimmerman, Marc. *U.S. Latino Literature: An Essay and Annotated Bibliography*. Chicago: March-Abrazo, 1992. 155 pp.

"Latino Literature: A Selected and Annotated Bibliography" (49–155) has the following major divisions: "I. General Latino Anthologies," "II. Chicano Literature," "III. U.S. Puerto Rican Literature," "IV. U.S. Cuban Literature," "V. Latino-Tending U.S. Latin American Writing," "VI. Chicanesque Literature," "VII. Secondary Materials." The individual items are well annotated. An author index would have added to the usefulness of this volume.

Cuban American Literature

1077. Lindstrom, Naomi E. "Cuban American and Continental Puerto Rican Literature." *Sourcebook of Hispanic Culture in the United States.* Ed. David William Foster. Chicago: American Library Assn., 1982. 221–45.
Classified, well-annotated bibliography of 61 items.

1078. Maratos, Daniel C., and Marnesba D. Hill. *Escritores de la diáspora cubana: Manual bibliográfico. Cuban Exile Writers: A Bibliographic Handbook.* Metuchen: Scarecrow, 1986. 391 pp.

URUGUAY

Dictionaries

1079. Penco, Wilfredo, ed. *Diccionario de literatura uruguaya.* 3 vols. Montevideo: Arca-Credisol, 1987–91.
Volumes 1 and 2 (1987) provide a biography of each author with a critical comment followed by a brief bibliography of works by and about the author. Volume 3 (1991) is subtitled *Obras, cenáculos, páginas literarias, revistas, períodos culturales* and concludes with a useful "Bibliografía de bibliografías sobre literatura uruguaya" (483–94).

1080. Rela, Walter. *Diccionario de escritores uruguayos.* Montevideo: La Plata, 1986. 397 pp.
Rela provides a biographical sketch of each author; his critical comments are quotations from literary critics. These biobibliographical sketches range from 1 to 7 pages. The bibliographical data add little to those found in his *Literatura uruguaya: Bibliografía selectiva* (no. 1082).

Bibliographies

1081. Rela, Walter. *Fuentes para el estudio de la literatura uruguaya, 1835–1968.* [Montevideo]: Banda Oriental, 1969. 134 pp.
Classified, unannotated bibliography of 930 items.

1082. ———. *Literatura uruguaya: Bibliografía selectiva.* Special Studies 26. Tempe: Center for Latin American Studies, Arizona State U, 1985. 86 pp.

The first part of this work is "Referencias críticas" and a classified bibliography of general critical studies, bibliographies, anthologies, and so on. The second part provides data on the book-length works of close to 100 authors along with book-length critical studies on their works.

1083. Welch, Thomas L. *Bibliografía de la literatura uruguaya.* Serie de documentación e información 10. Washington: OAS, 1985. xii + 502 pp.

Lists 9,329 items by Uruguayan authors in the Columbus Memorial Library. Includes translations of Uruguayan authors that are in the Columbus library. Title index.

Drama

1084. Rela, Walter. *Repertorio bibliográfico del teatro uruguayo, 1816–1964.* Colección Medusa. Montevideo: Síntesis, 1965. 35 pp.

Unannotated, classified bibliography.

1085. ———. *Diccionario de autores teatrales uruguayos.* Montevideo: Proyección, 1988. 138 pp.

Pages 7–33 are a "Breve historia del teatro uruguayo, siglo XIX–XX." Provides biographical, critical, and bibliographical sketches for Uruguayan dramatists.

Fiction

1086. Englekirk, John E., and Margaret M. Ramos. *La narrativa uruguaya: Estudio crítico-bibliográfico.* U of California Publications in Modern Philology 80. Berkeley: U of California P, 1967. 338 pp.

Provides data on 525 novels and 7,000 short stories by 265 authors. Gives quotations from critics for many of these works; locates copies in 9 United States, Spanish, and Uruguayan libraries.

Literary Journals

1087. Barite, Mario, and María Gladys Ceretta. *Guía de revistas culturales uruguayas 1895–1985.* Montevideo: "El Galeón," 1989. 101 pp.

Provides data concerning frequency, editors, dates of publications, and contributors for 239 Uruguayan cultural journals. Its indexes are "Indice alfabético cronológico" and "Indice de directores, redactores responsables y colaboradores." Extremely useful even when the compilers can supply only incomplete information.

Authors

1088. Rela, Walter. *Eduardo Acevedo Díaz: Guía bibliográfica.* Montevideo: Ulises, 1967. 83 pp.
Lists 397 items by and about Acevedo.

1089. ———. *Filoberto Hernández: Bibliografía anotada.* Montevideo: Ciencias, 1979. 50 pp.
Divided into works by Hernández, items 1–96, and works about him, items 96–190. Each section is subdivided, and some items are annotated.

1090. ———. *Horacio Quiroga: Repertorio bibliográfico anotado 1897–1971.* Buenos Aires: Pardo, 1972. 145 pp.
Classified bibliography of 915 items with several indexes. Items about Quiroga are not annotated. The annotations for material by Quiroga appear as notes at the end of each section.

1091. Blixen, Carina, and Alvaro Barros Lemez. *Cronología y bibliografía de Angel Rama.* Montevideo: Arca; Fundación Angel Rama, 1983. 203 pp.

1092. Rela, Walter. *Carlos Reyles: Guía bibliográfica.* Montevideo: Ulises, 1967. 62 pp.
Lists 325 items by and about Reyles.

1093. ———. *Repertorio bibliográfico anotado sobre Florencio Sánchez (1891–1971).* Guías bibliográficas 11. Buenos Aires: Facultad de Filosofía y Letras, Inst. de Literatura Argentina "Ricardo Rojas," U de Buenos Aires, 1973. 77 pp.
Classified bibliography of material both by Sánchez (items 1–168) and about him (items 169–520).

1094. Biblioteca Nacional de Montevideo. *Exposición bibliográfica y documental: Alberto Zum Felde en el cincuentenario de la publicación del* Proceso intelectual del Uruguay y crítica de su literatura. Montevideo: Biblioteca Nacional, 1980. 70 pp.
The 433 items by and about Zum Felde are divided into 3 periods: 1906–16, 1917–29, and 1930–76.

Women Poets

1095. Moratorio, Arsinoe. "La mujer en la poesía del Uruguay (Bibliografía 1879–1969)." *Revista de la Biblioteca Nacional* [Montevideo] 4 (1970): 43–63.
Presents data on the works of women poets published in book form as well as on reprints and translations of their books. Works under each poet are arranged chronologically.

VENEZUELA

Dictionaries

1096.   *Diccionario general de la literatura venezolana.* 2nd ed. 2 vols. Mérida: Editorial Venezolana, Consejo de Fomento, Consejo de Publicaciones, U de los Andes, 1987.
The prologue is signed by Ada Ojeda Briceño and Lubio Cardozo. The work is a revised, corrected, and updated version of the 1974 edition. It includes data through the end of 1982. Wherever possible, the entry for each author gives a brief biographical sketch, a critical note, a listing of the author's published books, and a listing of works about the author. This is an outstanding biobibliographical dictionary.

1097.   Miranda, Julio E. "Para un diccionario crítico de la nueva narrativa venezolana." *Revista iberoamericana* 166–67 (Jan.-June 1994): 381–93.
Biobibliographical critical discussion of 11 fiction authors, most of whom were born in the early 1950s.

Bibliographies and Surveys

1098.   Becco, Horacio Jorge. *Bibliografía de bibliografías venezolanas: Literatura, 1968–1979.* Caracas: Bello, 1979. 62 pp.
Classified bibliography of 250 items.

1099.   ———. *Fuentes para el estudio de la literatura venezolana.* 2 vols. Caracas: Centauro, 1978.
Valuable classified bibliography of 1,860 items.

1100.   Cardozo, Lubio. *Bibliografía de literatura merideña.* Mérida: Facultad de Humanidades y Educación, Escuela de Letras, Centro de Investigaciones Literarias, U de los Andes, 1967. 91 pp.
Bibliography of 275 books by writers from the state of Mérida.

1101.   Lovera de Sola, Roberto J. "La literatura venezolana en 1971." *Montalbán* 1 (1972): 541–84.

1102.   ———. "Producción literaria 1971. Bibliografía fundamental." *Libros al día* 1.15 (1976): 2–28.

1103.   ———. "La producción literaria en 1972." *Libros al día* 1.10 (1976): 21–28.

In nos. 1101–03 Lovera provides excellent surveys of the belles lettres for the periods covered.

1104. Niño de Rivas, María Lys. "Escritores actuales de Venezuela, una bibliografía." *ARAISA: Anuario del Centro de Estudios Latinoamericanos Rómulo Gallegos* (1975): 349–82.
Lists works published in the 1960s and early 1970s. Often indicates literary genre.

1105. Villasana, Angel Raúl. *Ensayo de un repertorio bibliográfico venezolano.* Colección Cuatricentenario de Caracas. 6 vols. Caracas: Banco Central de Venezuela, 1969–79.
Includes works published in or about Venezuela between 1808 and 1950. Concentrates on works of literature and history and on those of a general nature.

Afro-Venezuelan Literature

1106. Ramos Guédez, José Marcial. "IV. Literatura afrovenezolana." *Bibliografía afrovenezolana.* Serie bibliográfica 2. Caracas: Inst. Autónomo Biblioteca Nacional y de Servicios de Bibliotecas, 1980. 99–106.
Items 858–936 are an unannotated listing of material by black Venezuelans or material that discusses how blacks are presented in Venezuelan literature.

Drama

1107. Greymont, Sally J. "Hacia una bibliografía del teatro venezolano colonial." *Latin American Theatre Review* 8.2 (1975): 45–49.
Includes works that refer to pre-Columbian, colonial, and folk theater as well as to colonial dramatists.

1108. Rojas Uzcátegui, José de la Cruz, and Lubio Cardozo. *Bibliografía del teatro venezolano.* Mérida: Inst. de Investigaciones Literarias "Gonzalo Picón Febres," 1980. 199 pp.
The most extensive bibliography of the Venezuelan theater from 1801 to 1978.

1109. Salas, Carlos. "Bibliografía dramática venezolana." *Historia del teatro en Caracas.* Material para el estudio de Caracas 7. Caracas: Secretaría General del Cuatricentenario, 1967. 321–83.
Though this item is listed in earlier bibliographies, it is difficult to classify as a bibliography. It is an alphabetical list of Venezuelan dramatists whose works have been presented in the theaters of Caracas. Gives data concerning the plays' premieres, but apparently most of these plays were never published.

Fiction

1110. Coll, Edna. *Venezuela. Indice informativo de la novela hispanoamericana.* Vol. 3. Río Piedras: U de Puerto Rico, EU, 1978. 331 pp.
Bibliographical dictionary of novelists of Venezuela.

1111.   Larrazábal Henríquez, Osvaldo, et al. *Bibliografía del cuento venezolano.*
        Caracas: Facultad de Humanidades y Educación, Inst. de Investigaciones
        Literarias, U Central de Venezuela, [1975]. 315 pp.
        Provides data on 3,311 short stories by 332 authors.

1112.   *Bibliografía de la novela venezolana.* Caracas: U Central de Venezuela, Cen-
        tro de Estudios Literarios, Escuela de Letras, Facultad de Humanidades y
        Educación, 1963. 71 pp.
        Provides data on 324 titles by 187 authors whose works were published be-
tween 1842 and 1962.

Literary Criticism

1113.   Lovera de Sola, Roberto J. *Bibliografía de la crítica literaria venezolana,*
        1847–1977. Caracas: Inst. Autónomo Biblioteca Nacional y de Servicios de
        Bibliotecas, 1982. 489 pp.
        The 2 most important parts of this work are "Bibliografía de la crítica literaria
y temas conexos" and "Bibliografía de la crítica teatral en Venezuela." Includes
books and parts of books that deal with literary criticism in Venezuela and that
were published in this country. The annotations list the authors for whom critical
studies are given.

Periodical Index

1114.   Ziona Hirshbein, Cesia. *Hemerografía venezolana 1890–1930.* Caracas: Fac-
        ultad de Humanidades y Educación, Inst. de Estudios Hispanoamericanos,
        U Central de Venezuela, 1978. 574 pp.
        Useful classified index of literature that appeared in Venezuelan journals.

Poetry

1115.   Becco, Horacio Jorge, and Alberto Amengual. "Antologías poéticas ameri-
        canas y venezolanas en el siglo XIX." *Memoria del III Simposio de Docentes e*
        Investigadores de la Literatura Venezolana Vol. 1. Mérida: Facultad de Hu-
        manidades y Educación, Inst. de Investigaciones Literarias "Gonzalo Picón
        Febres," U de los Andes, 1981. 238–49.
        Divided into Spanish American poetry anthologies and Venezuelan ones. Gives
bibliographical details for each volume and lists Venezuelan writers included.

1116.   Querales, Juandemaro. *Estudio bibliográfico de la poesía larense.* El Libro
        Menor 14. Caracas: Acad. Nacional de la Historia, 1981. 94 pp.
        Classified bibliography that lists 203 books and anthologies from the state of
Lara. Not only lists the authors' works but also includes critical studies on them.

1117. Sembrano Urdaneta, Oscar. *Contribución a una bibliografía general de la poesía venezolana en el siglo XX.* Caracas: Facultad de Humanidades y Educación, Escuela de Letras, U Central de Venezuela, 1979. 367 pp.
Includes data on 2,068 volumes of poetry by 747 authors. Provides critical studies on Venezuelan poets.

Pseudonyms

1118. Castellanos, Rafael Ramón. *Historia del seudónimo en Venezuela.* 2 vols. Caracas: Centauro, 1981.
Includes not only pseudonyms of Venezuelan authors but also those used by foreign authors who have contributed to Venezuelan culture.

Authors

1119. *Contribución a la bibliografía de Antonio Arraiz, 1903–1963.* Colección bibliografías 3. Caracas: Gobernación del Distrito Federal, 1969. 199 pp.
Lists 1,042 items.

1120. Becco, Horacio Jorge. *Ediciones chilenas de Andrés Bello (1830–1893).* Caracas: Bello, 1980. 87 pp.
Classified bibliography of Bello's works published in Chile.

1121. Millares Carlo, Agustín. *Bibliografía de Andrés Bello.* Biblioteca histórica hispanoamericana 2. Madrid: Fundación Universitaria Española, 1978. 237 pp.
This classified bibliography devotes a section to works by Bello and a section of 1,070 items to material about him and them. It is the fullest bibliography of Bello, but many items published outside Venezuela are missing.

1122. *Contribución a la bibliografía de Eduardo Blanco, 1838–1912.* Colección bibliografías 9. Caracas: Gobernación del Distrito Federal, 1971. 82 pp.
Lists 176 items.

1123. Rivas Dugarte, Rafael Angel. *Fuentes para el estudio de Rufino Blanco Fombona, 1874–1974.* Colección Manuel Landaeta Rosales. Caracas: Centro de Estudios Latinoamericanos Rómulo Gallegos, 1979. 244 pp.
Lists 1,722 items by and about Blanco Fombona.

1124. *Contribución a la bibliografía de Manuel Díaz Rodríguez, 1871–1927.* Colección bibliografías 2. Caracas: Gobernación del Distrito Federal, 1970. 156 pp.
Lists 667 items.

1125. *Contribución a la bibliografía de Ramón Díaz Sánchez, 1903–1968.* Colección bibliografías 5. Caracas: Gobernación del Distrito Federal, 1970. 249 pp. Lists 1,131 items.

1126. *Contribución a la bibliografía de Rómulo Gallegos, 1884–1969.* Colección bibliografías 1. Caracas: Gobernación del Distrito Federal, 1969. 405 pp. Lists 2,041 items.

1127. Shaw, Donald L. "Rómulo Gallegos: Suplemento a una bibliografía." *Revista iberoamericana* 37.75 (1971): 447–57. Supplements list of critical studies in no. 1126.

1128. Bencomo de León, Guadalupe. *Bibliografía de Augusto León y otras fuentes para el estudio de su obra.* Caracas: U Central de Venezuela, Rectorado, 1981. 189 pp.

1129. *Contribución a la bibliografía de Enrique Bernardo Núñez, 1895–1964.* Colección bibliografías 6. Caracas: Gobernación del Distrito Federal, 1970. 203 pp. Lists 962 items.

1130. *Contribución a la bibliografía de Teresa de la Parra, 1895–1936.* Colección bibliografías 7. Caracas: Gobernación del Distrito Federal, 1970. 133 pp. Lists 473 items.

1131. Calvo de Elcor, Miren Zorkunde. *Contribución a la bibliografía de Fernando Paz Castillo, 1893– .* Colección bibliografías 11. Caracas: Gobernación del Distrito Federal, 1974. 322 pp. Lists 1,477 items.

1132. *Contribución a la bibliografía de José Rafael Pocaterra, 1890–1955.* Colección bibliografías 4. Caracas: Gobernación del Distrito Federal, 1970. 96 pp. Lists 360 items.

1133. *Contribución a la bibliografía de Luis Manuel Urbaneja Achepohl, 1873–1937.* Colección bibliografías 8. Caracas: Gobernación del Distrito Federal, 1971. 113 pp. Lists 335 items.

1134. *Contribución a la bibliografía de Arturo Uslar Pietri.* Colección bibliografías 10. Caracas: Gobernación del Distrito Federal, 1973. 396 pp. Lists 1,882 items.

The Colección bibliografías (nos. 1119, 1122, 1124–26, 1129–34) is a series of classified bibliographies of Venezuelan authors that provide data both by and about the authors. The research for these volumes was developed by Efraín Subero, head of the Seminario de Literatura Venezolana of the Universidad Católica Andrés Bello, Facultad de Humanidades y Educación, Escuela de Letras.

With the eighth volume of this series the seminario's title was changed to Centro de Investigaciones Literarias. Though these bibliographies were compiled by Subero's students, usually only Subero's name appears on the title page.

Women Authors

1135. *La mujer en las letras venezolanas: Homenaje a Teresa de la Parra en el año internacional de la mujer, 5–26 octubre de 1975.* Caracas: Congreso de la República, 1976. 176 pp.
Extensive bibliography of Venezuelan women authors.

1136. Rodríguez-Arenas, Flor María, and Raúl Neira. *Guía bibliográfica de escritoras venezolanas.* Bogotá: Codice, 1993. vii + 220 pp.
An important attempt at a bibliography of Venezuelan women authors with many incomplete citations. Includes material both by and about the authors. Pages 217–20 list pseudonyms.

TRANSLATIONS

Brazilian (Portuguese)

1137. Wogan, Daniel S. *A literatura hispano-americana no Brasil 1877–1944: Bibliografía de crítica, história literária e traduções.* Baton Rouge: Louisiana State UP, 1948. 98 pp.
Critical studies are briefly annotated and are arranged in chronological order. Translations are arranged by author.

Danish

1138. Larsen, Jørgen Ingemann. *Bibliografi over latinamerikansk skønlitteratur pa dansk samt over danske bidrag til den latinamerikanske litteratur historia.* 2nd ed. København: n.p., 1982. 122 pp.
Spanish American and Brazilian authors whose works have been translated and published in Denmark between 1940 and 1979 are arranged by countries. Often gives the title in the original Spanish or Portuguese. Also gives the contents of anthologies.

Dutch

1139.   Steenmeijer, Maarten. "Bibliografía." *Literatura hispanoamericana en traducción holandesa. Spaansamerikaanse literatur in nederlandse vertaling, 1946–1977.* Vol. 2. Leiden: Inst. de Estudios Hispánicos de la U, 1978. 54 pp.

English

1140.   Christensen, George K. "A Bibliography of Latin American Plays in English Translation." *Latin American Theatre Review* 6.6 (1973): 29–39.
Attempts to list both published and manuscript translations of plays. Arranged by country.

1141.   Freudenthal, Juan R., and Patricia M. Freudenthal. *Index to Anthologies of Latin American Literature in English Translation.* Boston: Hall, 1977. xxxvi + 199 pp.
Indexes almost 120 books and issues of periodicals devoted to Latin American literature in translation. Lacks original titles in Spanish or Portuguese.

1142.   Hulet, Claude L. *Latin American Poetry in English Translation.* Basic Bibliographies 2. Washington: Pan American Union, 1965. 192 pp.
Arranged by country. Often provides Spanish or Portuguese titles.

1143.   ———. *Latin American Prose in English Translation.* Basic Bibliographies 1. Washington: Pan American Union, 1964. 191 pp.
Divided by literary genre and then, within each genre, by country.

1144.   Shaw, Bradley A. *Latin American Literature in English Translation: An Annotated Bibliography.* New York: New York UP, for Center for Inter-American Relations, 1976. x + 144 pp.
Arranged by genre and then by country. Includes only books and anthologies and almost always gives the titles in the original language.

1145.   ———. *Latin American Literature in English 1975–1978.* Supp. to *Review* [Center for Inter-American Relations] 24 (1979): 1–23.
Provides data on 111 annotated entries that supplement and update no. 1144. Entries are arranged alphabetically by author or editor and are divided into anthologies, individual works, additions to the original volume, and reprints published before 1975.

1146.   Wilson, Jason. *An A to Z of Modern Latin American Literature in English Translation.* London: Inst. of Latin American Studies, 1989. 95 pp.
A checklist of fiction, drama, and poetry in translation arranged by author. Includes a list of anthologies in translation in chronological order and a bibliography of translation sources.

French

1147. Horn-Monval, Madeleine. *Répertoire bibliographique des traductions et adaptations françaises du théâtre étranger de XVème siècle à nos jours.* Vol. 4. Paris: CNRS, 1963. 8 vols.
Contains a section entitled "Théâtre de l'Amérique latine."

1148. Villegas, Jean-Claude. *La littérature hispano-américaine publiée en France.* Etudes, guides et inventaires 4. Paris: Bibliothèque Nationale, 1986. 260 pp.
Contains 1,166 titles. Bibliography suffers from the fact that the compiler has not personally examined all items. It is, however, the fullest attempt yet at a bibliography of French translations of Latin American writers.

German

1149. Reichardt, Dieter. *Schöne Literatur lateinamerikanischer Autoren: Eine Ubersicht der deutschen Ubersetzungen mit biographischen Angaben.* Bibliographie und Dokumentation 6. Hamburg: Inst. für Iberoamerika-Kunde, 1965. 270 pp.
Provides brief biographies of authors as well as German translations of their works found in 38 anthologies or published as books.

1150. Strausfeld, Michi. "Ausgewählte Bibliographie lateinamerikanischer Literatur im der BRD." *Die Horen* 28.29 (1983): 183–89.

Greek

1151. Rokas, Nicholas W. "Latin American Literature in Modern Greek: A Bibliography." *Revista interamericana de bibliografía* 41 (1991): 589–600.

Italian

1152. Bellini, Giuseppe. "Bibliografia dell'ispanoamericanismo italiano: Le traduzioni." *Rassegna iberistica* 6 (1979): 3–42.
Divided into general anthologies (subdivided by genres), authors, and original texts. 585 items.

Polish

1153. Sarnacki, John. *Latin American Literature and History in Polish Translations: A Bibliography.* Port Huron: Privately printed, 1973. ix + 84 pp.

Arrangement is by country. Almost always provides the title in the original language. Lists critical studies on the authors as well as Polish book reviews of their books.

Russian

1154. Biblioteca de Estado de Literaturas Extranjeras de la U.R.S.S. *Literatura latinoamericana en la imprenta rusa. Bibliografía de las obras traducidas al ruso y ensayos críticos 1765–1959.* Moscú: Cámara del Libro, 1960. 290 pp.
Provides data on Russian translations of Latin American authors but also lists monographs, reviews, and articles dedicated to Latin American literature and published in the Russian press in the nineteenth and twentieth centuries. The 1,519 entries are first arranged by country and then by author. Translations precede critical studies on the author.

DISSERTATIONS

1155. "Relación de tesis doctorales y memorias de licenciatura preparadas en el Departamento de Literatura Hispanoamericana de la Universidad Complutense desde marzo de 1986 hasta marzo de 1988." *Anales de literatura hispanoamericana* 17 (1988): 209–10.

1156. Sullivan, William M. *Dissertations and Theses on Venezuelan Topics, 1900–95.* Metuchen: Scarecrow, 1988. 284 pp.
Pages 196–217 list dissertations and theses on Venezuelan Spanish, literature, and art. Dissertations from the United States are annotated; dissertations accepted at universities outside the United States are included but not annotated; the same is true of MA theses.

1157. *Thèses sur l'Amérique latine soutenues en France, 1980–1984: Répertoire bibliographique en sciences sociales et sciences humaines.* [Paris]: CNRS, 1987. 540 pp.
See also nos. 599–604.

NATIONAL BIBLIOGRAPHIES

General

1158. Woodbridge, Hensley C. "Latin American National Bibliography." *Encyclopedia of Library and Information Science.* Vol. 36. New York: Dekker, 1983. 270–342.

This article gives the fullest discussion of national bibliographies, both retrospective and current, that has yet been produced.

Argentina

1159. *Libros argentinos. ISBN—1982.* Buenos Aires: Cámara Argentina del Libro, 1984. 350 pp.

This work is the latest attempt at a current Argentina bibliography. The advertisement announcing its publication stated, "A principios del año 1982 la República Argentina se unió al sistema ISBN que permite la identificación bibliográfica de cada libro publicado. . . . La Cámara . . . ofrece un volumen que contiene los primeros 9,335 títulos registrados por los editores argentinos hasta el fin del año 1982. Toda la producción editorial de ese año se encuentra incluída, además de los fondos de catálogo de varias editoriales.

". . . se encuentran libros no solamente de editoriales comerciales, sino también de instituciones y de ediciones particulares. El cuerpo principal del libro consiste en un ordenamiento por temas. . . . Además contiene un índice por autores y un índice alfabético de temas, con números que corresponden a la numeración correlativa del cuerpo principal. También aparece una lista de las editoriales con sus direcciones respectivas y sus códigos de ISBN."

The volume for 1984 appeared in 1985 (570 pp.).

For many years, the best current guides to Argentine publications were the classified lists issued by Fernando García Cambeiro and Librería del Plata, both book dealers in Buenos Aires.

Bolivia

1160. *Bio-bibliografía boliviana del año.* Comp. Werner Tichauer. La Paz: Amigos del Libro, 1975– (1976–).

Formerly entitled *Bibliografía boliviana del año* . . . , 1962–74, this work is chiefly a listing of books published in Bolivia, with occasional notes on the authors or volumes. Bibliographies of various kinds are sometimes special features of individual volumes. Some issues provide data on books published on Bolivia outside Bolivia. Well indexed.

Chile

1161. *Anuario de la prensa chilena.* Santiago: Biblioteca Nacional, 1877–1975.

The *Anuario* is a catalog of books deposited in Chile's Biblioteca Nacional. Since 1891 it has included books by Chilean authors or works about Chile published outside the country. From time to time it has included other types of printed materials.

1162. *Bibliografía chilena.* Santiago: Biblioteca Nacional, 1976– .

Colombia

1163. *Anuario bibliográfico colombiano "Rubén Pérez Ortiz."* Comp. José Romero
Rojas. Bogotá: Inst. Caro y Cuervo, 1963– (1966–). Formerly *Anuario
bibliográfico colombiano*, 1951, 1956–62 (1958–64).
Classified bibliography of Colombian publications and those published outside
Colombia by Colombians or about the country. The volume covering 1991–92
was published in 1995.

Cuba

1164. *Bibliografía cubana*. La Habana: Biblioteca Nacional "José Martí,"
1959–62– .
Annual classified bibliography of Cuban books, pamphlets, and periodicals
that also includes, in more recent volumes, postage stamps, records, posters, films,
and exhibition catalogs. Became a monthly in 1983.

Dominican Republic

1165. *Anuario bibliográfico dominicano, 1980–1982, de contenido retrospectivo al año
1979 y anteriores.* Santo Domingo: Biblioteca Nacional, 1984. 236 pp.
A classified subject bibliography of 2,537 items with subject and author indexes.

Ecuador

1166. *Anuario bibliográfico ecuatoriano*. Quito: Biblioteca General, U Central de
Ecuador, 1975– .
This classified list of books appears annually as the sixth issue of *Bibliografía
ecuatoriana*, which is a classified bibliography of material published in periodicals.
Has an author, title, and subject index.

Honduras

1167. Argueta, Mario. *Anuario bibliográfico hondureño 1980*. Ciudad Universitaria:
U Nacional Autónoma de Honduras, 1982. 33 pp.

Mexico

1168. *Bibliografía mexicana*. México: Biblioteca Nacional de México, Inst. de Investigaciones Bibliográficas, UNAM, 1967– .
This classified bibliography of separately published Mexican works appears 6
times a year. There is an author index. A list of publishers with their addresses is a
useful feature of each issue.

Nicaragua

1169. Hemeroteca Nacional "Manolo Cuadra." *Catálogo de periódicos y revistas de Nicaragua (1830–1930).* Managua: Biblioteca Nacional "Rubén Darío," Inst. Nicaragüense de Cultura, 1992. 197 pp.

Jorge Eduardo Arellano is listed in the unpaginated preliminary matter as the director of this remarkable compilation, which provides data on 615 Nicaraguan magazines and journals. A second volume is planned to cover 1931 through 1989.

1170. ———. *Catálogo de periódicos y revistas de Nicaragua (1979–1994).* Managua: Biblioteca Nacional, Inst. Nicaragüense de Cultura, 1994. 36 pp.

Contains 277 entries.

1171. *Nicaraguan National Bibliography, 1800–1978.* 3 vols. Redlands: Latin American Bibliographical Foundation, 1986.

Gives locations of copies of over 20,000 entries. Includes author, title, and subject indexes. "A comprehensive bibliography of works published in Nicaragua, of works by Nicaraguan authors, regardless of where published, and of works on Nicaragua, regardless of where published. It includes broadsides, rare imprints, annuals, and irregular serials" (advertisement).

1172. Biblioteca Nacional "Rubén Darío." *Bibliografía nacional de Nicaragua (1979–1989)."* Managua: Inst. Nicaragüense de Cultura, 1991. 452 pp.

Has 4,667 entries with author and title indexes.

1173. ———. *Bibliografía nacional de Nicaragua (1990–1992).* Managua: Inst. Nicaragüense de Cultura, 1993. 152 pp.

1174. [Arellano, Jorge Eduardo]. "Tres años de revolución sandinista (contribución a la bibliografía nicaragüense de julio 1979 a junio 1982)." *Boletín informativo* 2nd ser. 2 (July 1982): 9–73.

Section D, "Lingüística, literatura," comprising items 78–134, 288–99 (31–37, 67–68), is a bibliography of literary and linguistic works published in Nicaragua and of works on Nicaraguan literature and language published outside the country.

Paraguay

1175. *Bibliografía nacional paraguaya.* Asunción: U Nacional de Asunción, 1978– . The 1978 volume covers 1971–77.

Peru

1176. *Anuario bibliográfico peruano.* Lima: Biblioteca Nacional, Centro Bibliográfico Nacional, Inst. Nacional de Cultura, 1943– (1945–).

The first several volumes cover a single year; later volumes cover 2 or 3 years. The volume for 1970–72 was published in 1979. Includes publications of all kinds (books, pamphlets, newspapers, periodicals) and bibliographies of authors who died during the period covered. Thorough and comprehensive.

1177. *Bibliografía nacional: Libros, artículos de revistas y periódicos.* Lima: Biblioteca Nacional, 1978– .
Attempts to bring Peru's national bibliography up to date.

Uruguay

1178. *Anuario bibliográfico uruguayo.* Montevideo: Biblioteca Nacional, 1946–49, 1968 (1947–51, 1969).
A classified bibliography of books and pamphlets.

Venezuela

1179. *Anuario bibliográfico venezolano.* Caracas: Biblioteca Nacional, Centro Bibliográfico Venezolano, 1942– .
Appeared annually 1942–46; 1947–48, 2 vols. (1950); 1949–54, 2 vols. (1960); 1967–68 (1977); 1969–74, A–G (1979); 1975 (1977). The Biblioteca Nacional is working to complete this bibliography for the years missing. Items are arranged by author. There are sections on periodical publications and data on authors who died during the years covered. Includes dictionary-catalog of authors, titles, and subjects.

BIBLIOGRAPHIES OF
BIBLIOGRAPHIES

General

1180. Gropp, Arthur E. *A Bibliography of Latin American Bibliographies.* Metuchen: Scarecrow, 1968. ix + 515 pp.

1181. ———. *A Bibliography of Latin American Bibliographies: Supplement.* Metuchen: Scarecrow, 1971. xii + 277 pp.

1182. ———. *A Bibliography of Latin American Bibliographies Published in Periodicals.* 2 vols. Metuchen: Scarecrow, 1976.

These classified bibliographies (nos. 1180–82) are continued by nos. 1183–98.

1183. Cordeiro, Daniel Raposo. *A Bibliography of Latin American Bibliographies: Social Sciences and Humanities.* Metuchen: Scarecrow, 1979. vii + 272 pp.

1184. Piedracueva, Haydée. *A Bibliography of Latin American Bibliographies, 1957–1979: Social Studies and Humanities.* Metuchen: Scarecrow, 1982. xiii + 313 pp.

1185. ———. "Bibliography of Bibliographies: 1981 Supplement." *Papers of the Twenty-Sixth Seminar on the Acquisition of Latin American Library Materials.* Madison: SALALM Secretariat, 1984. 305–44.

1186. ———. "Bibliography of Bibliographies: 1982 Supplement." *Papers of the Twenty-Seventh Seminar on the Acquisition of Latin American Library Materials.* Madison: SALALM Secretariat, 1984. 179–208.

1187. Loroña, Lionel V. *Bibliography of Latin American Bibliographies 1982–1983.* Bibliography and Reference Series 10. Madison: SALALM Secretariat, 1984. 33 pp.

1188. ———. *Bibliography of Latin American and Caribbean Bibliographies, 1984–1985.* Bibliography and Reference Series 15. Madison: SALALM Secretariat, 1986. 128 pp.

1189. ———. *Bibliography of Latin American and Caribbean Bibliographies, 1985–1986.* Bibliography and Reference Series 17. Madison: SALALM Secretariat, 1986. 54 pp.

1190. ———. *Bibliography of Latin American and Caribbean Bibliographies, 1986–1987.* Bibliography and Reference Series 20. Madison: SALALM Secretariat, 1987. 64 pp.

1191. ———. *Bibliography of Latin American and Caribbean Bibliographies, 1987–1988.* Bibliography and Reference Series 23. Madison: SALALM Secretariat, 1988. 69 pp.

1192. ———. *Bibliography of Latin American and Caribbean Bibliographies, 1988–1989.* Bibliography and Reference Series 25. Madison: SALALM Secretariat, 1989. 66 pp.

1193. ———. *Bibliography of Latin American and Caribbean Bibliographies, 1989–1990.* Bibliography and Reference Series 27. Albuquerque: SALALM Secretariat, 1990. 48 pp.

1194. ———. *Bibliography of Latin American and Caribbean Bibliographies, 1990–1991.* Bibliography and Reference Series 30. Albuquerque: SALALM Secretariat, 1992. 125 pp.

1195. ———. *Bibliography of Latin American and Caribbean Bibliographies, 1991–1992.* Bibliography and Reference Series 31. Albuquerque: SALALM Secretariat, 1992. 59 pp.

1196. Williams, Gayle Ann. *Bibliography of Latin American and Caribbean Bibliographies, 1992–1993.* Bibliography and Reference Series 34. Albuquerque: SALALM Secretariat, 1993. 81 pp.

1197. ———. *Bibliography of Latin American and Caribbean Bibliographies, 1993–1994.* Bibliography and Reference Series 35. Albuquerque: SALALM Secretariat, 1994. 110 pp.

1198. Loroña, Lionel V. *A Bibliography of Latin American and Caribbean Bibliographies, 1985–1989: Social Sciences and Humanities.* Metuchen: Scarecrow, 1993. xiv + 314 pp.

After each annual SALALM meeting the organization produces a collection of its working papers. For many years, one of these working papers was an unannotated bibliography of bibliographies; later the works were issued separately as annual reports. These bibliographies should be used to supplement those by Gropp (nos. 1180–82), Cordeiro (no. 1183), Piedracueva (nos. 1184–86), Loroña (nos. 1187–95, 1198), and Williams (nos. 1196 and 1197). They have the following sections that could be of value to students of Spanish language and Spanish American literature: national bibliographies, personal bibliographies, language and literature, and theses and dissertations. They include bibliographies published as books and as articles.

Argentina

1199. Geoghegan, Abel Rodolfo. *Bibliografía de bibliografías argentinas: 1807–1970.* Buenos Aires: Pardo, 1970. 130 pp.
Classified bibliography.

Bolivia

1200. Siles Guevara, Juan. *Bibliografía de bibliografías bolivianas.* N.p.: Ministerio de Cultura, Información y Turismo, 1969. 38 pp.
Classified bibliography of 103 items, almost none of which deal with Bolivian Spanish or Bolivian literature. Items 73–99 are "Bibliografías colectivas" and "Bibliografías individuales."

Colombia

1201.   Giraldo Jaramillo, Gabriel. *Bibliografía de bibliografías colombianas.* 2nd ed., rev. and updated Rubén Pérez Ortiz. Publicaciones del Inst. Caro y Cuervo, serie bibliográfica 1. Bogotá: Inst. Caro y Cuervo, 1960. xvi + 204 pp. Classified bibliography.

Cuba

1202.   Robaina, Tomás F. *Bibliografía de bibliografías cubanas 1859–1972.* La Habana: Dept. de Hemeroteca e Información de Humanidades, Biblioteca Nacional "José Martí," 1973. 340 pp. Classified and annotated bibliography with author and subject indexes.

Dominican Republic

1203.   Florén Lozano, Luis. *Bibliografía de bibliografías dominicanas.* Ciudad Trujillo: Roques Román, 1948. 66 pp. Classified bibliography.

Honduras

1204.   Argueta, Mario R. "Bibliografía de bibliografías hondureñas." *Revista de la universidad* [Universidad Nacional Autónoma de Honduras] 6.21 (1984?): 55–62.

Mexico

1205.   Millares Carlo, Agustín, and José Ignacio Montecón. *Ensayo de una bibliografía de bibliografías mexicanas (la imprenta, el libro, las bibliotecas, etc.).* México: Biblioteca de la II Feria del Libro y Exposición Nacional de Periodismo, 1943. xvi + 224 pp.

1206.   ———. *Ensayo de una bibliografía de bibliografías mexicanas (. . .). Adiciones.* México: Feria del Libro y Exposición Nacional de Periodismo y I de Cine y Radio, México, 1944. 46 pp.

Although there is a later bibliography of Mexican bibliographies, nos. 1205 and 1206 continue as the best of their type for Mexico. Each is a classified bibliography with an excellent index.

Peru

1207.   Lostaunau Rubio, Gabriel. *Fuentes para el estudio del Perú (Bibliografía de bibliografías)*. Ed. and pref. Miguel Angel Rodríguez Rea. Lima: n.p., 1980. 500 pp.
Classified bibliography of bibliographies published in books or as articles.

Uruguay

1208.   Musso Ambrosi, Luis Alberto. *Bibliografía de bibliografías uruguayas, con aportes a la historia del periodismo*. Montevideo: n.p., 1964. vii + 102 pp.
A classified bibliography of 637 entries, with an index.

Library Catalogs and Union Lists

Many of the sources listed in the section on Spanish literature belong here as well. See in particular nos. 615–31.

France

1209.   *Catalogue collectif des périodiques sur l'Amérique latine disponibles en France*. 2nd ed., rev. and enl. Paris: CNRS, 1984. xv + 590 pp.
"Les périodiques sont présentés par pays d'édition. Chaque titre de revue, classé par ordre alphabétique, est accompagné d'une notice munie d'un numéro séquentiel comprenant: le numéro ISSN de la revue lorsqu'il existe, la ville d'édition, l'éditeur intellectuel, l'éditeur commercial et l'addresse, le (ou les) organisme(s) possédant la revue avec indication, pour chacun d'entre eux, de la cote et de l'état de la collection" (prepublication announcement).

Germany

1210.   Ibero-Amerikanisches Institut, Berlin. *Schlagwortkatalog des Ibero-Amerikanischen Instituts*. 30 vols. Preussicher Kulturbesitz in Berlin. Boston: Hall, 1977.
A subject catalog.

United States

1211.   Nelson, Bonnie F. "Spain, Portugal, Latin America, and the Caribbean." *A Guide to Published Library Catalogs*. Metuchen: Scarecrow, 1982. 123–35.

Items 170–92 list and annotate the library catalogs that deal with the countries and regions named in the title.

1212.   Charno, Steven M. *Latin American Newspapers in United States Libraries: A Union List.* Austin: U of Texas P, 1978. xiv + 619 pp.
Indicates the locations of 5,500 Latin American newspapers in 70 libraries of the United States.

1213.   Downs, Robert B. *American Library Resources.* . . .
See nos. 623–26.

1214.   University of Florida, Gainesville, Libraries. *Catalog of the Latin American Collection.* 13 vols. Boston: Hall, 1973. First supp. 7 vols., 1979.
Reproduces almost 210,000 cards from the university library.

1215.   Harvard University Library. *Latin American Literature.* Widener Library Shelflist 21. Cambridge: Harvard U Library, 1969. 498 pp.
Catalogs a portion of the largest university library in the United States. Includes "Classification Schedule," "Classified Listing by Call Number," "Author and Title Listing," and "Chronological Listing."

1216.   University of Miami, Coral Gables. *Catalog of the Cuban and Caribbean Library.* . . . 6 vols. Boston: Hall, 1977.
"The geographical area included would be Cuba and the rest of the Greater and Lesser Antilles, the Guyanas, Venezuela, Mexico, Colombia, and Central America except El Salvador" (1: iii).

1217.   University of Texas Library. *Catalog of the Latin American Collection.* 31 vols. Boston: Hall, 1969. First supp. 5 vols., 1971. Second supp. 3 vols., 1973. Third supp. 8 vols., 1975. Fourth supp. 3 vols., 1977.
The catalog of one of the largest collections of material on Spanish American culture in the United States.

1218.   *Bibliographic Guide to Latin American Studies, 1979–* . Boston: Hall, 1980– .
Annual supplement to the catalogs of the University of Texas. It "consists of publications catalogued by the Latin American Collection (LAC) of the University, with additional entries from the Library of Congress for thorough subject coverage" (1980: iv).

1219.   Tulane University Library. *Catalog of the Latin American Library of the Tulane University Library, New Orleans.* 10 vols. Boston: Hall, 1970. First supp. 2 vols., 1973. Second supp. 2 vols., 1975. Third supp. 2 vols., 1978.
The catalog of an outstanding collection that for a long time specialized in material on Mexico and Central America.

National Encyclopedias

There seem to be few national encyclopedias, that is, encyclopedias dealing entirely with the culture of a single country. Data are provided on two of this type.

1220.   Abad de Santillan, Diego. *Gran enciclopedia argentina*. 9 vols. Buenos Aires: Ediar, 1956–64.
Provides biographies on many Argentine writers and defines many argentinisms and *lunfardismos*. Volume 9 is a supplement.

1221.   *Enciclopedia de México*. 12 vols. México: Inst. de la Enciclopedia de México, 1966–67.
"Se ha tratado de lograr un justo equilibro en el espacio dedicado a cada disciplina: 'todo lo mexicano,' pero en una síntesis de lo que tiene validez permanente; y todo visto con una perspectiva actual, serena, sin partidarismos trasnochados. . . ." (1: x). Deals with all aspects of Mexican culture and provides biographies of Mexican authors. It is a shame that the longer articles do not include bibliographies.

Miscellaneous Works That May Be Useful

1222.   *Fichero bibliográfico hispanoamericano*. 1961– .
The frequency of this publication, the place of publication, and the publisher have varied; since October 1964 it has appeared monthly except for a combined January-February issue. Currently published in San Juan, Puerto Rico, by Melcher Ediciones, it is a classified list of current publications in Spanish regardless of place. Over the years some countries have been considerably better covered than others.

1223.   Foster, David William, and Virginia Ramos Foster. *Modern Latin American Literature*. 2 vols. New York: Ungar, 1975.
A "compilation of international commentary on Latin American literature" that presents "twentieth-century Latin American writers through the eyes of leading critics in their own country and abroad, with their particular stress on their reception in the United States" (1: v). Many of the comments on these 183 authors have been translated into English from other languages (Spanish, German, French).

1224.   Hilton, Sylvia-Lyn, and Amancio Labandeira Fernández. *Bibliografía hispanoamericana y filipina: Manual de repertorios bibliográficos para la investigación de la historia y la literatura hispanoamericanas y filipinas*. Madrid: Fundación Universitaria Española, 1983. 311 pp.
The most important sections of this classified, unannotated bibliography are "Bibliografía de bibliografías," "Repertorios biográficos por lugar de nacimiento,"

"Repertorios por profesiones y otras características personales," "Tipobibliografías hispanoamericanas y filipinas retrospectivas," "Indices de publicaciones periódicas," "Catálogos de bibliotecas hispanoamericanas y filipinas, y bibliotecas extranjeras con fondos hispanoamericanos y filipinos," "Catálogos de archivos hispanoamericanos y filipinos," "Indice de bibliotecas españolas con fondos hispanoamericanos y filipinos," "Indice de archivos españoles con fondos hispanoamericanos y filipinos," "Bibliografías de la literatura hispanoamericana," and "Bibliografías de la historia hispanoamericana y filipina."

1225.　*Libros en venta en Hispanoamérica y España.* 5th ed. 3 vols. San Juan: Melcher, 1990.
　　Equivalent to *Books in Print* in the United States. Includes publications in Spanish published in Spain, Puerto Rico, and the Spanish-speaking countries of the Western Hemisphere. Volume 1 is "Autores con guía de editores." Volume 2 is "Títulos," and volume 3 is "Materias."

1226.　*Quién es quién en el teatro y el cine español e hispano-americano.* 2 vols. Barcelona: Centro de Investigaciones Literarias Españolas e Hispanoamericanos, 1990.
　　An extremely useful *Who's Who*–type dictionary of individuals connected with the Spanish and Hispanic American theater and cinema. A short biographical note (2 or 3 lines) is followed by a "Cronología."

1227.　Sable, Martin H. *A Guide to Latin American Studies.* 2 vols. Los Angeles: Latin American Center, U of California, 1967.
　　Sable seems to prefer material in English, including English translations of works originally in Spanish and Portuguese. Items 2881–3112 deal with literature. There is also a section on language.

1228.　———. *Latin American Studies in the Non-Western World and Eastern Europe: A Bibliography of Latin America in the Languages of Africa, Asia, the Middle East, and Eastern Europe with Transliterations and Translations in English.* Metuchen: Scarecrow, 1970. xxiii + 701 pp.
　　Of little value for the study of literature. Arranged first by country of publication and then by Latin American country.

1229.　Wilgus, A. Curtis. *Latin America, Spain and Portugal: A Selected and Annotated Bibliographical Guide to Books Published in the United States.* Metuchen: Scarecrow, 1977. xv + 910 pp.
　　Classified and annotated bibliography of books published in the United States between 1954 and 1973. Items are arranged by country or region. Each large section is divided into smaller sections, one of which is almost always on culture.

1230.　Woods, Richard D. *Reference Materials on Latin America in English: The Humanities.* Metuchen: Scarecrow, 1980. xii + 639 pp.
　　The 1,252 entries, arranged by author, have excellent annotations. Includes author, title, and subject indexes.

Index of Authors, Editors, Compilers, and Translators

Entries are alphabetized letter by letter; numbers refer to entry numbers.

Index to Author Bibliographies, Glossaries, Concordances, and Anonymous Works

Index of Titles

Diccionario de autores teatrales argentinos,
1950–1980, 771
Diccionario de autores teatrales uruguayos, 1085
Diccionario de bolivianismos, 133
Diccionaro de concordancias del Poema de mío
Cid, 285
Diccionario de concordancia y frecuencias de uso en
el léxico poético de César Vallejo, 1058
Diccionario de costarriqueñismos, 149
Diccionario de cubanismos más usuales: Como habla
el cubano, 157
Diccionario de escritores colombianos, 872
Diccionario de escritores gaditanos, 242
Diccionario de escritores granadinos (siglos
VIII–XX), 247
Diccionario de escritores hondureños, 967
Diccionario de escritores mexicanos, 978
Diccionario de escritores mexicanos del siglo XX:
Desde las generaciones del Ateneo y novelistas de
la Revolución hasta nuestros días, 977
Diccionario de escritores uruguayos, 1080
Diccionario de expresiones malsonantes del español:
Léxico descriptivo, 66
Diccionario de gestos: España e Hispanoamérica,
80
Diccionario de la expresión popular guatemalteca,
166
Diccionario de la lengua castellana, 54
Diccionario de la lengua española, 61
Diccionario de la literatura boliviana, 816
Diccionario de la literatura chilena, 841
Diccionario de la literatura cubana, 903
Diccionario de la literatura ecuatoriana, 949
Diccionario de la literatura latinoamericana:
Argentina, 762
Diccionario de la literatura latinoamericana:
Bolivia, 815
Diccionario de la literatura latinoamericana: Chile,
837
Diccionario de la literatura latinoamericana:
Colombia, 873
Diccionario de la literatura latinoamericana:
Ecuador, 950
Diccionario de la literatura paraguaya (I parte),
1025
"Diccionario de las letras nicaragüenses.
Primera entrega: Escritores de la época
colonial y el siglo XIX," 1008
Diccionario de las vanguardias en España
1907–1936, 489
Diccionario del español medieval, 45, 47
Diccionario de literatura española, 235
Diccionario de literatura española e
hispanoamericana, 236
Diccionario de literatura hispano-americana:
Autores, 670

Diccionario de literatura puertorriqueña, 1059
Diccionario de literatura uruguaya, 1079
Diccionario del lenguaje campesino rioplatense.
Contiene alrededor de tres mil voces y locuciones,
aclaradas y comentadas, 208
Diccionario del Quijote, 355
Diccionario de mejicanismos, 180
Diccionario de métrica española, 558
Diccionario de movimientos y grupos literarios
chilenos, 859
Diccionario de nombres vulgares de la fauna
argentina, 130
Diccionario de retórica, crítica y terminología, 557
Diccionario de seudónimos literarios españoles, con
algunas iniciales, 249
"Diccionario de seudónimos peruanos," 1047,
1048
Diccionario de siglas e inicialismos nicaragüenses,
186
Diccionario de sinónimos, 71
"Diccionario de sobrenombres literarios
peruanos," 1049
Diccionario de términos literarios, 556
Diccionario de términos panameños, 192
Diccionario de uso del español, 59
Diccionario de uso. Gran diccionario de la lengua
española, 58
Diccionario de venezolanismos, 217
Diccionario de voces coloquiales de Puerto Rico, 202
Diccionario de voces de uso actual, 57
Diccionario de voces usadas en Guatemala, 169
Diccionario de voces y expresiones argentinas, 127
Diccionario ejemplificado de chilenismos, 141
Diccionario enciclopédico de las letras de América
latina, 672
Diccionario enciclopédico del país vasco, 650
Diccionario enciclopédico ilustrado de la Provincia
de Cádiz, 641
Diccionario etimológico comparado de los apellidos
españoles, hispanoamericanos y filipinos, 39
Diccionario etimológico latinoamericano del léxico
de la delincuencia, 122
Diccionario general de americanismos, 121
Diccionario general de la literatura venezolana,
1096
Diccionario histórico de la lengua española, 41
Diccionario ideológico de la lengua española desde la
idea a la palabra, desde la palabra a la idea, 56
Diccionario literario del Perú: Nomenclatura por
autores, 1030
Diccionario lunfardo y de otros términos antiguos y
modernos usuales en Buenos Aires, 128
Diccionario manual de americanismos, 119
Diccionario manual de literatura peruana y
material afines, 1031

"The Literature of Outsiders: The Literature
of the Gay Community in Latin America,"
743
*The Literature of Spain in English Translation: A
Bibliography*, 565
"Literature of the Renaissance," 300
"Littérature espagnole," 554
*La littérature hispano-américaine publiée en
France*, 1148
Lope de Rueda: Bibliografía crítica, 372
Lope de Vega: Nuevos estudios (adiciones . . .), 381
*Lope de Vega Studies 1937–1962: A Critical
Survey and Annotated Bibliography*, 378
*López Albújar, narrador de América: Bibliografía
general*, 1054

*Malas y peores palabras: Diccionario del argot
caraqueño*, 214
*Manual bibliográfico de cancioneros y romanceros.
Impresos durante el siglo XVI*, 315
*Manual bibliográfico de cancioneros y romanceros.
Impresos durante el siglo XVII*, 316
Manual bibliográfico de estudios españoles, 654
"Manual de bibliografía de la literatura
boliviana," 819
Manual de bibliografía de la literatura española,
238, 240
Manual de bibliografía perediana, 435
*Manual de investigación literaria (Guía
bibliográfica para el estudio de la literatura
española)*, 233
*Manual del librero hispano-americano: Bibliografía
general española e hispano-americana desde la
invención de la imprenta hasta nuestros tiempos*,
608
*Manual de proverbios en Chile, frases, dichos y
refranes de uso muy corriente in Chile. Incluye:
Más de cinco mil trescientas expresiones*, 137
Manual of Hispanic Bibliography, 232
Manuel de l'hispanisant, 652
"Mariano José de Larra: A Tentative Critical
Bibliography," 433
Masterpieces of Latino Literature, 677
Métrica española, 559
*Mexican Autobiography: An Annotated
Bibliography. La autobiografía mexicana: Una
bibliografía razonada*, 982
"Mexican Autobiography: An Essay and
Annotated Bibliography," 983
*Mexican Literature: A Bibliography of Secondary
Sources*, 979
*Mexican Theatre of the Twentieth Century:
Bibliography and Study*, 984
Mexico, 975

"Miguel Angel Asturias: Anticipo
bibliográfico," 960
*MLA Directory of Periodicals: A Guide to Journals
and Series in Languages and Literature*, 633
*MLA International Bibliography of Books and
Articles on the Modern Languages and
Literature*, 8
"Modern Drama Studies: An Annual
Bibliography," 448
*Modern Iberian Language and Literature: A
Bibliography of Homage Studies*, 5
Modern Latin-American Fiction Writers, 734, 735
Modern Latin American Literature, 1223
Modern Spanish and Portuguese Literatures, 446
"Morfosintaxis del moderno español
peninsular: Ensayo bibliográfico de estudios
descriptivos (1950–1972)," 85
Mozárabe. Elementos de bibliografía, 49
"La mujer en la poesía del Uruguay
(Bibliografía 1879–1969)," 1095
*La mujer en las letras venezolanas: Homenaje a
Teresa de la Parra en el año internacional de la
mujer, 5–26 octubre de 1975*, 1135

"Namelore in Latin America," 102
*La narrativa uruguaya: Estudio crítico-
bibliográfico*, 1086
*The National Union Catalog, Pre-1956 Imprints:
A Cumulative Author List Representing
Library of Congress Printed Cards and Titles
Reported by Other American Libraries*, 629
*El negro en la literatura hispanoamericana:
Bibliografía y hemerografía*, 706
"Neuere Literatur zu Humanismus und
Gelehrsamkeit im Spanien des 16.
Jahrhunderts," 306
*New Serial Titles: A Union List of Serials
Commencing Publication after December 31,
1949, 1950–1970 Cumulation*, 630
Nicaraguan National Bibliography, 1800–1978,
1171
Noticiero Alfonsi, 274
*La novela barroca. Catálogo biobibliográfico
(1620–1700)*, 336
"La novela colombiana, 1960–1974: Una
bibliografía," 882
"Novela, cuento y artículo literario," 897
"La novela española, 1700–1850," 400
La novela española, 1700–1850, 399
La novela española en 1961 y 1962, 483
"La novela española en 1979," 485
"La novela española en 1980," 486
"La novela española en 1981," 487
"La novela española en 1984," 488